D1450900

'Bitter with the Past but Sweet with the Dream':
Communism in the African American Imaginary

Historical Materialism Book Series

The Historical Materialism Book Series is a major publishing initiative of the radical left. The capitalist crisis of the twenty-first century has been met by a resurgence of interest in critical Marxist theory. At the same time, the publishing institutions committed to Marxism have contracted markedly since the high point of the 1970s. The Historical Materialism Book Series is dedicated to addressing this situation by making available important works of Marxist theory. The aim of the series is to publish important theoretical contributions as the basis for vigorous intellectual debate and exchange on the left.

The peer-reviewed series publishes original monographs, translated texts, and reprints of classics across the bounds of academic disciplinary agendas and across the divisions of the left. The series is particularly concerned to encourage the internationalization of Marxist debate and aims to translate significant studies from beyond the English-speaking world.

For a full list of titles in the Historical Materialism Book Series
available in paperback from Haymarket Books, visit:
www.haymarketbooks.org/category/hm-series

'Bitter with the Past but Sweet with the Dream': Communism in the African American Imaginary

Representations of the Communist Party, 1940–1952

by
Cathy Bergin

Haymarket Books
Chicago, IL

First published in 2015 by Brill Academic Publishers, The Netherlands
© 2015 Koninklijke Brill NV, Leiden, The Netherlands

Published in paperback in 2016 by
Haymarket Books
P.O. Box 180165
Chicago, IL 60618
773-583-7884
www.haymarketbooks.org

ISBN: 978-1-60846-639-9

Trade distribution:
In the US, Consortium Book Sales, www.cbsd.com
In Canada, Publishers Group Canada, www.pgcbooks.ca
In the UK, Turnaround Publisher Services, www.turnaround-uk.com
In all other countries, Publishers Group Worldwide, www.pgw.com

Cover design by Jamie Kerry of Belle Étoile Studios and Ragina Johnson.

This book was published with the generous support of
Lannan Foundation and the Wallace Global Fund.

Printed in Canada by union labor.

10 9 8 7 6 5 4 3 2 1

Library of Congress Cataloging-in-Publication data is available.

This book is dedicated to the memory of Johnny Bergin
(1938–2014)

∴

Contents

Acknowledgements

This book, like any intellectual endeavour, and particularly any socialist intellectual endeavour, has not been a solo project. I have enjoyed endless support. My colleagues in the Humanities Programme at Brighton have been instrumental in providing the intellectual and pedagogic atmosphere where interdisciplinary work is not merely tolerated or paid lip service to but is positively and actively promoted. It is a wonderful environment in which to research and teach. My thanks to my colleagues, Mark Abel, Bob Brecher, Graham Dawson, Mark Devenney, Paul Hopper, Peter Jackson, Andy Knott, Anthony Leaker, Paddy Maguire, Victoria Margree, Eugene Michail, Michael Neu, Lucy Noakes, Jason Porter, Gill Scott and Jon Watson. In particular, both Anita Rupprecht and Tom Hickey have been helpful, engaged and encouraging well beyond the call of duty. For their intellectual input, political incisiveness, comradeship and friendship I am extremely grateful.

Marcus Wood, who supervised my doctoral work on Communism and African-American writing, did so with great enthusiasm and encouragement. My year three seminar groups on African-American Writing have provided lively and incisive spaces for unpicking this rich literary and cultural field. My doctoral students Nicola Clewer, Jessica Hamlin and Jason Porter's very different research projects have enriched my understanding of my own work.

Over the years Patricia McManus has afforded me time, insights, numerous conversations and constructive criticism about my work which proved invaluable. Moreover all of the above were offered in a spirit of intellectual enthusiasm and generosity. Her valued friendship and her unflagging interest in my work transformed the final stages of writing this book.

Naomi Ashman, Brendan Donohoe, Theodore Koulouris and Sallie Richards have been excellent friends throughout this process, often providing much needed avenues of escape. I apologise for occasionally boring them to tears. I would also like to thank Daisy Asquith, Clare Baker, Jim Casey, Debbie De Wit, Amira Driscoll, Ann Duffy, June Du Halgouet, Steve Edwards, Danny Hayward, Brian Hanley, Melissa Halpin, Geetha Jayaramen, David Johnson, Brian Kelly, Shad Khan, Ian McDonald, Meredith Miller, Ken Mulkearn, Eleanor Norman, Chantelle Norton, Louise Purbrick, Kevin Reynolds, Lucy Robinson, Ian Sinclair, Brid Smith, Christine Smith, Mary Smith, and Aaron Winter.

My sisters Fiona, Susan and Barbara Bergin, and my aunt Clare Murphy have been enthusiastic and supportive of my work, if somewhat surly about my emigrant status. Along with my two nieces Kit and Ella Connolly they have provided the appropriately female-centred family from which to write about 'masculinity.'

John Duffy sustained me in a myriad of ways during the 'difficult' times and provided a near perfect environment in which to conduct research. For his love, patience, wit and wisdom and much more besides I am in his debt.

To my parents Johnny and Marie Bergin no thanks are fully adequate. I would not have been able to complete this book or indeed my studies more generally without their help. Their consistent and seemingly endless resources of love, support and encouragement in this, as in all else, have been immeasurable. Johnny's death in the summer of 2014 robbed our family of a unique and wonderful man. This book is dedicated to him.

Introduction

> I speak in the name of the black millions
> Awakening to Communism.
> Let all others keep silent a moment
> I have this word to bring,
> This thing to say,
> This song to sing...
>
> ... For now
> In many mouths
> Dark mouths where red tongues burn
> And white teeth gleam
> New words are formed
> Bitter with the past
> But sweet
> With the dream.[1]

Langston Hughes's demand for silence so he can articulate his vision where 'the Black/ and Red world/ Now are one', expresses a distinctive African American Communist voice which can speak both from and beyond the boundaries of race.[2] In Depression and post-Depression America, this voice did not emerge in silence but competed with a cacophony of voices vying for the allegiance of African-American communities. This struggle to win the hearts and minds of black America generated powerful models of black political identity which impacted upon a generation of African-American writers.

Given the diversity of political formations with which African-American writers could have engaged (emigrationist, integrationist, separatist, socialist), their engagement with Communists raises a question. Why is it in this particular historical period that writers concerned with the construction of modern African-American identity engage with the Communist Party to such a degree?

The tension between race and class as sites and vehicles of both oppression and resistance has shaped the nature of that resistance for over 250 years. That tension comes to us via the class fissures that characterise both the struggles and the self-identities and objectives of the African independence

---

1 Langston Hughes, 'A New Song' in the *Liberator* 15 October 1932, p. 5.
2 Ibid.

movements in the twentieth century. It comes to us via the USA in post-bellum sharecropping struggles in the South, and the fight for unionisation in Northern cities, in the principles of Wobbly organisation and those of DRUM against the institutional racism of the AFL-CIO. It also comes to us in the eruption of Black Panther resistance as a strategic alternative to the 'moral force' orientation of the Civil Rights movement. This study is concerned with this tension in a particular historical moment and through a rendering of its articulation in three literary texts.

In the USA in the 1930s and 1940s, the intricate ideological and political currents swirling around the Communist Party, black politics and race history, constitute a difficult and shifting terrain. This book is a Marxist analysis of that terrain undertaken in order to comprehend the discursive field which generated the literary responses of African-American novelists.

The influence of Communism in early- and mid-twentieth-century America has been the source of extensive historiographical research. From the 1950s on, and intensifying during the Cold War, historians claimed that American Communism was essentially a doomed foreign project and that the CPUSA was merely a tool of Soviet foreign policy and the dictates of the Comintern. Theodore Draper is a major exponent of this view, as are Howe & Coser, while Harvey Klehr's *The Heyday of American Communism* explicitly states his indebtedness to Draper's methodology.[3] From the 1950s onwards a series of writers concerned with Communism and race also concentrated on the presumed 'alien' nature of American Communism. In 1951 Wilson Record's influential *The Negro and the Communist Party* cast Marxism as an opportunist interloper which preyed on the hardship of black Americans. Harold Cruse's *Crisis of the Negro Intellectual* concentrated on how Communist influence 'smothered' and 'choked' black cultural expression.[4]

This interpretative tradition, however, has recently been challenged by an extensive body of work published by writers who emphasise a history from 'below'.[5] Important work by a range of scholars has overturned both the historical and aesthetic truisms which governed understandings of Communist activism during the Cold War. These works acknowledge the effects of Stalinism but stress equally the activities of rank-and-file Communists in day-to-day struggles against racism and poverty. Philip Foner's exhaustive studies detail the nature

---

3 Draper 1957 and 1960; Howe and Coser 1962; Klehr 1984.

4 Cruse 1969, p. 187.

5 'Below' here is not a technical or theoretical term but rather a descriptive one, although Kelley has written precisely about the importance of the tradition of history from below. See Kelley 1993, pp. 75–112.

of black working-class struggle and in particular the way in which industrial struggles generated a particular type of black yet working-class consciousness.[6] Paul Buhle focuses on the ethnic diversity which characterises the American Communist movement and enables an understanding of Communism as far from monolithic or homogeneic. Mark Naison and Robin Kelley have both written intricate histories of black Communist experiences during the Depression, histories which stress the day-to-day activities of African American Communists.[7] Mark Solomon has also written about rank-and-file black Party members and the continually contradictory relationship between Party dictates and Party practice.[8] This latter historical approach is largely consistent with the theoretical trajectory of this book. I am not writing a *history* of this period but my methodological approach necessarily incorporates a strong emphasis on the social and political history of the CPUSA's relationship to race in the United States.

Whilst the historiography of this period, as traced briefly above, has been challenged in the post-Cold War years, the literary-critical field is a more recent site of contestation. As Bill Mullen has observed, two influential and valuable anthologies of African-American writing periodise twentieth-century African-American literature in such a way as to erase the relationship between black writers and the Left – a relationship which arguably dominated African-American culture during the Depression.[9] Yet works in the field of literary history indicate a shift towards a reinterpretation of black culture in this period. To take two examples, James Edward Smethurst's *The New Red Negro: The Literary Left and African American Poetry, 1930–1946* and William J. Maxwell's *New Negro Old Left: African–American Writing and Communism Between the Wars*.[10] Smethurst addresses the lack of literary scholarship on black Communist poetry of the era, and conducts a dynamic re-reading of important black poets, within the context of CPUSA politics.[11] Maxwell's book focuses on the interracial collaborations, mainly of the Harlem Renaissance period, and argues that the 'history of African-American letters cannot be unravelled from the history of American Communism without damage to both'.[12] Both these texts are valuable studies

---

6   Foner 1974, and 1987.

7   Buhle 1991; Naison 1985; Kelley 1990, and 1994.

8   Solomon 1998.

9   Mullen 2001, pp. 148–9.

10   Other recent work on African-American literature and the Left include Mullen and Smethurst (eds.) 2003; Morgan 2004; Lubin (ed.) 2007.

11   Notably Langston Hughes, Sterling Brown and Countee Cullen.

12   Maxwell 1999, p. 2.

of the period and offer critical interpretations which, like this study, stress historical overlaps between the CPUSA and black Americans.

These texts are illustrative of the interpretive productivity of a return to a close reading of history in the examination of mid-century African-American cultural production. Unlike the dominant literary tradition which evades, underplays, or devalues the impact of American Communism on black writers of the period, these more recent studies scrutinise the influence of American left-wing politics on the African American cultural milieu.[13] The re-configuration of the political relationship between race and class in mid-century African American letters is the subject and ambition of this book.

Three seminal novels written by African-American men in the mid-twentieth century are dominated by representations of the Communist Party. Richard Wright's *Native Son* (1940), Chester Himes's *Lonely Crusade* (1947) and Ralph Ellison's *Invisible Man* (1952) generate very different black male subjectivities; notwithstanding the differences of these subjectivities, they are all predicated on encounters with the Communist Party. These literary representations of the Communist Party neither simply vindicate nor indict Marxism. Despite the wildly different interpretations of the CPUSA in the novels, all are structured on a remarkably similar model of race/class dynamics produced by the encounter between Communists and African Americans in the 1930s. Wright's, Himes's and Ellison's Communists may appear to conform to later narratives of Communist 'exploitation' of black activists, writers and artists. This appearance is only persuasive, however, if these representations are read through the *post-history* of these texts' circulation rather than the *pre-history* of their production.

This study provides a contextual framework through which to read these novels, a framework which maintains a detailed focus on the historically specific Communist milieu out of which these texts operated. The polemical purpose of this book is to make legible the black subjectivity which structures the work of these three African-American writers, a subjectivity, I argue, which is contingent on particular models of Communist identity. Moreover, this discursive subject is remarkably alert to the complexity of black history and black possibility in a society infected with the legacy of slavery.

I should draw attention to how this discursive subject is unambiguously 'masculine'. The reasons for black male writers' elision of black female subjectivities are complex but result in these black male authored texts operating a rigid gender dichotomy. Arguably none of the three novels can afford to complicate or render contingent their models of black subjectivity by bringing the

---

13   See Chapter 3.

latter into any close relation with the 'feminine'. The discursive struggle these novels are involved in sets out the terrain of subjectivity as always already masculine: Wright, Himes and Ellison do not disrupt this terrain on gender terms. Whilst I do draw attention to local instances in which the novels need to exclude black women so as to keep black masculinity absolute, my focus on the imbrication of race and gender in American racism remains within the paradigms of 'masculinity'.[14]

By concentrating on the representation of the Communist Party in black male authored texts, I explore the models of agency (political and aesthetic) in the repertoire of African American male writers of the period. The working hypothesis involved here is that certain Communist models of black identity structured and informed the black literary imagination in these texts. This phenomenon has not been *ignored* by literary criticism, but its significance needs to be disentangled from other dominant critical paradigms which assume that Communism was *apriori* an alienating interloper which negated 'true' forms of black identity. Larry Neal, for example, writes of Ellison: 'But luckily for us, his work never took on the simplistic assertions of the literary Marxist. Therefore Ellison's clearly articulated break with naturalism must also be seen in light of his previous awareness that hardcore ideologues, particularly Communists, represented an awesome threat not only to his artistic sensibility, but to his "national" sensibility as well'.[15]

This formulation of Communism as 'threatening' modern black subjectivity pervades literary critical approaches to mid-century African-American writing and will be examined in the discussion of my subject novels. The various literary critical interpretations of Wright, Himes and Ellison, albeit belonging to no coherent movement or adhering to no overt ideological agenda, are informed and affirmed by relevant work within the field of cultural and identity politics. Within this field, a formative paradigm can be traced at work in the understanding of the structures and symbolic systems constitutive of discourses of African-American identity. This approach to identity posits it as a fragmented and marginal site which resists Marxist appropriation. To take one example:

> It is precisely this essentialist privileging of the working class, the radical (male) intellectual, and later the Party as the agents 'making history' – and the attendant deployment of Marxism as an all-inclusive, self-sufficient

---

14   For an illuminating study of a contemporary female author, Anne Petry, see Lubin (ed.) 2007.

15   Neal 1990, p. 107.

grand narrative of social revolution – that radical post modernism and
the new identity politics . . . have worked to deconstruct.[16]

This stress on marginality and fragmentation, coupled with a determination
to construe Marxism as homogeneous and inflexible, results in a theoretical projection of black identity as incommensurate with the political subject
demanded by the totalising logic of Communist discourses of the era. These
particular formulations of identity construction form less of an academic project or movement than they do an underlying logic in African American and
post-colonial literary criticism, a logic which privileges the 'politics of discrete
exclusivities and localisms'.[17]

In terms of certain variants of racial identity politics, understanding race
as the exclusive matrix of any group's *experience* radically limits the political forms available to those groups: as Manning Marable has pointed out:
'The prism of a group's racial experiences tends to blunt the parallels, conti-
nuities and common interests which might exist between oppressed racial
groups, and highlights and emphasises areas of dissension and antagonism'.[18]
The inter-war Communist Party concentration on the common interests of
African-American workers, black workers internationally *and* the black and
white American proletariat, is consequently distinctly unfashionable within
the context of identity politics. Dominant interpretations of these novels insist
on the inability of class-based politics to comprehend racial oppression; such
interpretations cannot account for the sheer scale of the textual engagement
with Communism, or for the dominance of the Communist Party in the structuring of black identity in the novels.[19]

The assumption at work in many literary critical approaches to the novels
is that Wright, Himes and Ellison renounce the supposed self-cancellation
demanded by Marxist determinism in their quest for black subjectivity. I
argue, however, that none of these novels suggest that black identity is a site of
experiential exclusiveness predicated on *difference*. Wright, Himes and Ellison
all present models of black identity which challenge concepts of transhis-
toric 'blackness' – whether that 'blackness' is imagined either as an inherently

---

16   Soja and Hooper 1993, p. 201.

17   Ahmad 1992, p. 65. For a lively historical account of the dominance of identity politics in
      the US academy in the 1990s, see pp. 43–71.

18   Marable 1993, p. 118.

19   One critic of *Lonely Crusade*, for example, insists that 'frequent allusion to the Communist
      Party and Communism in the novel serve *only* as a technical device' (my emphasis). Carl
      Hughes 1967, p. 48.

oppositional self-positioning or as an objectified state of persistent marginality. Rather, African-American identity in these novels is a site of possibility which is unashamedly connected to agency, emancipation, ideology and history.[20] The *experience* of blackness here is not the sum of black identity. The latter is rather the meaning ascribed to this experience, the possible solidarities and alliances which arise out of this experience and the shaping of this experience into a meaningful struggle to transform both self and the wider world.

Although Wright, Himes and Ellison produce different modes of black identity, difference for them is not a post-modern site of play, 'blackness' is not emptied of historically contingent power relations, nor does race serve as an inter-textual 'trope' of difference.[21] 'Blackness' is historical, dynamic and material. Historically determinate structures inform both black identities and black resistance. All three writers insist on the possibility, and desirability, of interracial collaboration as a condition of meeting the demands of challenging racist discourses and practices. The solution which each of the subject novelists arrive at in order to combat racist projections of 'blackness' are, of course, very different, but the struggle of the fictional antagonists is conducted within a context saturated with Communism.

This study dislocates the novels discussed from modes of criticism which sublimate the significance of the fictional representation of Communism. The point is to reinscribe the dialectic between the texts and their *pre-history* in order to access a historically specific model of African-American identity. This model resisted both separatism and race blind assimilation, and was informed by a political prioritisation of interracial *class* solidarity.

I have structured the book in two parts which, taken together, trace a historical trajectory. The first part focuses on the genesis of the Communist policy on the 'Negro question,' and concentrates on key political interventions around race which transformed the CPUSA's relationship with black Americans during the 'Third Period'. Within this historical context I conduct a reading of the black Communist newspaper the *Liberator* and Richard Wright's 1941 novel *Native Son*. The second part of the book interrogates the effects of the Popular Front and the Second World War on the Communist intervention in black communities. This historical moment, in which American Communism attempted

---

20   This vision stands in direct contention with a variety of models of identity. For example Patricia Huntington tells us: 'The post-modern world we inhabit is enveloped by a social climate of retrenchment to local forms of life that do not, in actual fact, adhere to any broader moral obligation or humanist vision that transcends a local set of interests'. Huntington 1997, p. 190.

21   See Gates Jr. 1988, p. xxiv.

to fuse with the national war effort, has informed much of the hostility to the CPUSA's engagement with anti-racism; a hostility apparent in both Himes's *Lonely Crusade* (1947) and Ellison's *Invisible Man* (1952).

This structure may seem to reflect a literary-historical convention which separates all pre-War from post-War work. To pre-empt this worry, I want to emphasise the conviction which animates the following chapters, which is that a rich set of purposes and resources unify pre- and post-War black writing. At one level the Second World War obviously provided a break in historical narratives, but no historical moment is composed of one totalising narrative. The challenges faced by Himes and Ellison, as writers concerned with con- structions of black identity in the post-War period, are marked by the sense of 'betrayal' engendered by Communist activity during the Second World War. This study is also concerned, however, to demonstrate the many ways in which Communist discourses of the 1930s provided all three writers with models of identity against which a black subject could be defined. This focus demon- strates the endurance of both the desire of black writers to remodel a black self, and the power of Communism in the collective imaginary of the writers dedicated to this task.

Chapter One focuses on specific moments of Communist anti-racist theory and practice in the late 1920s and early 1930s. The aim is to examine the impact of a radical political ideology which sought to disturb the traditional dialectics of race and class. Communist Party praxis in this era generated key models of black political identity, models which are drawn upon in the fictional repre- sentations of the subject novels.

Chapter Two is a study of the African American Communist newspaper the *Liberator*. This newspaper, which ran for just under five years, is very much a text of the Comintern's Third Period, not least in its ruthlessly sectarian yet powerful critiques of the African-American bourgeoisie. Such attacks enabled the paper to construct an alternative model of black identity. This model was resistant to compromise and reached back into a radical black history as well as contemporary Communism for its origin and purpose. My focus is on how the *Liberator* delineated the discursive models used by Communist activists to create a representational space in which race and class could coincide to produce a convincing model of black Communist agency.

Chapter Three places my analysis of *Native Son* in relation to the theoreti- cal framework of the proceeding chapters in order to access a historically- specific African-American consciousness of race and class. As with the *Liberator*, and indeed my other subject novels, competing models of African-American identity are produced in order to define a resistant black identity. In *Native Son* that resistant identity is formed in opposition to both white supremacist projections and accommodationist passivity. In this novel, black subjectivity is a process rather than an essence.[22] It is precisely the question of political solidarity, the articulation of common interests, which allows for the articulation of a tremulous and painful black self-identity.

Chapter Four maintains a thematic focus on specific historical events which illuminate the representations of the Communist Party in the core novels. The chapter looks at the move away from the Third Period to the Popular Front and the impact of this on the centrality of African-American cultural forms to Communist politics. It also examines the war-time activities of the CPUSA and its increasing commitment to 'Americanisation'. This complex period of CPUSA history, which often saw a rise in black membership of the Party, is one which necessitates a careful engagement with the often contradictory elements of CPUSA politics during the War.

Chapter Five is a reading of *Lonely Crusade*. It takes issue with the argument that Himes's negative portrayal of the Communist Party in the novel is a simple repudiation. Rather, attention is focused on the potent models of black male identity that are circulated through his representation of the Communist Party. These models are central to the assertion of a black masculine identity which structures *Lonely Crusade*. Much standard reception of the novel is flawed by the fact that Himes is often read through a Cold War paradigm. Many of Himes's criticisms of the Party, however, are historically and politically contingent on Communist politics in the 1940s, and the models of black political identity which proliferate in the text echo the politics of the Communist Party of the 1930s. Thus, the anti-Communist invective in the novel differs from what was to become generic anti-Communist dogma in the 1950s and 1960s.

Chapter Six provides a textual analysis of *Invisible Man* which locates Ellison's representation of the Communist Party within its cultural and historical moment. The focus of the chapter is on Ellison's early theoretical writings rather than his later anti-Communist aesthetics which often form the framework for literary critics of *Invisible Man*. The chapter is an investigation of how Ellison textually constructs the Communist Party as a barrier to both African-American identity and American responsibility: thus there is a repudiation of Communism as a coercive co-opter of black self-hood. While *Invisible Man* marked a decisive break between black writers and Communism, I argue that the earlier models of black Communist identity identified in this study also structure the text.

Bringing historical and literary critical discourses into dialogue can be a fraught and clunky business. The pitfalls are numerous and no doubt this book

---

22   Hall 1994, pp. 392–401.

has fallen into some of them. However, this study is founded upon a commitment to examining the local and specific historical context in which these
texts were produced. The textual analysis of the three novels which follows is
informed by the complex formations of black political agency presumed and
reproduced by American Communism in the 1930s and 1940s.

PART 1

Radical Alliances

∵

Introduction to Part 1

In June 1931, Ada Wright, an African-American working-class woman from Alabama, with no history of political activism, addressed a mass meeting in Amsterdam on the subject of racism and American Imperialism. In addition to appealing for support for her son who was framed on a rape charge in Scottsboro Alabama, her speeches attacked the 'social fascism' of the European social democrats and urged 'mobilization of the masses against the imperialist war'.[1]

This unusual spectacle of a desperate mother reading what seemed to be set speeches written by Communist ideologues is suggestive of how the CPUSA cynically used African-American victims of racism to swell their ranks, and give credibility to their sectarian attacks on reformist movements. However, the example of Ada Wright is significant on many levels and exemplifies the contradictory politics not only of the CPUSA, but also of the era. The history of the CPUSA and its relationship to African Americans is also a history of the contemporary political climate and the battle for the hearts and minds of a new generation of African-American workers and activists. The very fact that a political organisation would seek credibility by having a southern black working-class woman speak for them immediately estranges them from other organisations concerned with 'race' and class in the United States in the 1930s. That Ada Wright and the other parents of the Scottsboro boys put their trust and their sons' lives in the hands of the Communists, the American nation's pariah, is enormously significant. The story of US Communism and black struggle in the Depression years is the account of an intense struggle against American racism and a deep commitment to interracial class solidarity.

It is not my intention to give an empirical or uncritical account of Communist intervention in black struggles. Part 1 of this book is an interrogation of the claims which the CPUSA made for itself. I will focus on specific moments of Communist anti-racist practice in the late 1920s and early 1930s in order to examine the impact of a radical political ideology which sought to disturb the traditional dialectics of race and class. The relations between the CPUSA and the Comintern have structured much of the historiography of this period. In the 1920s it was often the politics of liberation encapsulated in Bolshevism, rather than the compulsion to defend Mother Russia, which attracted African-American radicals. The Bolshevik tradition cannot be sublimated into the failures of Stalinism.

---

1 Carter 1969, p. 172.

This point is key. The ultimate failure of the Stalinist CPUSA to secure its position as vanguard of the black working-class is often posited as illustrative of the inability of Marxism, as a 'European Enlightenment' ideology, to divest itself of its white ethnocentric presumptions. In this rubric, Marxism's original sin is its dualism: a fixation on the dialectic of class struggle which eschews the ambivalences and dislocations of race, a methodological move which, it is argued, guarantees that it is deeply implicated in the very traditions which ensure the continuation of racist oppression.[2] While obviously this was not the view of those early black communists who were attracted to the Party, it was also not, as I argue in Part 2, the perspective of those disillusioned African Americans who broke with Communism. There is no suggestion here of a 'before and after Stalin', or of positing a 'true' Marxist tradition. Rather, I investigate the genealogy of black Communist political identity whose heyday was realised under the Stalinist hegemony of the working-class movement worldwide but whose theoretical roots cannot be reduced to that legacy.

For African-American Communists the act of resistance in articulating the nature of racist oppression was also an act of relocating that voice into an international movement against all oppression, whilst simultaneously maintaining the specificity of racism. This internationalist framing of American racism, not only as an element of the global class struggle but also into a worldwide movement of the racially oppressed, was an overriding element of Communist praxis in the early 1930s. The CPUSA strove to create a movement which would redefine the American racial landscape. It was a battle on three fronts – against white supremacy, against black reformism and against black separatism. The CPUSA attempted to unite white and black workers and tried to separate the black working class from its traditional leaders.[3]

If the CPUSA was successful in convincing a sizeable minority of black workers that Marxism could eradicate racism, it is essential to investigate exactly what type of Marxism they were proposing. What were the theoretical foundations of the CPUSA's radicalism on race? That the limitations of the CPUSA were the limitations of Marxism is a truism which dominated Cold War histories of the period and many literary-critical engagements with my core writers. This assumption has severely obscured our understanding of African American involvement with the CPUSA. The historical and theoretical underpinnings of the Third International are necessary to comprehend the particular brand of

---

2 For a comprehensive overview of the debates about the *ability* of Marxism to speak to issues of 'race' see Bakan 2008, pp. 238–66.

3 'Black reformism' here, is a term directly related to the specific organisations of the time (especially the NAACP) which sought to agitate for racial reforms within the system.

Marxism which dominated the CPUSA. This question is more pressing given the proposition that Marxism as a Eurocentric, alien economism is ill-suited to even comprehend the complexities of racism.[4]

---

4 This characterisation of Marxism is true even of more sympathetic theorists like Cedric Robinson, who identifies Marxism as an important and influential but irredeemably European philosophy which was responsible for the 'cultural debilitation' of the black radical tradition. See Robinson 1983.

CHAPTER 1

'Towards Soviet America'

1.1   Determinations and Determinism: Lenin, Stalin and the Comintern

> Lenin is our teacher
> We shall not be moved
> Just like a tree that's standing by the water
> We shall not be moved![1]

Communists in the 1930s held a particular worldview in which struggles against injustice were part of a world-wide revolutionary movement which sought the destruction of capitalism. Yet this movement was also dominated by a 'Socialist' state which far from being the instrument for international revolution, consistently sacrificed revolutionary possibilities to secure its national interests. The contradiction between global Party orthodoxies and daily activities, between Party doctrine and local contingencies, mirror the complexity of the history of twentieth-century Marxism. A detailed analysis of this complexity is beyond the scope of this study. The activities of the CPUSA, however, cannot be understood in isolation from the impact of both the Russian Revolution, and the hegemonic status of the Soviet Union. Traditional histories of the CPUSA often concentrate exclusively on the internal political structures of the Party and its relationship to the Comintern under Stalin.[2] Here, I am more concerned with the impact of the Bolshevik revolution on questions of self-determination, not least because the models of black identity generated by American Communism found embryonic expression in the Communist definitions of self-determination in the wake of the Russian Revolution.

From its early days the American Communist Party had voiced a commitment to ending racial oppression in the United States. The Party declared at their 1922 convention that:

---

1   Sung by Eula Gray, the niece of murdered black share-cropper Ralph Gray at the CPUSA convention 1934; see Haywood 1978, p. 418.

2   See Draper 1960 and Klehr 1984 as examples of this historical approach. More recently Eric Arnesen has suggested that the revisionist historians from below have overstated the significance of rank-and-file Party activity: see Arnesen 2006, pp. 13–52.

The Negro workers of this country are exploited and oppressed more ruthlessly than any other group. The history of the Southern Negro is the history of brutal terrorism, of persecution and of murder ... the Worker's Party [later CPUSA] will seek to end the policy of discrimination followed by the labour unions. It will endeavour to destroy altogether the barriers of race prejudice that have been used to keep apart the Black and white workers and weld them into a solid mass for the struggle against the Capitalists who exploit them.[3]

Yet prior to the 1930s the Party was isolated from the majority of black workers. It was reluctant to engage with specific black demands and its abstract anti-racist sentiments existed in a vacuum. Apart from recruiting a small militant black cadre, they had made no serious impact in terms of black membership.[4] A turning point came in 1928 at the Sixth Congress of the Third International, when the Party adopted the self-determination of the Black Belt thesis. This argued that black Americans in the Southern States constituted an oppressed nation possessed of the right to self-determination, and that Northern blacks constituted a national minority who were denied social, political and economic equality.

Although the policy of self-determination for the Black Belt was both controversial and ambiguous, occupying a fraught space within Leninist orthodoxy, this unambiguous recognition of African Americans as a specifically oppressed group with particular demands, emerged out of the Party's determination to demonstrate its commitment to black struggle. It was a theory of autonomy and solidarity, which placed black Americans within the brotherhood of the exploited working class and simultaneously positioned them as racially oppressed subjects of the American State. This, as Paul Buhle points out, was of enormous significance; the 1928 resolution introduced a new imperative for Americans to support Black struggles as 'black race consciousness was identified as revolutionary in and of itself'.[5]

The genesis and effectiveness of self-determination in this context, has been debated extensively in the historiography of the period. I do not wish

---

3   Quoted in Foner and Shapiro 1987, p. 20.
4   Although notably in the early 1920s the Communists attracted a sizeable section of the black nationalist African Blood Brotherhood (ABB) discussed below. For a detailed analysis of the influence of Caribbean radicals in Harlem in the 1920s and the relationship between the ABB and the Communist Party, see Solomon 1998, pp. 3–22.
5   Buhle 1991, p. 139.

to reproduce those arguments here.[6] Mark Solomon's meticulous work on the Sixth Congress gives a fascinating account of how the thesis was born from a combination of factional battles within the CPUSA, black Communists' frustration with the Party's inaction on the Negro question, Comintern directives about the nature of the period, and debates over Lenin's theory of self-determination of oppressed nations. Solomon's work refutes the belief, commonly held amongst Cold War historians, that the self-determination for the Black Belt thesis was simply foisted on American Communists by the Comintern. While Solomon shows that Moscow was instrumental in the adoption of the thesis, he also attempts to unravel the complex relationship between national, international, Soviet and black interests which informed the adoption of the thesis.[7]

The Black Belt thesis was initially rejected by all but one of the black delegates at the Sixth Congress of the Comintern. Only Harry Haywood, who had co-drafted the original document, accepted the proposition that blacks in the Southern States constituted a nation. As late as 1930 he was attempting to convince other black cadre of the necessity of the thesis.[8] As Solomon points out:

> Ironically, the power of self-determination lay not in its theoretical validity, but in its pragmatic implications. It undercut those who subordinated the struggle for Negro rights to the class question, or who equated the two – thus devaluing the centrality of Negro liberation for revolutionary change... The theoretical and programmatic elements of self-determination may have been painfully hard to define, but the concept nevertheless drove Communists into a frenzy of struggle for equality and black liberation.[9]

The key lay in the organisational implication of the new analysis of the 'Negro question,' yet the fact that the impetus for this change came from Moscow is not inconsequential. By identifying the 'Negro question' as a national question, American Communists could recognise the specificities of the local situation while drawing on a wider theoretical framework. The Communist tradition

---

6 The self-determination thesis has been the subject of much debate, see Record 1951, pp. 55–119; Kanet 1971, pp. 86–123; Naison 1985, pp. 18–22; Solomon 1998, pp. 68–91; Allen 1974, pp. 207–45; Klehr and Tompson 1989, pp. 354–66; Zumoff 2012, pp. 53–89.

7 Solomon 1998, pp. 38–52.

8 Foner and Shapiro 1987, pp. 17–35.

9 Solomon 1998, p. 87.

could now 'own' the national question and reformulate it to specific local needs. As Harry Haywood states it, the revolutionary implications fired the young black Communists of the period:

> Thus, the new line brought the issue of black equality out of the realm of bourgeois humanitarianism. It was no longer the special property of the philanthropists and professional up-lifters who sought to strip the black struggle of its revolutionary implications.[10]

The adoption of the Black Belt thesis was not merely illustrative of the relationship between Moscow and the CPUSA; as argued by Cold War historians, it also provided a specific 'ownership' of 'the Negro question' in the Party in opposition to philanthropic demands. The assertion that American racism in the 'black belt' constituted African Americans as a national minority located them clearly within Lenin's theory of self-determination, for an understanding of which attention needs to turn, however briefly, to the Second International.

At the onset of the First World War the Second International's professed internationalism was revealed to be an illusion, infamously summed up by the remark of the leader of the German Social Democrats, Karl Kautsky, that the 'International is an instrument for peace, not for war'.[11] As the major Social Democratic parties lined up opportunistically to support their own ruling classes in the War, only the Bolsheviks, the Serbs and the Bulgarian Socialists had a majority of their parties opposed to the War.[12] Although there were major debates about the status of nationalism within the Second International, particularly between Lenin, Rosa Luxemburg and Otto Bauer, they had never had a unified formal position on the national question. The depressing haste with which the major European socialist parties embraced jingoistic patriotism in an imperialist war constituted an abandonment of any solidarity with those fighting colonial oppression. Even among the anti-war Socialists remaining in the International, the general call was a pacifist one. Lenin was in a minority when he called for a revolutionary defeatist position – that Socialists should call for the defeat of their own ruling classes and turn the imperialist war into a civil war.[13]

---

10   Haywood 1978, p. 279.
11   Quoted in Munck 1986, p. 36.
12   Nimni 1991, pp. 44–70.
13   Gankin and Fisher 1940, p. 151.

Lenin ceased to be a minority voice on the national question with the victory of the Bolshevik Revolution. The fact that the Revolution had occurred
not, as expected, in the advanced West, but in the vast, largely un-industrialised
East, was of particular significance. The national minorities had played a major
part in the break up of the Tsarist Empire in 1917, and as the Revolution failed
to spread to the West, the Bolsheviks turned their attentions to the East.[14] The
experience of the Bolsheviks had illustrated that for a proletarian revolution to
be successful in an industrially undeveloped country, non-proletarians – the
peasantry and those suffering nationalist oppression – had to be mobilised
and won over to a Marxist perspective. Lenin insisted that far from being a
European phenomenon, capitalism was a globalised system and national racial
oppression was intrinsic to the workings of that system.[15] Therefore, even
prior to the Revolution, the Bolsheviks represented a new internationalism.
Lenin's theory of self-determination (1916), which emphasised that the 'bourgeois nationalism of any oppressed nation' had a 'general democratic content
that is directed *against* oppression' which Communists must 'unconditionally
support', represented a seismic shift away from the narrow nationalism of the
Second International.[16] Lenin stressed that the support of anti-imperialism
was fundamental to the Socialist cause, stating in 1916 that:

> Socialist parties which did not show by all their activity, both now, during
> the revolution and after its victory, that they would liberate the enslaved
> nations and build up relations with them on the basis of a free union –
> and free union is a false phrase without the right to secede – these parties
> would be betraying socialism.[17]

The emphasis on the *right* of oppressed nations to secede from oppressor
nations was a radical departure. However, Lenin's theory of the right of nations
to self-determination was articulated within the context of a revolutionary
politics seeking to destroy the capitalist order. Support for national struggles
was *strategic* insofar as those struggles were understood in terms of a wider
working-class struggle.

Consequently support for national movements against oppression was not
an endorsement of *nationalism* but a commitment to fighting imperialism.

---

14   Smith 1999, p. 51.
15   Allen 1974, p. 210.
16   Lenin 1964a, p. 412.
17   Lenin 1964b, p. 143.

Central to the theory was the belief that, in the event of a revolution, national minorities would associate themselves with the world-wide proletariat. The instrument for furthering the cause of world revolution was the Comintern or the Third International, which was born in 1919 in the euphoric aftermath of October when international revolution seemed imminently possible. This was the first Socialist movement which attempted to link the cause of the industrial proletariat with anti-colonial struggles. The Comintern insisted on anti-imperialism as a condition of membership; the Conditions of Admission to the Communist International in 1920 demanded that:

> Every Party... is obliged to expose the tricks and dodges of 'its' imperialists in the colonies, to support every colonial liberation movement, not merely in words but in deeds, to demand the expulsion of their own imperialists from these colonies.[18]

The early years of the Comintern saw a series of critical debates about the relationship between anti-colonial struggle and socialism, debates that were held in an atmosphere of urgent anticipation.[19] The question of race in the United States was debated in this atmosphere. As early as 1920 Lenin warned American Communists that they ignored racism at their peril and emphasised that blacks were 'a strategically important element in Communist activity'.[20] The Fourth Congress of the International in 1922 saw the formation of a 'Negro Commission' and lengthy discussions on the status of black workers in the States, including a speech by the Jamaican-American writer Claude McKay, who stated baldly that there was a 'great element of prejudice among the Socialists and Communists of America' who were simply 'not willing to face the Negro Question'.[21] McKay addressed a series of questions on the matter to Trotsky, whose response was representative of general frustration with the CPUSA's inactivity on the 'Negro question': 'Every 10 Negroes who gather around the flag of revolution, and unite to form a group for practical work among the

---

18 Eighth condition for affiliation to the Comintern, quoted in Degras 1971, Vol. 1, p. 170.

19 The Second Congress of the Comintern in 1920 was the scene for intense debates on nationalism, especially between Lenin and the Indian Marxist M.N. Roy: see Communist International, 1920, pp. 117–35.

20 Draper 1960, p. 322.

21 Cooper 1973, p. 95.

Negroes, are worth a hundred times more than dozens of the resolutions establishing principles, so generously passed by the Second International'.[22]

There was widespread impatience with the American comrades' lack of progress in recruiting black workers. The Comintern was instrumental in forcing the issue of race to the forefront of Party activity, and as has been widely noted, the American Party was particularly dependent on Moscow for their political direction. This dependence became more troublesome in later years as the Comintern itself was transformed from a Soviet-dominated mechanism for international revolution into an international mechanism for Soviet domination.

The history of the Comintern is a hotly debated area of study, and its demise as an instrument of international revolution is too complex to detail here. However, to collapse the Bolshevik tradition around the national question into the national imperatives which structured the Comintern in the 1930s is to negate the influence of the Bolshevik revolution on the first generation of black Communists who came within the Party's orbit.[23] Significantly, the consolidation of Stalinism meant that revolutionary political identity was no longer stateless, a point that becomes enormously significant for black political identity in the Second World War.[24] The Bolshevik Revolution had offered the promise of political and social liberation that could be imagined across borders and nations. Such a possibility had fired early black Communists such as Cyril Briggs in their dream of a Pan-African revolutionary class consciousness. Stalinism relocated political identity from the realm of international solidarity into the circumscribed space of the nation (Soviet) state.[25]

Even before Lenin's death, the Comintern was increasingly dominated by the imperative to protect the gains of the Revolution, as the expected victory of the working class in other countries, especially Germany in 1923, failed to materialise. The prospect for international socialism looked bleak, but not hopeless. The triumph, however, of the Stalinist bureaucracy in the bitter power struggle following the death of Lenin had disastrous consequences for international socialism. Stalinism did not signify the continuation or even distortion of the October Revolution, but its demise. This point can be illustrated

---

22   Trotsky 1974, p. 101.

23   Zumoff 2012, p. 63.

24   See chapter 4.

25   For a discussion of Briggs and the early black Communists see pp. 28–30 below; for a discussion of the re-nationalisation of the race question during the Second World War see pp. 130–7 below.

by Stalin's theory of 'socialism in one country' – a theory which marked a decisive break with all previous Marxist orthodoxy. The Trinidadian Trotskyist and intellectual C.L.R. James indicated the effects of this theory as early as 1937:

> The theory of Socialism in A Single Country was the final triumph of the bureaucracy. For if Russia could build Socialism by herself, then for Russian Socialists the world revolution was a matter not of necessity but of gratuitous benevolence, and gratuitous benevolence has no force in the calculations of governments, Capitalist or Socialist. Henceforth the main business of the Communist International would be not revolution but 'the defence of the U.S.S.R.' The future development of the Soviet Union was not of necessity, but only incidentally a threat to world Capitalism.[26]

The consequences of the failure of the Revolution to spread – particularly Russian dominance of the Comintern – were theorised into a political philosophy which transformed the function of the Comintern. As the spreading of the Revolution was no longer essential, the defence of 'existing socialism' became the priority for the international workers' movement. As early as 1926 the Comintern had become an instrument of Russian foreign policy.[27] Even formally, the Comintern under Stalin barely resembled the body set up to further international revolution. The organisation became increasingly dogmatic and hierarchical. As McDermott and Agnew note in their far from eulogising account of the early Comintern, 'without idealising the Comintern under Lenin, we can conclude that this process of hyper-bureaucratisation and ossification is one of the main differences between, say, 1920 and 1928'.[28]

While the stereotype of Communist Parties worldwide slavishly following the Comintern line has been challenged in recent years in the US context, particularly in the work of Mark Naison and Robin Kelley, the imperative to defend Soviet interests impacted directly, if not mechanically, on the activities of Communists the world over, including the CPUSA. The Party in the 1930s attracted thousands of black and white workers to a revolutionary Marxism which the country of revolution had abandoned. Yet the example of that revolution, and the hostility of the capitalist powers to the Soviet Union, secured

---

26 James 1937, p. 202.

27 The Chinese Communist Party had been effectively sacrificed to the strategic alliance between the Soviet state and the nationalist Kumingtang. See Bianco 1971 and Trotsky 1976.

28 McDermott and Agnew 1976, p. 61.

the unwavering loyalty of generations of working-class activists. The meaning of this loyalty is clouded unless it is placed beside the stark factual evidence of the economic conditions and political polarisation of the 1930s, a point at which Stalinist hegemony of the Communist movement was consolidated. In the face of severe capitalist crisis the existence of a 'Socialist' state, which seemed to escape the ravages of the market, was not insignificant. The growth of fascism in Europe appeared to confirm Rosa Luxemburg's declaration that the choice society was facing was between 'socialism or barbarism'.[29] As Eric Hobsbawm explains, the Soviet state offered a haven to Communists as the subjective and objective centre of revolution:

> The young who thirsted to overthrow capitalism became orthodox Communists and identified their cause with the Moscow-centred international movement; and Marxism, restored by October as the ideology of revolutionary change, now meant the Marxism of Moscow's Marx-Engels-Lenin Institute, which was now the global centre for the dissemination of the great classic texts. Nobody else within sight offered both to interpret the world and to change it, or looked better able to do so.[30]

The Soviet Union still *represented* the promise of international socialism, the confirmation that capitalism could be challenged and that the working class could take power. Its sheer iconic status cannot be overestimated.

This unwavering loyalty to the Soviet Union is well expressed in African American Communist Harry Haywood's autobiography *Black Bolshevik* (1978). Haywood spent all of his adult life as a member of the CPUSA. From the early 1920s to the mid-1950s he was a committed Communist and an enthusiastic defender of the thesis for self-determination in the Black Belt. Unlike other celebrated black Communists, Hosea Hudson or Ned Cobb, for example, Haywood was a professional Party activist working at the highest levels of the Party. Many of his 36 years with the Party were spent as a full-time organiser and at one time as a member of the Politburo. From early on he was primed as a leading black Party member – he spent three years with the Lenin School in Moscow in the 1920s, returning to the USA as a prominent proponent of the self-determination thesis. Haywood spent the early 1930s working for the Party in New York, Chicago and Pittsburgh before falling from grace after accusations of cowardice in the Spanish Civil War.

---

29   Luxemburg 1915, http://www.marxists.org/archive/luxemburg/1915/junius/cho1.htm.
30   Hobsbawn 1995, pp. 74–5.

Throughout *Black Bolshevik*, Haywood always contextualises events within the framework of internal Party politics; it is factional disputes which for Haywood sow the seeds for the CPUSA's decline. It is lack of political will, the general rightward shift, the *abandonment* of Stalin, the accommodation to bourgeois nationalism, and personal and political opportunism that are to blame for the Party's abandonment of the 'Negro question'.

His unquestioning loyalty to the Soviet Union is not an example of political naiveté (Haywood possesses a heightened, almost belligerent, awareness of the subtleties of political manoeuvring), but stems from a genuinely held belief, based on personal experience of Russia and the United States, as much as political doctrine, that the Soviet Union is the centre of world revolution and anti-imperialist struggle. Haywood's experiences cannot be generalised in a haphazard manner, however, the intricate relationships between local conditions and the wider imperatives of the Soviet Union which are visible in his interpretation of Marxism are at work generally in this period. Celebrating the 13th anniversary of the October Revolution the *Southern Worker* proclaimed:

> It was a revolution which not only changed the entire structure of Russia, but is having a tremendous effect throughout the world. It is the bearer of light of the exploited and suppressed masses in every capitalist and colonial country. Today Soviet Russia rises above the world as a tremendous proletarian force, an inspiration and guiding example. It covers one-sixth of the earth's surface – just a beginning – for it will not be finally complete until the other five sixths of the earth are included in the International Soviets.[31]

The complex relations between rank-and-file activism, bureaucratic Stalinist hierarchy and the example of 'existing Socialism' in the Soviet Union cannot be understood by negating any of the terms of the equation. Neither can these contradictions be investigated by abstracting them from the specific historical context of the Depression. Perry Anderson emphasises this essential element of Communist Party historiography:

> Any decent history of a Communist Party must take seriously a Gramscian maxim, that to write a history of a political Party is to write the history of the society of which it is a component from a particular monographic standpoint. In other words, no history of a Communist Party is finally intelligible unless it is constantly related to the national balance of forces

---

31   *Southern Worker*, 8 November 1930, p. 4.

of which the Party is only one moment, and which informs the context in which it must operate.[32]

Thus, in order to investigate the legacy of the CPUSA in articulating models of black identity, a legacy Wright, Himes and Ellison had to confront, it is necessary to keep in mind the wider discursive field of a society infected with racism, yet one which was simultaneously engaging with the possiblity of social emancipation named by the Marxism of the Second and Third Internationals. The tightly packed coherence of a racially specific class politics is of particular significance when reading Wright, Himes and Ellison. Before considering how African-American writers and activists were informed by and informed this legacy, it is necessary to touch upon two other models of black identity which were politically potent in this period. The following two sections of this chapter will look at two of those models: Garveyism and reformism.

1.2   Swearing Allegiances: Garveyism and Communism

The Soviet Union is the one country in the world where race discrimination is a crime that is punished by the courts. The whole experience of the Soviet Union shows us that the white workers of the U.S. can gain their freedom only by helping to gain freedom for the oppressed Negroes.

Southern Worker, 15 November 1933

Thy voice thro' the dim past has spoken,
Ethiopia shall stretch forth her hand,
By Thee shall all fetters be broken,
And Heav'n bless our dear fatherland.

The Universal Ethiopian Anthem, 1920

In the 1930s Communists attempted to organise a section of the population who had rarely been the focus of black reformist groups. However, the black *working class* had not been untouched by all political movements and Communists were not the only voice demanding the allegiance of the black working class. Garveyism offered a potent and active form of black agency which could not be easily dismissed.

For Communists in the 1930s, black workers had the power to become agents of their own liberation, not by narrowing the focus of their struggle, but by

---

32   Anderson 1981, p. 148.

broadening it. Although race remained a determining factor, active political identity did not reside in ethnic particularity alone but in class-conscious racial awareness. Black proletarian identity in this context bears little relationship to the model of identity posed by Garveyism; a model premised on racial exclusiveness. Nor was black Communist identity productive of a broad universalism, which seeks assimilation into existing society; after all, smashing the prevalent social order was the objective. The differences between Garveyites and Communists lay in the different ways in which their respective models of blackness negotiated with and inhabited the historical, political, and philosophical contradictions engendered by the legacy of slavery. Did the origins of black subjugation lie in the system of white-capitalist oppression or with whites *as* oppressors? Was the African diaspora connected by a shared history of exploitation or by a shared history of origin? Was it conceivable that black workers could ever trust the white American working-class to fight for black liberation? What were the terms of cross-class solidarity within the black communities?

Communist engagement with black nationalism arose in the early 1920s. It was the Comintern, rather than American Communists, who saw the significance of Garveyism. The small and fractious organisations that emerged from the splits in the American Socialist movement in the early 1920s were ill-equipped, organisationally and politically, to inspire the new generation of black militants who inhabited the ghettos of the Northern cities.[33] It was Garvey's Universal Negro Improvement Association which harnessed the new black militancy that followed upon the First World War.[34] Previous black-led anti-racist organisations, such as Du Bois's Niagra movement, had appealed to the 'talented tenth' of black intellectuals. In contrast, the UNIA based itself in the black working class and claimed 350,000 members in New York alone. With branches throughout the United States, as well as the Caribbean, Central and South American, Asia, Europe and Africa, the movement had between two and six million members in 900 chapters around the world.[35] It offered race pride and militant anti-assimilationism and was a mass movement capable of articulating the anger and frustration of black communities. Garvey 'dramatized, as no one before had done, the bitterness and alienation of the black masses'.[36] Garveyism, like Communism, saw black rage as a position of strength. The impact of Garveyism constitutes a tremendously important chapter of black

33   Zumoff 2012, pp. 56–8.
34   The UNIA was founded by Garvey in Jamaica in 1914. See Robinson 1997, p. 118.
35   Garvey's own figure of six million has been disputed by scholars, who put the figure closer to one or two million. See Pinkney 1976, p. 44.
36   Meier and Rudwick 1976, p. 248.

militancy in the twentieth century, but it is the specific relationship between Communists and the UNIA and the ideological divergence between radical black nationalism and Marxism which is significant here. I am concerned to recreate the model of black identity assumed and reproduced by Communism *in relation* to Garveyism so as to better highlight the specificity of the model enabled by the activities of the CPUSA. In the 1920s how did Communists produce a model of radical black agency which stressed an interracial proletarian identity in relation to the *mass* movement of Garveyism which held that white workers were inherently racist?

Initially in the US, the left-wing challenge to Garveyism came not from the Communists officially but from Communist-inspired black nationalists around the African Blood Brotherhood (ABB). In comparison to the UNIA, the ABB was a modest organisation whose membership peaked at around 3,500.[37] The ABB was founded in 1919 by Cyril Briggs, a Caribbean journalist from Nevis and gifted Marxist, who later became the editor of the black Communist paper *The Liberator*. The organisation also included Richard B. Moore, who was to become a powerful Communist orator and the flamboyant Lovett Fort-Whiteman, who was known as the 'black Cossack' due to his penchant for wearing Russian clothes. Harry Haywood, author of *Black Bolshevik*, his older brother Otto Hall and the poet and writer Claude McKay were also members of the ABB. By autumn 1923, the organisation had merged into the CPUSA, but in the early 1920s, the ABB was a significant independent radical nationalist organisation which attempted to influence the Garvey movement.[38] It was a secret black revolutionary organisation, inspired by both the Bolsheviks and Sinn Fein in its revolutionary and nationalist aspirations. Harry Haywood recounted the impact of meeting Irish revolutionaries:

> As members of oppressed nations, we had a lot in common ... But what impressed me most about them was their sense of national pride – not of the chauvinistic variety, but that of revolutionaries aware of the international importance of their independence struggle and the role of Irish workers.[39]

A national 'pride'—articulated here in opposition to chauvinism—which sought to inspire across national boundaries was what impressed Haywood

---

37   Solomon 1998, p. 14.
38   The ABB were ousted from the UNIA convention in 1921: see Solomon 1998, p. 24.
39   Haywood 1978, pp. 205–6.

and the ABB. The ABB programme focused on 'the fostering of racial self respect . . . organised and uncompromising opposition to the Ku Klux Klan and anti-Negro organizations' and 'co-operation with those other Darker Races and with those white workers who are fully class-conscious and are honestly working for a United Front of all Labour'.[40] Most explicitly at the centre of the ABB's vision was an interracial solidarity built on an 'identity of interests' within the working class:

> The A.B.B. believes in inter-racial co-operation – not the sham co-operation of the oppressed Negro workers and their oppressors, but the honest co-operation of colored and white workers based upon mutual appreciation of the fact of the identity of their interests as members of the working class. This is the only inter-racial co-operation the A.B.B. believes in.[41]

The ABB envisioned a federation of all black organisations which would constitute an international mass movement. The organisation saw itself as a vanguard which could *influence* the massive UNIA. Whilst both groups scorned the assimilationism of the black moderates, the differences between the two organisations were considerable. Garvey's mass movement was premised on the notion of a proud black empire. The African diaspora was connected by culture and 'blood,' rather than by colonial legacy. Briggs's black nationalism was wedded to an equally fierce commitment to Socialist internationalism. Whilst from its inception the ABB was concerned with race pride and armed self-defence, it also took its inspiration from the Russian Revolution. The ABB publication, the *Crusader*, called on African Americans to:

> affiliate yourself with the liberal, radical and labor movements. Don't mind being called 'Bolsheviki' by the same people who call you 'nigger'. Such affiliation in itself won't solve our problems, but it will help immensely.[42]

In the absence of a coherent intervention from American Communists on the 'Negro question,' the ABB and the Comintern provided the political response to Garveyism. The ABB was successful in recruiting a number of leading

---

40   Quoted in Hill (ed.) 1985, vol. 1, pp. 523–4.
41   Quoted in Aptheker (ed.) 1973, p. 419.
42   From the *Crusader* 1920, quoted in Van Deburg (ed.) 1997, p. 36.

Garveyites, including the Rev. James D. Brooks, who had been the UNIA secretary general. In the early days, relations between Garveyites and Communists were cordial. The Comintern saw the movement as a significant, if mistaken, response to racism and Garvey himself made approving comments about the Russian Revolution. No less a figure than J. Edgar Hoover warned that the Garveyist *Negro World* contained 'an open avocation of Bolshevism'.[43]

Initially, the Party was interested in gaining control of the Garvey movement; their failure to do so and the fundamental differences between radical black nationalism and radical anti-racist Communism ensured that relations deteriorated rapidly.[44] Communists may have invested the black radical past with revolutionary significance, but it was a specifically anti-separatist tradition. It was Frederick Douglas rather than Martin Delaney who was accorded iconic status.[45] The argument about separatism was not a qualitative one in terms of commitment to anti-racism; as Manning Marable has observed, the radical nature of black struggle is not articulated by *either* separatism or integrationism, as both traditions have included conservative and revolutionary positions.[46] The difference was a question of political ideology. Communists were unequivocal that black workers could not achieve liberation without smashing capitalism and capitalism could not be destroyed without the mobilisation of the entire working class, black and white. Anti-racism was held as a prerequisite to any class unity, but both the possibility and desirability of interracial solidarity were categorical. Garvey's dismissal of white workers as racially bound to their white masters was equally unambiguous; in fact, according to Garvey, 'the only convenient friend the Negro worker or laborer has, in America at the present time, is the white capitalist'.[47]

Garvey's militant race pride and his ability to articulate the frustrations and aspirations of millions of black Americans was essential to the success of the 'Back to Africa' movement. But the radical desire for a black homeland free from racial oppression was conceived in conjunction with other more traditional Washingtonian beliefs of self-help and black capitalism. While on the one hand Garveyism succeeded in relating to vast numbers of the black poor who had been ignored by the traditional reform movements, on the other it advocated that black workers should accept lower wages in order to appease

---

43   From the *Crusader* 1920, quoted in Van Deburg (ed.) 1997, p. 33.

44   The attempts of the Party to infiltrate the UNIA are detailed in Solomon 1998, pp. 33–7.

45   For a discussion of the Communist relationship to radical black history see pp. 57–64 below.

46   Marable, 1993, p. 182.

47   Garvey 1967a, vol. 1, p. 69.

white capital.[48] The contradictions which pervaded this populist movement were transcended by an increasing emphasis on racial purity; the UNIA's overtures to the Ku Klux Klan (KKK) on the basis of racial separation were the hideously logical result.[49] In the early 1920s African-American social-ists and reformers were horrified that Garvey had agreed a deal with the KKK on the basis of its continued opposition to the National Association for the Advancement of Colored People (NAACP). NAACP founder Du Bois was appalled, and the socialists A. Phillip Randolph and Chandler Own joined with NAACP members William Pickens and Robert Bagnall to form a 'Garvey Must Go' campaign. Garvey responded to the outrage his alliance with the Klan engendered by stating plainly: 'I regard the Klan, the Anglo-Saxon Clubs and White American societies, as far as the Negro is concerned, as better friends of the race than all other groups of hypocritical whites put together'.[50]

Garvey's supposed Bolshevik sympathies were never consistent and he regarded Communists with deep suspicion, declaring that 'capitalism is neces-sary to the progress of the world'.[51] Garvey warned that 'those who unreason-ably and wantonly oppose or fight against [capitalism] are enemies of human advancement'.[52] Briggs claimed that, although Garveyism was an impressive response to racism, there was nothing automatically radical about the move-ment. Writing in 1931 he recognised that 'Garveyism, or Negro Zionism, rose on the crest of the wave of discontent and revolutionary ferment which swept the capitalist world as a result of the postwar crisis'. Yet he insisted that 'from the very beginning there were two sides inherent to the movement: a democratic side and a reactionary side'.[53] By 1932 any gestures of solidarity from Garvey had long evaporated:

> We claimed then and we claim now that a European Communist will be no different, when he gets into power, to the Southern Cracker of the United States. The Cracker has in his blood the desire to kill and brutalize the Negro because of his vaunted image of superiority based upon the difference of color. When you scratch the Communist beneath the sur-face, you will find him the same vicious Southerner whose political belief will not surmount his racial prejudices and for this, we have always kept

48   Allen 1974, p. 240.
49   See Solomon 1998, pp. 23–35.
50   Garvey 1967b, vol. 2, p. 71.
51   Garvey 1967b, vol. 2, p. 72.
52   Ibid.
53   Briggs 1931, pp. 174, 176.

Communism at bay; hence no one will mistake us for having any sympa-
thy for the Communists as far as bringing the Negro into Communism is
concerned.[54]

At the core of this argument was the question not only of how you achieve
black liberation, but the nature of that liberation. Economic liberation meant
two entirely different things for Communists and black nationalists. While the
former insisted on the need to smash capitalism, the latter were concerned to
shift the economic benefits of capitalism to black communities. Black nationalists sought to encourage the growth of black owned and controlled business,
to redress the historical legacy of black slavery and discrimination by ensuring
that black Americans were in a position to benefit from capitalism. While the
nature of American racism ensured that such a demand was immediately a
radical one, in Marxist terms it was another version of the racial uplift ideology,
in which the aim was not political and social change through working-class
struggle, but social advancement through demanding the means to escape the
heightened oppression of class. This belief in capitalism as progress, which
Garveyism pre-supposed, presented a model of identity antithetical to the
CPUSA's insistence on attaining liberation through smashing capitalism.

Garveyism, despite Garvey's own intellectual debt to Booker T. Washington,
could hardly be perceived as an accommodationist movement, even in the
heyday of Stalinist ultra-leftism, but the black nationalist demands for black
economic self-sufficiency were in direct contradiction with the anti-class-
collaborationist position of the Communists. The CPUSA were insistent that
the interests of all black people were neither philosophically, politically nor
socially analogous. These ideological differences had direct consequences in
terms addressing black workers. The Party's insistence on the conflicting class
interests within black communities and the centrality of working-class unity
consistently placed them in a minority position when it came to localised battles against white (mostly Jewish) owned businesses in black areas. These campaigns were of central importance to black nationalists in the 1920s and 1930s.[55]

Increasingly Communists and Garveyites were in direct competition, seeking the allegiance of the newly politicised black-northern working class, and
by the early 1930s differences between black Communists and Garveyites in

---

54   Garvey 1932, p. 319.
55   Of the many successful cults and street corner movements led by grass roots leaders
      in the 1930s, Sufi Abdul Hamid's campaign for 'Jobs for Negroes' against discriminatory
      employment practices of white shop owners was particularly successful. See Muraskin
      1972, pp. 361–73.

Harlem occasionally ended in physical confrontation.[56] Yet the Garvey movement still attracted militant young workers and had also supplied the CPUSA with some of its more experienced and effective agitators.[57] Whilst the leadership of the Garveyite movement was dismissed as 'degenerate,' rank-and-file members were seen as potential converts to Communism, and the paper approached them as militant radicals who were being deceived by reactionary politics. The Party's black vice-presidential candidate James Ford was 'convinced that many Garveyites are sympathetic with Communism'. In an 'Open Letter to the People of Harlem' in October 1933 Ford insisted that 'the world program of Communism will accomplish the freedom of Africa'.[58] In the same year Briggs wrote an extensive article on the imperative of treating rank-and-file black nationalists with respect and patience.

> In our approach to the Garveyites it is necessary to bear in mind the origins and source of the Garvey movement. Garveyism rose on the crest of the wave of discontent and revolutionary ferment which swept the capitalist world as a result of the post-war crisis. The masses who joined the Garvey movement were sincerely seeking a way of struggle against imperialism, a way out of national oppression, subjugation and degradation.... It is the duty of every L.S.N.R. [League of Struggle for Negro Rights] member to strive patiently and intelligently to win the Garvey masses to the revolutionary struggle – the only way out of imperialist oppression, unemployment, job discrimination and growing mass misery. We must approach these masses with the greatest sympathy, We must overcome the mistakes we have made in the past of antagonizing them – mistakes from which the *Liberator* has not been free.[59]

This passage is significant because it reveals that in its approach to Garvey *supporters* the Party showed uncharacteristic flexibility and restraint, yet still insisted on the centrality of class differentiation within the black community. Communists maintained that Garvey was wrong, not only because his racial insularity blinded him to the capacities of interracial unity, but because it led him to unholy alliances with the bastions of American white supremacy. Consequently, a purely racial solution to the problem of racism was not only

---

56 Naison 1985, p. 40.
57 Prominent Harlem Communist spokesmen like Steve Kingston, Louis Campbell and William Fitzgerald were all ex-UNIA members. See Naison 1985, pp. 38–41.
58 *Harlem Liberator*, 21 October 1933.
59 *Harlem Liberator*, 23 September 1933.

anti-working-class, but was a dangerous capitulation to the most menacing of political forces. The Party was relentless in its insistence that a solution to American racism could not be found solely within the parameters of the minority black community. Ethnic particularity was historically created by capitalism, it was the starting point for radical political identity, not the end point of political radicalism. As James S. Allen wrote in 1936:

> The Negro question is not isolated or self-contained, any more than the creation of this problem is the result of a course of development which affected only the Negro and left un-touched other sections of the population. It is necessary to relate the tasks of Negro liberation to the most pressing problems of the present period.[60]

No movement, however, had more of an impact on the black working class than Garveyism. The UNIA had inspired millions of African-American workers precisely through an appeal to common identification and racial particularity. Communists needed to harness this ability of race pride to mobilise black workers, while retaining their insistence on inter-racial class struggle. Its ability to mobilise in large numbers and to establish their credibility was secured during the early 1930s.

1.3   Trials on Trial: Yokinen and Scottsboro

> I am with the Party as long as I live ... I don't care who likes it or who don't like it ... I like it because it believes in every man or woman to have a right to a decent living ... I tell the world I want to be somebody but I can't understand this government. This so called government has put many a good woman in the garbage can, and put the lid on it, But I tell the world I will fight like hell to stay out and I want the rest of my comrades to do the same[61]
>
> VIOLA MONTGOMERY, Mother of 'Scottsboro Boy' Olen Montgomery (1934)

In spring 1931 two trials transformed the fortunes of the Communist Party in their attempt to win black working-class support. One was an internal Party matter, which was publicised in every Communist publication, the other was a

---

60   Allen 1936, p. 8.
61   Quoted in Goodman 1994, p. 237.

trial in Alabama which became an international event. The Communist intervention around these two trials, Yokinen and Scottsboro, provided concrete examples of the Party's commitment to anti-racist practice. More specifically they provided opportunities to formulate a class conscious anti-racism which set itself up in opposition to competing forms of *both* (white) working class identity and (black) racial identity. The Yokinen trial provided the prototype American Communist as the best fighter against racism. The Scottsboro trial assumed the moral and political right to speak exclusively to the concerns of black workers. These prototypes are both lauded and ridiculed in the fictional representations of Communism which I examine and a detailed examination of these events are an illustrative example of the models of African-American identity with which the novels engage.[62]

In February 1931, a Finish Communist named August Yokinen was put on trial in a Communist Party 'court'. Yokinen was a janitor at the Finnish Workers Club who had stated that black Communists were unwelcome at the club, as they would 'soon be coming into the bathroom' and he 'did not want to bathe with Negroes'.[63] From its inception the American Party had been dominated by foreign-language federations, and the Yokinen trial demonstrated the Party's commitment to expunge racism from its ranks, even at the expense of its core membership. At his trial Yokinen was defended by the veteran black Communist Richard B. Moore, while the white Communist editor of the *Daily Worker*, Clarence Hathaway, acted as prosecutor. Yokinen had admitted his guilt, and Moore's defence centred around the hitherto lax Party attitude to race, and its poor record in educating Party members about the malignant effects of white chauvinism. He asked that Yokinen be spared the humiliation of expulsion, stating that he himself would 'rather have my head severed from my body by the capitalist lynchers than to be expelled in disgrace from the Communist International'.[64] The 'jury' of seven whites and seven blacks returned a verdict of guilty. Yokinen was expelled from the Party, but could apply for re-admission on the condition that he carried out anti-racist work, including selling the black Communist newspaper *The Liberator* in Harlem.

---

62   Trials and purges predominate in the fictional representations of Communism I discuss in this book. For Wright's characterisation of the lawyer Max in *Native Son*, as the exemplary anti-racist, see pp. 105–7; for a discussion of *Lonely Crusade's* pivotal section on Party 'purges' for racism see pp. 105–1; Ellison's portrayal of the Brotherhood is also structured by internal trials at which Party members must account for their commitment to anti-racism.

63   Naison 1985, p. 47.

64   Foner and Shapiro 1987, p. 168.

Expulsions from the Party for 'White Chauvinism' have been the source of much scepticism.[65] The Party saw its anti-Chauvinist purges as essential to its anti-racist work: General Secretary Earl Browder remarked that if it hadn't been for the Yokinen case there could have been no Scottsboro campaign.[66] The dark history of the purges in Stalinist Russia in the mid-1930s offer a sobering context for reviewing these events and certainly throughout the 1930s dissenting comrades were expelled from the American Party under a variety of pretexts. However, as with so much of this history, there is a contradictory element. By taking an uncompromising stand on racism and *privileging* black experience of discrimination, the Party signalled that it was a unique force on the Left. When Hosea Hudson attended a Communist Party educational, a small incident regarding borrowed face cream became a major event. Two white girls were disciplined for white chauvinism after accusing a black comrade of stealing their moisturiser. Hudson was convinced that 'that one battle of how the Party handled discrimination, white chauvinism against Negroes, ... gave me the double determination that I had somewhere I could fight for against oppression'.[67]

Expulsions for white chauvinism were widely and favourably reported in the African-American press and helped to establish the Party's credibility among black workers. The *Chicago Defender* favourably reported at the close of the trial:

> Thereupon the 'court' arose, and the audience sang the 'Internationale'. And Harlem, throbbing capital of change and excitement, talked through the night of justice, at least as it is done in a political Party that challenges the established order.[68]

The anthem of the International workers' movement at the centre of Harlem political debate was the expression of a vigorous commitment to racial justice within a specific theoretical context. The Yokinen trial was an active instance

---

65   The fate of Yokinen is lamented in much Cold War history of American Communism. Cruse maintains that the trial was little more than a stunt which victimised an unsubtle racially prejudiced foreigner in order to cover up more subtle racism (see Cruse 1967, pp. 144–6). The *Liberator* covered the trial, and later set up a campaign to stop Yokinen's subsequent deportation by the authorities who were alerted to his illegal status by the publicity surrounding the trial. The Party maintained that it was his newly acquired anti-racism that made him an 'undesirable citizen'. See *Liberator*, 18 July 1931.

66   See Solomon 1998, p. 140.

67   Painter 1979, p. 212.

68   *Chicago Defender*, 7 March, 1931, quoted in Foner and Shapiro 1987, p. 181.

of the centrality of black dignity to Communist political identity. In his auto-biography Harry Haywood emphasised that:

> The Trial was a living political demonstration of our program on the Afro-American question and had tremendous repercussions on the Black liberation front as a whole – for the first time, the Communist Party was seen by the broad masses as a serious contender for hegemony of the movement.[69]

The Party had demonstrated they would fight racism inside their own ranks, but a yet bigger test lay outside. Within weeks of the Yokinen trial they seized the opportunity to prove that they had the ability and commitment to fight institutional racism on its own grounds.

The most famous campaign of the CPUSA in the early 1930s was the Scottsboro case. The details of the case are well known – on 29 March 1931, nine young black men between the ages of 13 and 21 were arrested in Alabama. Haywood Patterson, Ozie Powell, Charlie Weems, Olen Montgomery, Clarence Norris, Willie Roberson, Andrew and Roy Wright, and Eugene Williams were dragged off a freight train in Paint Rock, after a fracas with a group of white boys. By 9 April eight of them were on the way to the electric chair for 'forcefully ravaging' Ruby Bates and Victoria Price, two white women who had been on board the train. Their speedy trials constituted a barely concealed frame-up. The defence lawyer called no witnesses whilst the medical evidence, which concluded that no rape had taken place, was ignored. This was hardly newsworthy in the Southern states, where hysterical defences of 'white womanhood' had long provided the justification for lynch law.[70] As Scottsboro defendant Haywood Patterson related, 'what happened in the Scottsboro case wasn't unusual. What was unusual was that the world heard about it'.[71] Scottsboro was a *public* articulation of black rights to justice in which the defendants themselves and their families were encouraged to articulate the meaning of their plight.

The most startling fact was that the men had survived the lynch mob long enough to stand trial at all, a source of pride to Alabamian liberals. But it was

---

69   Haywood 1978, p. 358.
70   In the 1930s 115 black men were sentenced to death for rape as compared with 10 white men during the same period. Between 1930 and 1959 90 percent of all Americans executed for rape were black; the South was the locale for all but two of those executions. See Marable 1983, p. 320.
71   Patterson and Conrad 1950, p. 182.

not Alabamian liberals who dictated the course of events over Scottsboro. The Communist Party seized on the case as the perfect example of the race hatred of the 'boss class'. It was the headline story of the *Daily Worker* on 2 April and the *Southern Worker* on 4 April, and dominated Party activity in the early 1930s. Every week Communist papers carried the story, giving pride of place to letters from the defendants and their parents. By 10 April the International Labor Defense (ILD), the Party's legal defence organisation, had taken over the defence case and secured the confidence of the Scottsboro parents. The intervention of the Communist Party was critical. Scottsboro became an international cause célèbre, threw a spotlight on Southern 'justice' and became the test case for the Party's commitment to anti-racism.

It is not necessary here to detail the intricacies of the court cases. The trials have been adequately documented, particularly the unseemly struggle between the CPUSA and the NAACP to gain control of the legal defence.[72] The significance of Scottsboro for the purpose of this study lies in how it illustrates the wider balance of forces that enabled the Communists to work so effectively in the previously indifferent, if not hostile, environment of the black communities. The question is not so much *why* the CPUSA took control of the Scottsboro case but how they did so as Scottsboro became the defining moment for black and white Communists in the 1930s.[73] During the campaign the Party's understanding and validation of black rage was key to its success.

From the beginning the Party launched an aggressive attack on Jim Crowism as an irreformable bastion of racism and privilege. They did this in terms of both class and race:

> We understand the dirty device that the lynchers are using in this case. They have gone through a sham trial – a hideous mockery of a few hours in court – in order to give a legal varnish to the most cold-blooded murder of the children *of our class and people*. We declare that there is no difference between the way these boys are being murdered and the customary method of southern white ruling class lynching, lynching on the public square, except that the boys are rushed through the court house on the way to the lynching and are to be burned in the electric chair instead of the stake. We denounce this outrageous case as a 'court house lynching'.[74]

---

72   The most comprehensive study of the Scottsboro case remains D. Carter 1969.

73   'It was the ILD's handling of the Scottsboro and Herndon cases which first propelled the Communist Party into national and international notoriety as the self-professed defender of Afro-Americans against oppression'. Martin 1979, pp. 131–42.

74   *Harlem Liberator*, 25 April 1931 (emphasis mine).

The Party was adamant that there could be no compromise with the Southern lynchers, that Alabama was the centre of home-grown fascism and that the trial of the Scottsboro boys was legalised murder. They expressed a trenchant loathing for the Southern legal system that struck a chord with other African Americans. Langston Hughes had written in 1923 'that Justice is a Blind goddess, is a thing to which we blacks are wise,' and the open Communist disregard for the authority of the Southern state met an enthusiastic response in black communities. Rarely had the institutions of the South been so contemptuously and publicly disparaged, not just by Communists but by black Communists. The *Baltimore Afro-American* approvingly related how Communists had broken up a session of the State legislature:

> [T]he spectacle of black men impolitely breaking up a legislative session, is just too precious for words. The usual delegation kow-tows, begs for aid or relief on sentimental, moral or religious (seldom legal) grounds. The legislators listen with ill-concealed impatience and when the petitioners have departed, calmly kick them in the pants by ignoring their requests and their rights. Just imagine the Reds marching into a session of hard-boiled legislative nuts, and a black spokesman urging them to be quiet and listen to a real programme for the people. Then picture the lawmaking boys being told 'if you don't listen today, we'll go back and bring down a bigger crowd'. Think of that and you'll understand why the AFRO is profoundly grateful that there is somebody in the state who can give the legislature a piece of his mind.[75]

This is an enthusiastic articulation of *relief* at an active repudiation of the authority of a Southern institution. Moreover, the fact that this scorn for Southern institutions was taking the place of a perceived supplication is key to understanding how Communist validation of black anger spoke to the wider African American community.

The Chicago Defender was even more unequivocal in its admiration for the Communist Party:

> An organisation distinguished for its love of justice, although unpopular among the wealth and power of the land, has come into the state to help these young men clear themselves. It came not by invitation from either the young men or their Race. It came simply because a wrong had been done and called for some agency to right it ... It is a source of boundless

---

75   Editorial in *Baltimore Afro-American* reprinted in the *Liberator* 25 Apr. 1931 p. 8.

gratification, not only that a powerful organization came to the young men when they were hopeless, or because of the retention of distinguished lawyers in their cause, but also because Alabamians not of their Race have established for them in public opinion the benefit of the doubt of both their guilt and that they had a fair trial at Scottsboro.[76]

Central to the Communist case was the argument that the Southern state could not offer black protection from the lynch mob, because it *was*, structurally and actively, the lynch mob. This was no sensitive legal manoeuvre in which the officials of the South had to be courted gently. This was a political fight to mobilise the mass of American workers against white supremacism and to expose the injustice at the core of Southern institutions. Alabama State officials were flooded with telegrams demanding the release of the suspects. The Scottsboro defence team did not attempt to hide their distrust of the legal system when they wired Governor Miller:

> We demand stay of execution and opportunity to investigate and prepare for new trial or appeal. We demand right for our attorney to interview defendants and to obtain formal approval of defence counsel, and, above all, we demand absolute safety for the defendants against lynching.[77]

This was a challenge to racism, not as a voluntary ideological prejudice, but as the institutional and legal foundation of the Southern states. For Communists it was not the defendants on trial, but the institutions of Southern racism and the economic base of the plantocracy. As ILD president William L. Patterson explained, their task was 'to destroy the illusions of a democracy and justice above class, and to expose their class character'.[78] Scottsboro offered a unique opportunity to put Jim Crowism in the dock. *Southern Worker* explicitly defined the nature of the Scottsboro case.

> The fight for the freedom of the boys has become a struggle of great significance. It is not a 'rape case' as both the Southern white ruling class and such Negro judases as the National Association of Colored People would like to make it appear. It is a case which typifies the most vicious oppression and persecution of the Negro workers and farmers in this

---

76   Editorial, *Chicago Defender*, reprinted in the *Liberator*, 16 May 1931, p. 8.
77   Patterson and Conrad 1950, p. 248.
78   Quoted in Martin 1985, p. 167.

country, the denial of every right to them by the white ruling class the whole system of virtual slavery on the plantations and in the cities.[79]

The CPUSA was going to war against Southern racism, but it was a war also against the NAACP. The NAACP consistently challenged American racism, but their gradualist and legalistic approach rarely rallied the black poor. Throughout the 1930s the NAACP was perceived as an organisation which represented the professional class of black Americans.[80] In the early 1930s the NAACP were the target of an unrestrained sectarian onslaught by the Communist Party. Again the rationale for Communist practice was rooted both in the concrete historical situation and in the Stalinist hegemony of the international workers' movement. To understand the dynamic it is essential to place the persistent and fanatical tirades against black moderates in a wider context, domestically and internationally.

The disastrous policies of the Third International during the Third Period (1928–35) decreed that the world was in a period of revolutionary upsurge and the only thing standing between the global proletariat and Communism was Social Democracy. According to this analysis of the period, these 'social fascists' merely prolonged the dying gasps of a system on the verge of collapse, indeed Social Democracy could even be construed as worse than fascism as its legitimising veil hid its true nature. The disastrous consequences of this in Europe are well known.[81] In the United States this policy was complicated by the lack of a mass Social Democratic party, a lack which saw Communists reserve their scorn for the Socialist Party. The leader of the Socialist Party, Norman Thomas, was a virtual hate figure for Communists in the early 1930s, 'a running dog of capitalism' according to the *Daily Worker*.[82] In the context of black struggles, Third Period ultra-leftism found its most concrete manifestation in the sectarian dealings with the NAACP over the Scottsboro defence; they conducted

---

79   *Southern Worker*, 18 July 1931, p. 4.

80   Reed 1997, p. 77.

81   The mass Communist parties of central Europe were disarmed in the face of fascism. The German Communists (KPD) were instructed to expose the 'social fascism' of the Social Democrats (SPD) at every opportunity while the Nazis were coming to power. This farce reached its nadir when German Communists in Prussia were instructed to turn a Nazi inspired referendum against the Social Democrats into a 'Red Plebiscite', effectively allying themselves with Hitler. The campaign found little support amongst Party members, yet the KPD declared when the referendum gained 26 percent of the vote that it was 'the greatest blow of all that the working class has yet dealt to Social Democracy'. See Rosenhaft 1983, p. 113.

82   *Daily Worker*, 28 October 1929, quoted in Evans 1964, p. 126.

what Charles Martin describes as 'national warfare against the association'.[83] However, this hostility towards black moderates was initially a significant factor in the Party's ability to mobilise black workers.[84]

In the sphere of American race relations during the Depression, the policies of the Third Period ironically seemed to reflect the growing division between an increasingly militant black working class and the cautious leaders of black reformism. A generation of black workers had had their illusions of Northern equality shattered upon reaching the ghettos of New York, Detroit and Chicago. To put it crudely, it was not political affiliation that threatened black workers' employment prospects, it was political and economic reality.[85] Recalling his first encounter with Communists in Alabama, Hosea Hudson remarked:

> I wasn't scared of the Reds, never was scared of the Reds, but I just wasn't interested. Other people were scared, said 'better not fool with that mess, you'll lose your job'. But I was never scared of losing a job. I lost five jobs.[86]

Communists increasingly filled a political vacuum where the demands of black workers could not be met by the politics of the moderates. There was palpable frustration with the conciliatory politics of the NAACP outside Party ranks. When American Communists launched blistering attacks on the credibility of black moderates they touched a raw nerve. The *New York News* welcomed Communist intervention in Scottsboro, not least because it showed up the intransigence of the NAACP:

> It takes gruesome outrages such as the threatened wholesale legal lynching of these nine black boys to arouse and break the shackles of a cruel caste system. It would be a revolution in the South today just as the freeing of the slaves was a bloody Civil War in 1861. If, too, the agitation of the Red organisation should serve to stir the National Association for the Advancement of Colored People from their selfish, social lethargy into sincere and efficient action, that too, would be a great and lasting gain for the race. The N.A.A.C.P. has recently become bloated with a silly pride and drunk with a little authority.[87]

---

83   Martin 1979, p. 134.

84   See 'The Communist Party's Zigzag on Negro Policy', in Mclemee (ed.) 1996, p. 117.

85   In 1931, about one-seventh of black men and one-twelfth of black women in the North were unemployed, see Foner 1974, p. 190.

86   Painter 1979, p. 85.

87   Editorial, *New York News*, reprinted in the *Liberator*, 4 July 1931, p. 4.

This growing polarisation within black communities compelled a sizeable minority of black workers to look to more radical politics. The Communist Party's aggressive opposition to both Southern racism and to the politics of moderation were crucial in the early 1930s. The Depression had not automatically heralded a new militancy, as the desperate conditions engendered by economic collapse often gave rise to passivity and desperation. Communist intervention was critical in directing anger at the institutionalised racism that many more traditional organisations saw as monolithic. It was precisely their belief that targeted *anger* was the crucial element in winning the Scottsboro case that differentiated the Communists from other models of black political identity. Angry politics needed angry political subjects. The discursive validation of black political rage underlined the mass mobilisations around Scottsboro.[88] This was in marked contrast to the major black reformist organisations. Dan Carter, who is often critical of CPUSA tactics in relation to Scottsboro, acknowledged that the NAACP:

> accepted the status quo for the most part and concentrated on limited goals. The moderates expected nothing sudden and saw no short cuts. The only thing 'radical' about the association was its opposition to racial proscription, and often this was soft-pedalled in order to work for short-term goals.[89]

The divergent political agendas of the CPUSA and the black moderates had concrete manifestations in terms of how they configured black political identity. In terms of the Scottsboro case, NAACP leader, Walter White, was reluctant to involve his organisation in a rape case before the full facts were known. As late as November 1931 the NAACP were still misreading the significance of the case:

> The N.A.A.C.P. is not an organisation to defend Black criminals. We are not in the field to condone rape, murder and theft because it is done by Black men...When we hear that eight coloured men have raped two white girls in Alabama, we are not first in the field to defend them. If they are guilty and have a fair trial the case is none of our business.[90]

---

88   For a discussion of Communist discursive models of black rage see pp. 66–9 below.

89   Carter 1969, pp. 62–3.

90   *The Crisis*, November 1931, cited in Haywood 1978, p. 360.

The Party had no such reservations regarding black 'criminality'. In terms of Scottsboro, compromise meant defeat when the terms and conditions were set by Southern racism.[91] Nor were the Communists in the least defensive about the 'articulacy' of the Scottsboro parents. For the CPUSA the parents were part of the struggle and as black southern workers they were essential to it; in return, the Party secured the unwavering loyalty of the majority of Scottsboro parents, who found a space in which to articulate their anger at the Southern institutions. In contrast the NAACP were, in the words of Walter White, exasperated with these 'humble folk' who had 'few opportunities for knowledge'.[92] William Pickens went further, proclaiming that the parents were 'the densest and dumbest animals it has yet been my privilege to meet'.[93]

The difference in approach was not just one of decency vs. snobbery, it was political.[94] The Communists had not merely placed race at the centre of their politics, they had placed it at the centre of their class politics. It was this fusion of race and class which gave black Communist subjectivity its particular character. Racial and social marginalisation were configured as the centre of revolutionary change. The Party had targeted the black working class as the catalyst for social transformation, consequently their interest was not just in representing black workers, but in mobilising them. As one ambivalent commentator states:

> The ILD was not just one additional voice speaking out on behalf of poor blacks; it was a movement composed of poor blacks. It not only provided free legal defense and sought to expose the 'class basis' of racism in the South, it gave black working people what traditional middle-class organizations would not – a political voice.[95]

---

91   This was also true of the other major trials the CPUSA were involved with, for example Euel Lee and Angelo Herndon. Euel Lee was a 60-year-old black farm worker from Maryland accused of murdering his employer. The ILD took his case, forced the state to stop excluding blacks from juries, and kept him off death row for two years. Lee was executed in October 1933. Angelo Herndon was a black Communist organiser who was sentenced to 20 years of hard labour for distributing Communist leaflets. Herndon was eventually released after an exhaustive campaign by the ILD.

92   Quoted in Carter 1969, p. 72.

93   Quoted in Carter 1969, p. 90.

94   See Martin 1985, although his pronouncement that it was the 'day to day behaviour of radicals, not Marxist theory' which secured the ILD's control of the case is questionable.

95   Klehr 1984, p. 91.

It was not Communists alone who challenged the NAACP's conservatism, A. Phillip Randolph consistently attacked the organisation as elitist and 'hat-in-hand' in the *Messenger*.[96] It is also pertinent to note that the CPUSA's sectarian hostility to the NAACP was more than matched by the NAACP's attitude to the Communists. The Party was attacked for preying on the desperation of poor blacks, for duping the uneducated into supporting a cause they knew little about, for jeopardising the case by antagonising the Southern judiciary, for being insensitive to the precariously balanced structure of Southern race relations and for using blacks as the agents of a foreign (Soviet) power. The Party was further accused of stirring up a lynch mentality and a willingness to see the defendants martyred for the cause. The main charge was that they used prisoners and their families in order to gain publicity. In the political discourse of the moderates the only place for black workers was as objects, either of *their* benevolence or of Communist cynical manipulation. In contrast, Communists saw racism, not as a matter of custom, but as part of a system which was susceptible to destruction. Black workers, then, had positions available to them – through Marxism – which posited them as black and as workers and hence as political agents capable of bringing about *their* own emancipation. This complex of activity, policy and factionalism generated positions which confirmed colour and class not as vehicles for oppression alone, but also, and simultaneously, as vehicles for liberation.

The Communist strategy of mass protest and their legal challenges to Southern racist legislation were significant factors in saving the Scottsboro defendants from execution.[97] While Scottsboro was the most notorious intervention, the Party was instrumental in many other legal cases, as well as mounting campaigns against police brutality.[98] The Party had established the Sharecroppers Union (SCU) in the South which boasted over 6000 (mostly black) members in 1934.[99] They used their credibility in the fight for racial justice to launch blistering attacks on their political opponents. While the Party grudgingly admitted (though not frequently) that the black middle-class were victims of racism, their 'complicity' in the capitalist system meant that

---

96   Meier and Rudwick, 1976, p. 245.

97   The Party won the right to have black representation on juries. The Scottsboro boys were not released together, and the cases dragged on for over a decade. The final defendant to be released was Andy Wright, who was eventually freed in 1950.

98   Communist campaigns against police brutality are detailed in Naison 1985, pp. 116–17.

99   Marable 1983, p. 35. For detailed analysis of the SCU see Kelley 1990, pp. 34–56; for a first-hand account see Ned Cobb's recollections in Rosengarten, 1974.

they, unlike black workers, could negotiate the terms of their oppression. As Langston Hughes stated in 1932, 'if the Communists don't awaken the Negroes of the South, who will? Certainly not the race leaders whose schools and jobs depend on white philanthropy'.[100] Communists were seeking nothing less than complete hegemony within the black community. Their exaggerated attacks on the integrity of other black organisations may have had its roots in the debacle of Third Period politics, but local conditions turned the potentially dead-end sectarianism of ultra-left anti-reformism into an explosive discourse of defined and oppositional black agency. Sectarian principle here translates, because of concrete conditions, into effective political mobilisation. The Party sought to present a radical model of black agency, a model whose impact was echoed in narratives of black identity which are the focus of this book.

The Scottsboro trials and the Yokinen trial transformed the fortunes of the Communist Party's anti-racist work. From a handful of black members in the 1920s, the Party had attracted just under 1000 black members by 1930 and by 1939 there were over 5000 black members.[101] The point about Yokinen and Scottsboro is not merely to stress the anti-racist credentials of the CPUSA, but to point to the historic elaboration of a model of an interracial political discourse which made race an active and angry position from which to speak. Moreover, black radicalism was also seen as the vehicle of liberation for the white working class.

I am stressing here that the Communist Party was not a monolithic puppet master, hovering opportunistically at the sidelines of black struggle, yet this is how it has often been characterised by both Cold War historians and black nationalists. Although the influence of Stalinist dogma and the requirements of Soviet foreign policy had negative and damaging effects on the legacy of the CPUSA, the Communist-led political battles of the early 1930s often led to the formation of new solidarities within the prism of class and race. Despite their sectarianism, the Communists were the first left-wing political organisation in the US to unconditionally support black self-determination. No other predominantly white political organisation had ever attempted to systematically organise black workers and no Party blueprint could predict the effects of their

---

100   Quoted in Robinson 1997, p. 121. Ralph Ellison's bitterly satiric characterisation of Bledsoe in *Invisible Man* draws on many of the Communist paradigms of the black bourgeoisie. See pp. 184–6.

101   See Draper 1960, pp. 551–2.

intervention. In order for the CPUSA to function it had to engage with local conditions and the concerns of the increasingly militant black working class. The Party did not impose bland dogma on an inactive black 'mass'. The black communities they encountered were not blank sheets waiting to be inscribed with Soviet interests. As Robin Kelley remarks in relation to the Southern states:

> Because the movement was built from scratch by people without a Euro-American left-wing tradition, Alabama's black cadre interpreted Communism through the lenses of their own cultural world and the international movement of which they were now a part. Far from being a slumbering mass movement waiting for Communist direction, black working people entered the movement with a rich culture of opposition that sometimes contradicted, sometimes reinforced the Left's vision of class struggle.[102]

The complex interplay born out of this dialectic informed the nature of 1930s American Communist anti-racist theory and practice. The relationship between Communists and black communities in the 1930s was just that, a *relationship*. Party mobilisations around anti-racist struggles effected the organisation in unpredictable and dynamic ways. This was a dialectical relationship where black political identity was no more static and unchanging than Communist praxis.

The CPUSA actually won few converts from the established reform movements of the early 1930s, as they concentrated their energies on organising poor African Americans who hitherto had been the object of white philanthropy and black reformism, but had rarely been addressed as the subject of their own liberation. In focusing on the agency of black workers themselves, the Party inspired a resolute loyalty from its activists, as Hosea Hudson, who joined the Party in Birmingham in 1931, recounted:

> I found this Party, a Party of the working class, gave me rights equal with all others regardless of color, sex, or age or educational standards. I with my uneducation could express myself, without being made fun of by others who could read well and fast, using big words. I was treated with *high respect*.[103]

---

102   Kelley 1990, p. 93.

103   Painter 1979, p. 180 (my emphasis).

Hudson's relationship to the Party here, as an organisation which he 'found' and in which he found a space of equality and respect, is also articulated as a space for black self-expression. In their paper specifically targeting black workers, *The Liberator*, the Party endeavoured to create a militant black radical journal that could both rally the African American proletariat and offer them a site for creative self expression.

CHAPTER 2

The *Liberator* (1929–35)

2.1 The *Liberator*: The Black Bourgeoisie and Revolutionary Tradition

Organize! Protest! Don't be meek
Read the Liberator every week[1]

The *Liberator* newspaper was launched in December 1929; it sought to bring Communist politics to the African-American working class and the black radical tradition into the orbit of Communist politics.[2] Its first editor was ABB veteran Cyril Briggs, a leading black Communist journalist and intellectual, whose contribution to the *Liberator* cannot be underestimated.[3] Prominent black Communists, Otto Hall, James Ford and Otto Huiswood, were all regular contributors. For any scholar interested in negotiating the matrix of black and Communist politics in the 1930s, the *Liberator* offers the most illuminating example of the effort to negotiate a new type of American Communism, one which appealed on a race specific, class conscious, populist level.[4] Although the *Liberator* has been used as a historical resource, it remains a relatively *uninterpreted* source. The attempt of the *Liberator* to fuse Communist theory, anti-racism, black history, interracial class solidarity and race pride produced a potent interventionist paper which focused on the role of black workers in anti-capitalist revolt.[5] While the tone and content of the paper changed

---

1   From 'Marching Forward' by E.S. published in the *Harlem Liberator*, 11 November 1933, p. 4.

2   The *Liberator* was launched in 1929, changing its name twice, to the *Harlem Liberator* in 1933 and the *Negro Liberator* in 1934.

3   Briggs's last editorial was 23/9/33, though he continued to write extensively for the paper. Maude White edited the paper from October 1933, Benjamin Davis became editor in the summer of 1934.

4   Although the *Liberator* had three different editors and the shifting editorial staff reflected the demands of the CP it is not my intention to offer a history of the factional differences which informed these changes, or to engage with the internal Party dynamics of the paper. This is covered by Naison 1985, pp. 109–11 and Solomon 1998, pp. 262–4. It is the generic tropes of black proletarian identity and interracial class solidarity which I explore here.

5   It is important to reiterate here that by the 1930s Stalinism had a firm grip on the worldwide working-class movement. The Marxism the *Liberator* engages is thus somewhat distorted by the imperatives of Soviet foreign policy and crude Stalinist determinism, which becomes

during its life (1929–35), it remained constant on three central questions; the institutional nature of American racism, the necessity of interracial working-class self-activity, and a deep hostility to cross-class alliances within the black community.

Although a Communist newspaper, the *Liberator* was never formally a paper of the Communist Party – officially it was the paper of the Communist-founded American Negro Labor Congress (ANCL)/ League of Struggle for Negro Rights (LSNR).[6] However, the paper's commitment to the Communist Party is consistent and is best summed up in a somewhat unconvincing assertion of independence by Cyril Briggs:

> While THE LIBERATOR sees nothing disgraceful in being a Communist newspaper, but on the contrary hails and salutes the Communist Party of the United States as the only Party in this country supporting the demands of the Negro workers and agricultural laborers and therefore the only Party worthy of the support and membership of Negro workers and tenant farmers, and hails and salutes the Communist International and its sections throughout the world, in South Africa etc., in the aggressive and relentless struggle for the overthrow of the system under which Negroes are oppressed and exploited, we deem it necessary to point out that THE LIBERATOR is not a Communist newspaper.[7]

If the paper was seriously attempting to distance itself from the Party, it was a spectacular failure. The achievements of Communists at home and abroad in fighting racism and imperialism dominate the paper. The example of the Russian Revolution and the perceived lack of racial prejudice in the Soviet Union are frequently cited. The *Liberator*, like the CPUSA in general, balanced its proclamations of Soviet supremacy against a strong commitment to local struggles against racism and exploitation. The *Liberator* was a black Communist paper of the 1930s and as such it fought a consistent battle against racism, revered Soviet Russia and engaged with the concrete material conditions of an economy in crisis. It drew on the writings of Marx, Lenin and Stalin,

---

more apparent during the Second World War. However, the paper's regular reports on the paradisiacal nature of the Soviet Union, and abstract campaigns against 'enemies of the Soviet Union', are printed side by side with accessible explications of Marxist and Leninist doctrines on class, imperialism and the nature of capitalist rule.

6   Originally the paper was the organ of the ANLC which was replaced by the LSNR in November 1930.

7   *Liberator*, 25 January 1930, p. 2.

on the traditions of black struggle from Toussaint L'Overture to contemporary black Communists like Angelo Herndon and sought to attract a new generation of black supporters to the Party.

The *Liberator*, in all its crusading, sectarian and self-conscious glory, set out to offer black workers a specifically black radical identity. Its prime role was to introduce the politics of the CPUSA to black workers, and it is the *way* the paper addressed its readership that I am focusing on in this chapter. What kind of class-specific race-conscious discourse did the *Liberator* employ in its attempt to promote and produce the discursive black Communist subject?

This book is an investigation of fictional representations of Communism in black American writing from 1940–52 and the historical milieu in which those representations operated. The earliest of the novels studied here was published five years after the *Liberator* ceased production, there is no suggestion that Ellison, Himes or even Wright came across this Harlem-based paper. *Native Son* portrays a symbiotic relationship between Communist and black identities, whilst in *Lonely Crusade* and *Invisible Man* identity is achieved in defiance of, what are presented as, prescriptive Communist projections of black identity. In including a non-fiction text for analysis here, the point is *not* to counterbalance black fictional representation of Communism with Communist factual representations of black American life. I am not using the *Liberator* to question the verisimilitude of the fictional representations of Communism in the novels. However, as a text which insisted on the primacy of Communism in structuring radical black identity, the *Liberator* presents us with an opportunity to investigate specific discourses of black radicalism in the Depression era. I am not suggesting any direct resemblances or antagonisms between black radical activism and black-authored representations of that activism. Rather, the historically-specific discourses of black Communism provide a necessary field within which to rearticulate how three novelists negotiated their own struggle to produce normative modes of black identity. The *Liberator* problematises our understanding of the repertoire of images and histories of the major literary texts analysed in this study. The model of black identity offered by the paper contradicts the tired stereotypes of black Communist political identity.[8]

---

8 Best summed up by Wilson Record's early articulation in 1951:

At times Communists have regarded the Negro as their burden, seeing themselves in the role of suffering missionaries lifting the black man to a higher plane. In shaking hands with a Negro, in sitting beside him at meetings, in participating with him in joint activities, and in calling him 'comrade', the white Party member frequently feels that he is responding to as basic a principle as that of conformity to Party leadership. For he prefers to think that he is Communist in the first place because of humanitarian impulses and

Indeed the *Liberator* constitutes an active instance of one attempt to produce
a coherent model of African American identity adequate to specific political and cultural goals. The purpose here, therefore, is twofold. Firstly, to read
the *Liberator* as a text steeped with traces of the discursive struggle to form a
model of black identity. Secondly, to point that discursive struggle forward so
that it can then inform the reading of the core novels of this study.

The historical material analysed in the previous chapter provided an
account of the political positions and strategies the CPUSA used to generate a powerful model of black class-conscious agency; this chapter looks at
the *Liberator*'s ambitious attempt to both reclaim and institutionalise black
radicalism within a discursive left-wing political framework. As a Communist
newspaper aimed specifically at African-American workers, the *Liberator* is a
critical site, revealing a black radical discourse crucial to understanding the
distinctively Communist discourse which the Party engaged to attract black
Americans. The *Liberator*'s attempt to marry black radical traditions to Soviet-
style Communism released a model of black agency which would echo through
the 1930s and 1940s.

The *Liberator*'s first editorial in December 1929 set out the parameters for
Communist engagement in the black community:

> The present condition of the Negro workers, the increasing attacks on
> their wages, the widespread unemployment crisis which, affecting all
> workers, affects Negro workers first and most extensively, the efforts of
> the landlords to raise rents at the same time that wages are being cut and
> large numbers of workers are being laid off; the betrayal of the working
> class by the bureaucratic leadership of the American Federation of Labor,
> the treachery of the Negro middle class leaders ... all these are reasons
> for a Negro working-class newspaper, voicing the demands of the Negro
> workers and fighting side by side with them against the wage-cutting
> bosses and the rent raising landlords. Such a paper is THE LIBERATOR.
> This is your paper if you are a worker.[9]

This declaration articulates the complex dialectic between race and class, a
dialectic the paper would struggle to keep productively active. The *Liberator*
addresses the 'Negro workers' *as* workers – as the subject of wage attacks unem-

---

    moral conviction; and he is inclined to resist the idea that he pays lip service to, and goes
    through the motions of racial equality because he is a Communist.
    Record 1951, p. 293.

9   *Liberator*, 7 December 1929, p. 2.

ployment, rent hikes, treacherous union bureaucrats *and* as black Americans. It addresses a working class which is here also a black working class; and it defines itself as a 'working-class newspaper'. Class and colour are equally constitutive components of a sharply defined identity which the paper sets out to politicise as a necessarily Communist identity. The pages of the *Liberator* are dominated by the virulence of American racism, the intransigence of American trade unionism and the duplicity of the aspirant black middle class. The paper's rhetoric insisted that what was needed was a strategy of resistance based on offensive working-class militancy rather than defensive negotiation. The *Liberator* reiterated that the politics of accommodation were not only undesirable but unavailable to the disenfranchised black masses; accommodation was the preserve of the black middle classes.

Early editions of the *Liberator* set out to create a radical space for the articulation of the specific demands of the black proletariat as a distinct force within both the black community and the wider ranks of the American working class. From the first, the paper launched a scathing attack on both the black bourgeoisie and the church 'apologists' as the cynical beneficiaries of black poverty:

> Damn it, we should be proud to sacrifice our babies and see our women starve and scrimp until their nipples run dry to support a Watt Terry and a St. Phillip's corporation. A Negro millionaire! A Watt Terry with his shining new automobile! A smug, well-fed pastor of the richest and softest Negro parish in the city, driving an expensive automobile on weekdays, living in a swell, well-kept house amid luxuries and comforts. And on Sunday? On Sunday preaching contentment to the starving and the dispossessed to the exploited and disinherited![10]

With its transgressive metaphoric evocation of the black wet-nurse used to nourish the aspirant *black* rich, here, in its first edition, the *Liberator* explicitly sets out its determination to forcibly articulate the parameters of its engagement with both slavery and class. Capitalism is posited as a 'new form of slavery'; 'wage slavery' as opposed to 'chattel slavery'.[11] The paper insists that the legacy of slavery does not unite the race, but divides it upon class lines. Moreover the *Liberator* places itself in the tradition of Garrison's abolitionist *Liberator*; despite Garrison being a 'hopeless pacifist,' the paper sees itself as the inheritor of the best abolitionist tendencies. In a 1931 article titled '100 years of the *Liberator*', the paper argues:

---

10   *Liberator*, 7 December 1929, p. 2.
11   *Liberator*, 21 February 1931, p. 5.

> We must inherit the 'fire' of Garrison, his uncompromising, unwavering attitude, his devotion to the cause of freedom, and the columns of the new *Liberator* must reflect an intensified struggle against the new forms of slavery, until wage slavery, like chattel slavery, is completely wiped out.[12]

The *Liberator's* discursive politics are crucial here. The paper wanted to speak its presence as the continuation of a radical voice that they feared black moderates would steal and suffocate. The *Liberator* here, as elsewhere, is reclaiming history even as it is competing for it. This rhetorical position and mode of address signals an intense discursive struggle as the paper strives to root itself simultaneously in the present and the past – as the natural inheritors of a black radical history which they produced as illustrative of black traditions of struggle. Moreover the paper attempted to naturalise Communist theory and practice so that Communism was embedded in the very fabric of black cultural and political history:

> And on the ruins of this system which they have destroyed, the Negro and white workers in firm alliance with the poor farmers, will erect a Socialist society where mankind be he in a black or white skin, will for the first time in all history be truly free. The leader of this final battle as of the immediate struggles of today can be none other than the Communist Party of the United States, the true guardian and bearer of the revolutionary heritage of the Negro people in America.[13]

The *Liberator* constantly ruptures narratives of racial solidarity with questions of class allegiance. It actively sought to shatter the pseudo-unity of a racial harmony which would silence social difference. This is apparent in the *Liberator's* construction of a radical emancipationist black history. The black middle class, the 'misleaders', have no claim upon the revolutionary traditions of black Americans and only cite black heroism for their own shadowy motives:

> Unlike the treacherous Negro intellectuals who bandy about his name to cloak their treachery Douglass exposed and repudiated the sinister motives of the white ruling class in cultivating race prejudice and hatred among the exploited classes ... [Douglass] stand[s] in sharp contrast to

---

12   Ibid.
13   *Harlem Liberator*, 7 April 1934, p. 7.

the servile, spineless policy of surrender and treachery of the Negro intellectuals under whose leadership masses have been consistently betrayed.[14]

This hostility to moderate black organisations was breathtaking, even within the context of Third Period sectarianism. When Du Bois made the modest suggestion in *Crisis* that the ANLC and the NAACP had much in common he was greeted with outrage and labelled as a 'prostitute intellectual' and 'agent and instrument of the imperialist oppressors'. The editorial in March 1930 went on to castigate the NAACP in no uncertain terms.

> With brazen bourgeois trickery, Du Bois presents, in parallel columns a list of 'against' and 'fors,' without the slightest mention of methods, i.e., whether of struggle or of petition. This is the rotten bourgeois basis on which he claims for the reformist petitionist program of his organization 'essential agreement' and similarity with the militant, uncompromising, class struggle program of the ANCL ... No worker who knows anything of the activities of the two organizations would for a moment swallow Du Bois' lying slander that the ANLC fight against lynching and mob violence, for instance, is on the same plane as the legalistic anti-lynching activities of the NAACP.[15]

This battle against black moderates was not restricted to editorial tirades, it informed the majority of articles in the paper. So stories of dire poverty in Harlem were not only topical reports, but were also part of an ideological battle with reformist leaders who were promoting Harlem as a showcase black city.[16] While the black press depicted the district as a thriving cosmopolitan centre which evidenced the creativity and capacities of the black community, the *Liberator*'s Harlem was a squalid ghetto of gross inequality:

> Here in Harlem death stalks at the heels of the children on their way to school, waylays them in their homes – homes bare of food, cold and even in darkness, for the light has been turned off because the bills haven't

---

14   *Liberator*, 8 February 1930, p. 3.
15   *Liberator*, 29 March 1930, p. 2, 4.
16   The paper's extensive coverage of tenant/landlord relationships was part of a programme of direct action in Harlem at this time. The Communist-inspired Harlem Tenants League was organising housing committees and calling for rent strikes. For details of the Tenants League's activities see Naison 1985, pp. 19–25.

been paid – poor mean shelters, that are breeding grounds of tuberculo-
sis and disease.[17]

This gothic cityscape, the paper's depiction of a Harlem on the brink of destruction, was a refutation of the reformers' vision, but it was also as Mark Solomon
notes a 'commitment to the most vulnerable and impoverished sectors of the
community'.[18] The rhetorical onslaught against the landlords and shopkeepers
of Harlem sought to establish the Party as the only alternative to destitution,
but it also sought to smash the myth of racial uplift. According to the *Liberator*,
in a capitalist world a black person could only achieve status by profiting on
the segregation and oppression of the rest of the black community. Far from
being examples to revere, black businessmen were 'Black Judases, whose only
wish is the destruction of this army of working class freedom'.[19]

Thus, it was constantly reiterated that the black bourgeoisie were not simply
removed from the concerns of the black masses but represented a conflicting class interest. If they did not embody the class enemy as white business
did, they certainly represented the race traitor; the 'true' tradition of the race
was uncompromising struggle against oppression. The invective that produces
the paper's presentation of black business is seeped in the imagery of parasitic, sycophantic self-interest. An article entitled 'Isolation and Oppression of
Masses a Boon to Negro Business' states unambiguously:

> Negro business want to widen its field of exploitation and to gain conces-
> sions from the imperialists; it becomes the faithful agent of imperialism.
> Under these conditions Negro business has a definite class interest in the
> continuation and perpetuation of the Negro segregated district. It can
> have little or no interest in the militant struggles of the Negro masses for
> solidarity with the revolutionary white workers ... [their] plea for racial
> solidarity becomes therefore a plea for the masses of toiling exploited
> Negroes to turn away from their natural allies, in the struggle for their
> democratic rights and to aid their exploiters for the sole reason that
> this group of exploiters making the appeal are also Negroes whose eco-
> nomic interests are bound to the interests of the white exploiters and
> oppressors.[20]

17   *Liberator*, 21 February 1931, p. 3.
18   Solomon 1998, pp. 95–103.
19   *Liberator*, 3 October 1931, p. 8.
20   *Liberator*, 6 June 1931, p. 5.

In the *Liberator* the political traditions of black workers had their roots in slave resistance and the fights against Jim Crow. The black middle class had no such history to fall back on. They belonged to a different history, to a long line of 'handkerchief heads,' and 'Uncle Toms' who had historically allied themselves with the politics of accommodation in order to achieve minimal advancement within the system. These 'contemptible Negro servants' had no interest in the proud struggles of the race, they 'forget the best traditions of the Negro People', and 'go to the white masters table as belly crawling serpents'.[21]

In order to underline this distinction, the *Liberator* ordered historical narratives into two specific and diametrically-opposed traditions within the race, rendering the idea of cross-class racial solidarity not only as counter-productive, but as a contrivance of the black bourgeoisie.[22] The polemical onslaught against black moderates peaked during the Scottsboro campaign, but from its first edition, the paper's inflated invective against the 'misleaders' of the black community was given precedence. These were the 'old Negro,' who, rather than fight for the future socialist society, spent their time 'licking the white bosses' boots and looking backwards'.[23] The *Liberator* delighted in attacking the black middle class, bringing their full rhetorical arsenal to bear in their vilification:

> With this issue, the NEGRO LIBERATOR begins the custom of naming the most prominent Negro misleaders to the ORDER OF THE BANDANNA. The members of this society may use the following title after their names: 'Loyal Uncle Toms,' 'High-Class Bootlicker,' 'Professional Kisser of Ruling Class Feet,' and 'Hat-in-Hand Clown, to his Majesty the White Boss'. The insignia of the new order will be a large bandanna handkerchief, which members may on occasions use to wipe away their crocodile tears over the suffering and oppression of the Negro masses. The password, by which fellow-members may immediately recognize one another, is 'Me too, boss!' Qualification for membership in the Order of the Bandanna is some act of service to the white ruling class. Such acts consist of betraying the struggles of the Negro masses, either for Judas silver or for a mere pat on the back from rich white masters.[24]

---

21   *Liberator*, 25 July 1931, p. 2; 22 August 1931, p. 5.

22   This line was of course modified with the rise of the Popular Front, but the *Liberator's* heyday was the Third Period and even the modest gestures made toward black moderates during the 'Hands off Ethiopia' campaign of 1935 were conducted in terms which emphasised the 'treachery' of the black middle class.

23   *Harlem Liberator*,13 May 1933, p. 5.

24   *Negro Liberator*, 29 December 1934, p. 8.

The style here is openly, joyously satiric, the black middle-class are characterised as willing *slaves* of capitalism. They are crudely drawn caricatures who embrace the racist stereotyping of the white rulers as a badge of honour. The *Liberator* frequently utilises the iconic images of plantation slavery in order to castigate black moderates and their relationship with capitalism. This focus on the plantation was simultaneously utilised to upbraid the moderates and to order the narratives of slavery into a story of black agency and rage. The black bourgeoisie are utilised to structure the *Liberator's* model of black identity; an identity defined by defiance, pride and anger and ultimately aimed at securing for black Communism an immanent identity between black history and Marxism. It is black workers alone whose interests are served by joining the international brotherhood of the proletariat; in order to do so, they have to separate themselves completely from the 'misleaders,' who would betray the Communist, and therefore the African-American, cause. This emphasis on divergent class interests, however, did not descend into the race-blind class reductionism of the traditional left.[25] The paper did not *negate* the idea of a black tradition but fought to relocate that tradition. 'Struggle' was the true heritage of the 'Negro race', and the black bourgeoisie had marginalised themselves from that history by their objective class interests. 'There are two roads, leading in opposite directions. Which one will you take?', demanded the editorial in 1931. And continued:

> The roads are now unmistakably clear. There is no getting away from them. Either you die on the roadside or you take one or the other. The sign posts on both roads claim that they lead to freedom. One says: via the white ruling class. The other: through working class solidarity to freedom for all workers black and white … The true road to freedom has its sign posts marked clearly. There is no deception here. The army that travels this road carries no chains. There are no signs like those to be found on the other: 'Centre of the road for members of the white race only – ditches for members of the colored race'. The army that travels this road consists of white workers travelling shoulder to shoulder with black toilers. They batter their way past the numerous obstacles thrown into the

25   The American hard Left had traditionally viewed racism as just one other aspect of class
      exploitation. Even the most militant class fighters like the Socialist Eugene Debs claimed:
      'We have nothing special to offer the Negro and we cannot make separate appeals to all
      the races. The Socialist Party is the Party of the working class, regardless of colour – the
      working class of the whole world'. Quoted in Sterling D. Spero & Abraham L. Harris, *Black
      Worker* (New York: Atheneum, 1968), p. 405.

path by the white ruling class and the Black Judases, whose only wish is the destruction of this army of working class freedom. For this is the army led by the Communist Party. This is the road marched by the League of Struggle for Negro Rights. It is the road that THE LIBERATOR rallies the working class.[26]

This political argument in the form of a parodic parable makes the discursive struggle with black moderates explicit; *both* roads claim they lead to freedom. The *Liberator* fights to give 'freedom' an entirely different form, origin and goal in relation to black moderates. The form is collective not individual, the origin is struggle not conformity, the goal is liberation of the entire class.[27] The paper presents a normative political subject in *competition* with other models. It is the black working class and their allies who were the true inheritors of the heroic line of resistance, a line which stretched from Toussaint L'Ouverture through to Angelo Herndon. Setting itself up as the antithesis of Washingtonian perseverance, the *Liberator* actively located itself in the revolutionary traditions of slave resistance. It enacted the elements which enabled that location by producing two competing narratives and a whole apparatus of 'true' and 'false,' 'heroes' and 'traitors' which could be read out of both history and the present.

Black revolutionary heroes were central to the *Liberator* and their significance cannot be overestimated.[28] The first edition of the paper declared its intention to 'revive the revolutionary traditions of the race and do honor to fearless leaders of the numerous slave insurrections in this country'.[29] The LSNR branches in New York took their names from black heroes past and present. As well as the Frederick Douglass, Toussaint L'Overture, Crispus Attucks and Harriet Tubman branches, there were also branches named after the Scottsboro defendant, Clarence Norris, murdered black sharecropper, Ralph Gray, and jailed Communist organiser, Angelo Herndon.[30] Black heroes were inscribed with an almost biblical sense of destiny enabling the proud black fighters of the past to pass down the legacy of rebellion to its natural heirs, the radical black workers of the present: 'The Liberator serves an important function in the organization of the Negro proletarians for their *historic role* of

---

26   *Liberator*, 3 October 1931, p. 8.

27   Boris Max, the Communist lawyer in *Native Son*, also demystifies the concept of 'freedom' in American politics in his defence of Bigger Thomas. See Chapter Three.

28   The *Liberator*'s evocation of black radical historical figures echoes the earlier celebratory histories of black radical achievement inaugurated by Brown 1968.

29   *Liberator*, 7 December 1929, p. 3.

30   The New York LSNR branches are listed in the *Harlem Liberator*, 9 June 1934, p. 7.

leadership of the Oppressed Masses'.[31] Even social events were occasions for celebrating the radical past, as an advert for a social in 1934 publicised:

> A swell time is in store for those who attend the entertainment and dance given by the downtown branch of the LSNR Saturday evening, June 2 ... Besides the prominent artists scheduled to appear at the entertainment, there will be a brief outline of the life and struggles of Toussaint L'Overture, Negro revolutionist.[32]

This blend of entertainment and celebratory history recalled the black cultural traditions of anti-slavery, thereby placing the paper within a rich cultural history of resistance.[33]

The *Liberator* concentrated on commemorating significant dates in black radical history. For instance, 15 February 1935 was the 'Fred Douglass Anniversary Issue'. This issue of the paper complained that Douglass's name 'was dragged through the back door – as a mere appendage' to Lincoln. Communists were the rightful heirs of Douglass's 'revolutionary fervor'. Moreover, the 'theory of militant action put forth by Douglass' was:

> carried out in accordance with present-day conditions by the League of Struggle for Negro Rights and by the International Trade Union Committee of Negro workers. It is these organisations, and not the reformists to which the Negro masses all over the world are turning for guidance and leadership.[34]

Douglass was rarely mentioned without a corresponding dig at Lincoln, who was cited as a racist. Readers were called upon to 'repudiate' Lincoln as an 'anti-Negro idol of the white ruling class'.[35] The *Liberator* was committed to a wholesale debunking of the 'myth' that Lincoln freed the slaves. Lincoln, the paper insisted, belonged to the 'so called Race leaders' who 'would much rather put forth the figure of Lincoln, the white president as a "savior of the race", than to

---

31   *Liberator*, 18 January 1930, p. 2 (my emphasis).
32   *Harlem Liberator*, 2 June 1934, p. 6.
33   For an account of African-American freedom festivals and commemoratory events in the nineteenth century see Wood 2000, pp. 250–6.
34   *Negro Liberator*, 15 February 1935, p. 5.
35   *Negro Liberator*, 1 February 1935, p. 1.

give credit for the emancipation to the revolutionary struggles of the Southern Negro slaves during and immediately after the Civil War'.[36]

Lincoln, thus, belonged to the moderates, the *Liberator* claimed Douglass for their tradition. 'Negro Workers!', it implored, two months after its launch, 'Honour your Revolutionary Heroes! Down with the myth of Lincoln the Emancipator. Celebrate February 12th [birthday of Lincoln and Douglass] as Frederick Douglass Day'.[37] In an overt challenge to other narratives of American history the *Liberator* chooses a heroic model of *black* agency as paradigmatic for present day struggles against black moderates:

> One of the first tasks facing the new Negro industrial proletariat which is today increasingly taking over the leadership of the masses from the treacherous intellectuals and stock-promoters is the fight against these illusions and against the Lincoln myth and for the reviving of the revolutionary traditions of the race and the honouring of its revolutionary heroes.[38]

The honouring of black revolutionary heroes in the paper was the configuration of a specific black radical tradition. Toussaint L'Overture, Nat Turner, Frederick Douglass, Harriet Tubman and black Communists Angelo Herndon and Ralph Grey were claimed as constituting a tradition of continuous struggle from the slave resistance to the contemporary fights of African-American workers. The paper attempted to delineate a specifically insurrectionary black tradition which stood intrinsically opposed to the black middle-class 'misleaders':

> The Frederick Douglass meetings are part of the general campaign of the American Negro Labor Congress, beginning with the celebration last year of Toussaint L'Ouverture and Nat Turner days, to revive the revolutionary traditions of race and mobilize the Negro workers to do honor to their revolutionary fighters and heroes. At these meetings the self sacrificing life of Frederick Douglass, and the courage and fearlessness with which he waged the struggle against the enemies of the Negro race, will be sharply contrasted with the cowardly, imbecilic leadership with which

---

36   *Negro Liberator*, 15 February 1935, p. 5.

37   *Liberator*, 1 February 1930, p. 2.

38   *Liberator*, 8 February 1930, p. 3. During the Second World War the 'Lincoln myth' was one adopted by the Party during their 'Americanisation' period.

the Negro intelligentsia and shop keepers have afflicted the race for the past several decades.[39]

While the 'despicable' Robert Moton of the National Negro Business League was reviled, along with the 'Faithful Slave' Booker T. Washington, the *Liberator* sought its own black heroes. From 12 December 1933 to April 1934, Jack Layton chronicled the history of slavery and slave rebellions from the Conquistadors to the recent murder of black Communist Ralph Grey at Camp Hill in his regular column 'The Revolutionary Traditions of the Negro People'.[40] This chronological series promised to relate the history of black America as a heroic narrative of sacrifice and struggle:

> No tale of fiction, no best selling romance is more thrilling than the story of the Negro people and their age long struggle against slavery and oppression in America. It is a tale that takes us back to the dawn of the fifteenth century . . . The back-breaking labor of African Negroes was now to supplement the rich soil of the Americas; their blood and sweat was to fertilize this earth; their labor was to lay the foundations of American wealth and power.[41]

African Americans are seen here as the first American Proletarians, their labour is responsible for the development of the US. The column consciously set itself up as the bastion of black revolutionary historiography fighting the revisionism of bourgeois accounts of slavery by placing black history at the centre of anti-capitalism. Moreover, black history not only provided examples of noble resistance, it offered the best examples of how to fight oppression. In his six-part column dedicated to the Haitian revolution, Otto Hall insisted that 'we must remember that the heroic Haitian slafes [sic] under the leadership of Toussaint L'Overture, in achieving their own freedom dealt a blow that was to shatter the system of chattel slavery in every part of the Western World'.[42]

The paper consistently pointed to the peerless nature of black radicals, with the names of Douglass, Vesey, Turner and L'Overture dominating each issue. There was far less interest in adapting white European radical traditions than in reclaiming revolutionary black history. Aside from articles dedicated to the

---

39   *Liberator*, 15 February 1930, p. 4.
40   For a detailed account of the Camp Hill shoot out, see Kelley 1990, Chapter Two.
41   *Harlem Liberator*, 16 December 1933, p. 5.
42   *Harlem Liberator*, 26 May 1934, p. 6.

gains of the Soviet Union and the odd piece on Lenin or the Paris Commune, the *Liberator* sought legitimation for Marxist politics in the black revolutionary past and the contemporary struggles of black workers.[43] This was more than a simple redressing of the balance, or an act of cultural reclamation. It was part of an ideological battle to place Communism at the centre of black resistance, to dislocate it from a strictly European tradition and to forge the link between slavery and capitalism:

> T]he struggle for Negro liberation began by the brave slave insurrectionists, continues today and reaches its highest form in the class struggle which, under the leadership of the vanguard of the working class, is uniting Negro and white workers, native and foreign-born in a revolutionary fight against the very roots of their exploitation and oppression, against the capitalist system with its new slavery.[44]

The history of black revolt in the *Liberator* evoked racism as historically specific, as ideological rather than ontological. Racism's roots lay in capitalism and therefore could be destroyed as part of the struggle against class society. For centuries black people had been forced into brutal confrontation with capitalism; the struggles of black workers, past and present were fights against capitalist modes of exploitation, both chattel slavery and wage slavery. According to Cyril Briggs both the 'American bosses' and the 'treacherous Negro petit bourgeoisie':

> have very nearly succeeded in wiping out of the consciousness of the Negro masses all memory of their glorious revolutionary traditions. For the bosses, whose oppression of the Negro masses is today as brutal as under chattel slavery, do not wish the exploited Negro masses to have any traditions of revolt and struggle against their oppressors.[45]

These questions of 'consciousness', 'memory' and 'revolutionary tradition' were key terms in the struggle to articulate a Communist model of black political

---

43   Even within its coverage of the Soviet Union the paper was concerned with race. They took a particular interest in Pushkin as a black Russian artist, offering: 'A Pushkin Bust in Every Negro Home! Attractive small busts of the great Negro Russian Poet will soon be ready. $1 each. Special price with subscription to the *Harlem Liberator*'. *Harlem Liberator* 13 May 1933, p. 5.

44   *Liberator*, 14 March 1931, p. 8.

45   *Liberator*, 6 June 1931, p. 2.

identity. The construction of black history in the *Liberator* was not intended to act simply as a counter-history to racism, it interwove the history of racism with the emergence of capitalism. The two were seen to be historically linked and had to be fought simultaneously. Racism was the 'boss ideology' and anti-colonial revolts therefore were intrinsic to the history of anti-capitalist protest. Such a historical construct could be made to provide a rich source of inspiration for contemporary black revolutionaries. The *Liberator* took command of a discursive field in which history/tradition formed a crucial site of symbolic structuring of black political identity. The paper ensured that, far from being a foreign import, Communism was the terminus of the black radical past and had an organic relationship to the black proletariat.

> We must remember the many slave rebellions in which our forefathers took part, arose in spite of severe persecutions, wholesale killings and the treachery of stool pigeons in the ranks ... If we honor the fighting traditions of our forefathers, if we claim the right to be their true sons and daughters, positively we must follow in their footsteps of struggle and not disgrace their heroic struggles and trample in cowardly passivity the courageous and fighting heritage that they have passed on to us.[46]

In the pages of the *Liberator* there were two Americas. The country of the slaveholders and their 'allies,' and that of the slaves and the inheritors of their traditions. The *Liberator*'s version of black radical history was essential to its class politics. The paper set out to delineate a specific revolutionary black tradition which could be utilised in the struggle against both American racism *and* black entrepreneurship; a strategy which was characterised by veneration of black heroes and sectarian hectoring of black moderates. Such a move was essential to a paper which insisted on the primacy of interracial solidarity in anti-racist struggle. I am concerned with black Communist radicalism here as illustrative of the model of black identity produced in the *Liberator*, not as one manufactured out of Stalinist theory alone, but one constructed out of a reworking of black history. However, the re-appropriation of black revolutionaries was not purely an act of cultural nationalism, for this history was only one element in the revolutionary process. Black workers needed to reclaim black radical traditions but they also needed the solidarity of white workers.

---

46   *Liberator*, 15 August 1931, p. 4.

2.2   The *Liberator*: Interracial Solidarity and Internationalism

> In the United States of America, every independent movement of the
> workers was paralysed as long as slavery disfigured a part of the Republic.
> Labour cannot emancipate itself in the white skin where in the black it
> is branded.[47]

While the *Liberator* was certainly not immune from formulaic sloganeering,
the paper retained a sophisticated theoretical understanding of the centrality
of race in the structuring of black political identity. For Communists in the
early 1930s race was more than just a prejudice, it was the axis upon which the
fate of the American working class turned. The *Liberator* strove to keep both
race and class as sites of political agency, yet they encountered difficulties in
this negotiation.

   While the rhetorical construction of the black bourgeoisie worked to delineate a counter-tradition of black radicalism, white American workers could
rarely be used un-problematically. As argued in Chapter One, what differentiates Communist politics at the time from the politics of black nationalism is not a lack of race pride or a dilution of the impact of racism, but the
question of interracial solidarity and the possibility of winning white workers
to anti-racism. With notable exceptions such as the Knights of Labor or the
International Workers of the World (IWW), this history rendered fewer heroic
examples than the black radical tradition.[48] Craft unionism, which dominated
the American labour movement, had an appalling record of racism and exclusion, and while the American Federation of Labour (AFL) was cited contemptuously in the paper, examples of interracial solidarity tended to focus on John
Brown and current Communist-led campaigns. American Communists aside,
within the paper the main historical referent for working-class anti-bigotry lay
outside the United States. While the centuries-old tradition of black resistance
pointed to Communism as its radical inheritor, the proletarian fight against
national and racial oppression was sourced in the Soviet Union. The Russian
Revolution had established that workers could break down centuries of deeply
held prejudices and Lenin had formulated a theory of anti-imperialism which
forged the alliance between Communism and anti-colonial struggle:

---

47   Marx 1983, p. 284.
48   The reasons for this are of course widely contested. For a critical overview of the historio-
      graphical accounts of the persistence of race divisions in the American working class see
      Kelly 2001, pp. 3–17.

It was Lenin who laid the basis for that whole-hearted support which Communist parties throughout the world have given to the nationalist movements in Turkey, China, Haiti, Morocco, India, Egypt, Korea and other oppressed countries, as well as for a free black republic of South Africa, self-determination for the Negro people of the Southern United States and complete racial, social and political equality for the Negro north and south.[49]

In terms of the United States, the *Liberator* carried articles every week pointing to examples of white Communists fighting for black equality. Typical articles concerning interracial solidarity stressed the danger white Communists faced in standing up for black rights, like 'White Worker On Trial for Negro Speech,' 'White Workers Jailed, Defending Negroes,' 'White Workers are Rallying to The Defence of Negroes Against Klan Terror' or 'White Workers Save Negro from Beating'.[50] It was *Communists* who were the driving force in fighting segregation, and white Communists specifically who most explosively shattered the racial boundaries of resistance.

However, white Communists were not representative of the white working class as a whole and initially the *Liberator*'s attitude to white workers in general was somewhat ambiguous. While the paper was in many ways a sophisticated and professional journal, it was also very much a work in progress. The paper frequently drew attention to its own theoretical and practical errors and the early editions were the site of a debate concerning the very nature of black resistance and the place of white workers within it. An early editorial entitled 'The Need to Hate' from January 1930 is worth quoting at length. Responding favourably to a black student's exhortation to '[l]et your motivating force be your hatred of white people', the editorial continues:

> This normal and necessary attitude of hating one's enemies will not be to the liking of either the white imperialist oppressors or their servile Negro middle-class tools. These like to point to the Negro as a spineless cowardly creature, constantly turning the other cheek and, like a yellow cur, licking the hand that abuses him. Such a conception is contrary to human nature and is tantamount to admitting the dictum of the imperialist oppressors that the Negro race is inferior, that it is scarcely human and more allied to the patient jackass than to red-blooded beings capable of passionate hatred against oppression and oppressors.

49   *Liberator*, 18 January 1930, p. 2.
50   *Liberator*, 28 December 1929, p. 3; 5 April 1930, p. 2; 25 April 1931, p. 3; 15 October 1932, p. 3.

It would be a good thing for the Negro race if all Negroes did hate all white people. It will be a better thing still when the Negro workers start differentiating between the white ruling class at whose hands we suffer the most terrific exploitation and brutal oppression and the white workers who are also oppressed and exploited by our oppressors, and whose hostility to us is deliberately fostered and inspired by the white imperialists in order to divide and weaken the working class and perpetuate their exploitation of both groups of workers.[51]

The rhetorical flourishes of this animated assertion of black proletarian militancy takes hatred as its source of strength, it harnesses 'hate' as a political weapon, it structures 'hate' as a dynamic aspect of black identity. Throughout the paper it is constantly reiterated that there is nothing so ineffectual as passivity, and here, *any* hatred is seen as a foundation on which Communism can grow. In theorising hatred as the embryo of revolutionary activity, the *Liberator* validated and celebrated black rage. This articulation of the 'right to rage' was enormously significant and set the *Liberator* apart from moderate black leaders who felt that such anger was a barrier to assimilation in the white community.[52] The paper's abhorrence of 'passivity' or 'non-resistance' was one of its most abiding tropes. This was most powerfully manifested in its *hatred* of Gandhi, who was constantly caricatured in small articles and cartoons, often with little contextual analysis of either his politics or indeed British colonialism in India. In the *Liberator* Gandhi is utilised as a potent symbol of supplication. His pacifism is a 'slavish principle of "non-violence" '; he uses the 'poisonus [sic] propaganda of non-resistance' in order to articulate the 'cowardice and apprehensions of the Indian bourgeoisie'.[53] 'Hate' is the active expression of black agency.

In the 'Need to Hate' editorial, racism is explained as an instrument of capitalist strategies of divide and rule, but any notion of white workers being part of the struggle is absent. Racist 'hostility' is explained as a contrivance of the ruling class, but though white workers should be differentiated from the powerful white ruling class, they are not seen as having an active role in black liberation. This ambiguity is illustrative of the difficulties the paper faced in building a model of black agency flexible enough to recuperate all black radical

---

51   *Liberator*, 18 January 1930, p. 2 (emphasis mine).

52   bell hooks sources this uncompromising hate in Malcolm X; it is significant to find the articulation of it some 30 years previously in the pages of the *Liberator*. See hooks 1996, p. 13.

53   *Liberator*, 5 April 1930, p. 4; 26 April 1930, p. 4; 3 May 1930, p. 4.

energies yet not to tip over into black separatism. The *Liberator*'s acknowledgement of 'hate' as a historical fact exhibits the discursive field's sensitivity to the materiality of its addressees, yet that materiality cannot be left unfocused. The next issue seized upon this point. Asserting the shared identity of interests between black workers and 'the class conscious revolutionary white workers of the imperialist countries', as well as the necessity for working-class solidarity, the editorial 'A Correction and Self Criticism' goes on to state:

> In the editorial 'The Need to Hate' which appeared in the January issue of THE LIBERATOR, the writer made an impermissible and absolutely incorrect statement in the sentence 'It would be a good thing for the Negro race if all Negroes did hate all white people'. While an attempt was made in the same editorial to develop this statement along the line of the A.N.L.C. said attempt was wholly inadequate. This statement is, of course, absolutely opposed to the line of the A.N.L.C., which, as explained above calls for solidarity and fraternization between Negro workers and class conscious white workers, as a prerequisite to effective struggle against the oppressing class. The writer fully repudiates this statement. Hatred there must be. Hot passionate hatred by the Negro workers against their oppressors, but that hatred must be directed solely against the brutal white imperialists of this and other countries … The A.N.L.C. while stimulating hatred of oppression and oppressors in the minds of the Negro workers and farm laborers, at the same time fights the attempt of the oppressing class and its tools in the A.F. of L and the Negro middle class to foster racial antagonisms among the workers in the deliberate efforts to split the ranks and divert their energies from the necessary struggle against their oppressors. The A.N.L.C. also fights the pacifist propaganda carried on among the Negro workers by the salaaming Uncle Toms and 'Mammies' of the Negro middle class.[54]

Solomon points to this retraction as an example of Party control of the paper, which it does indeed suggest. But the fact that the initial editorial *was* published and in the context of the *Liberator*'s self-critical reproaches elsewhere, also points to a certain amount of independence from Politbureau dictates.[55] The more salient point here is that the ambiguity surrounding the white working class is about the fight to present a normative model of black political identity which was more than an ideal. The 'interests' shared by black and

---

54   *Liberator*, 25 January 1930, p. 2.
55   See Solomon 1998, p. 165.

white workers are abstract; the hostility and hate are concrete and there is a tension, a difficulty in relating the two within the same model of identity. The self-correcting editorial is significant precisely because it is the last visible articulation of this ambiguity. Black hate in the *Liberator* is made a class issue; class was the basis for solidarity and identification, but a solidarity between *class conscious* blacks and *anti-racist* white workers. The challenge was to construct a model which would speak to the daily activities of black workers but also demand a leap of faith as to the ability or willingness of white workers to contribute to anti-racist struggle. It was an ambiguity that remains as a significant silence in the *Liberator*, save for the representations of future freedom predicated on interracial unity which dominated the poems and stories of the paper (discussed below). In general, henceforth the paper concentrated on reporting concrete examples of white Communist anti-racist activity.

The *Liberator*'s regular reports of discrimination, police brutality, white-on-black rape, and racial violence emphasised that working-class unity could not be premised on any diminishment of the pervasive nature of American racism. Unlike the black radical historical tradition, the commitment to working-class unity could not find expression in any ideal form. Given the tangible extremity, yet daily constancy, of American racism, white workers could not be presented as either actual or absolute allies. The paper had to negotiate 'racial' difference whilst proclaiming class identity. The *Liberator* constantly stressed the *ideological* function of racism; far from being endemic to American whites, racism was a dynamic and pernicious ideology which structured all social relations in the United States, not only between black and white, but North and South as well:

> The slave conditions which reign in the Southern Black Belt extend to the cities in the North, and enshackle the Negro industrial worker. The shackles that bind the Negro also bind the white worker. The Negro worker in the North cannot free himself as long as the Negro remains a slave in the South. The white worker cannot free himself as long as the Negro masses are chained. The blow that strikes the shackles from one must strike the shackle of the other... The terrific needs of the Negro people have dictated this program. It is based upon the experience and traditions of three centuries of struggle against oppression. Its sharpness has been tempered in the blood of Negroes murdered by the white ruling class oppressors.[56]

---

56   *Harlem Liberator*, 4 November 1935.

The *Liberator* focused on how the abuses heaped on the Communist Party were manifestly related to their record of anti-racist activity. Often this was done directly, as in the case of the Party's sexual politics. The claim that the CPUSA recruited black men through the sexual availability of white Communist women was a pervasive one. Indeed Wright, Himes and Ellison all comment on the sexual 'lure' of white Communist women in their fictional representations of Communism. The coroner in *Native Son* accuses the Communist Jan of using Mary Dalton to entice Bigger: 'You had never used Miss Dalton as bait before had you?' In *Lonely Crusade* Lee Gordon initially (and correctly) suspects that Jackie Forks has been instructed to seduce him into the Party: ' "Did they send you out?" ... "No we don't do that ... Not now, not since the war" '. In *Invisible Man* Ellison's satiric vignette on the narrator's position as spokesperson for women is summed up in the famous line, 'why did they insist upon confusing the class struggle with the ass struggle?'[57]

The *Liberator* went on the offensive when it came to the charge that the Party attracted black men to Communism by making white women sexually available:

> But to imply – as do the Negro fakers – that sexual intimacy with white women is the basis of the attraction of Negroes into the Communist Party, is to slander the Negro masses, and to strengthen an old lie put forth by the lynchers of Negroes. No 'sexual lure' is necessary to draw towards the Communist Party – the Party that fights for unemployment insurance and for Negro rights – the millions of starving, oppressed Negro workers. The fight for bread and for work, the fight against lynching and Jim-Crowism – these struggles are drawing the Negro masses away from the bosses' political parties and into Communist ranks. The white boss lynchers have diligently spread the lie that the Negro is especially prone to the crime of rape. To 'protect white womanhood,' Negroes must be lynched, disfranchised, jailed, and kept in the direst poverty. According to these 'theorists' the chief motive in the life of a Negro man is his longing for white women.[58]

Here, the attempt to smear Communism is inseparable from those racial myths that justify lynch law and, again, the fight against one myth is dialectically related to the other. However, while racism is connected to wider class questions, nowhere in the *Liberator* is it suggested that black workers sacrifice

---

57   Wright 1990, p. 359; Himes 1997, p. 99; Ellison 1965, p. 337.
58   *Liberator*, 1 August 1932, p. 8.

their specific racial demands to the demands of the working class as a whole. It was in the interests of the entire working class to fight racism. Anti-racism, as the Yokinen trial discussed in Chapter One demonstrated, was now a prerequisite for Communist Party membership, as the *Liberator* clarified conclusively in 1930:

> During the last three months, nearly a thousand Negro workers throughout the country have turned to the Communist Party... As the Negroes join in large numbers there have been outcroppings of race prejudice among some of the less advanced of the white membership of the Communist Party. The Party's answer to this manifestation is to expel all white members still under the influence of the imperialist ideology of white chauvinism, and to train the new Negro recruits for leadership in the Party.[59]

The demand for interracial struggle meant the *Liberator* was also conducting a polemic against black nationalism. The antipathy between Garveyites and Communists in Harlem often involved physical violence, as depicted in Ellison's *Invisible Man*, in the farcical climactic battle where the narrator is set upon by the Garveyite Ras the Exhorter. The *Liberator* reported such skirmishes with relish: 'Garvey Misleaders Allied with Police in Attack on Workers,' the paper reported in April 1931. Briggs, who was a veteran of the battles between Communists and the UNIA (he successfully sued Garvey for libel in 1922 over accusations that he was a white man who was 'Negro for convenience'), wrote bitterly of the 'misdeeds' of Garveyism:[60]

> Is it not a fact that Garveyism shamelessly shares the reactionary philosophy of the fascist Ku Klux Klan that the United States is a white man's country? Has not Garveyism consistently surrendered the struggle for Negro rights within the United States and the West Indies? Has not Garveyism turned into a reactionary slogan the essentially progressive demand for a free Africa by preaching the surrender of Negro rights in the United States and the West Indies and a peaceful return to an Africa still enslaved by the imperialists? A demand further negated by Garvey's infamous statement that 'the Negro must be loyal to all flags under which he lives'. Has not Garveyism betrayed even the struggle for a free Africa

---

59   *Liberator*, 22 February 1930, p. 3.
60   For details of the Briggs libel case see Hill 1985, pp. 107–41.

by peddling illusions of imperialist charity and co-operation in the establishment of a Negro homeland.[61]

This pseudo Pan-Africanist vision permeated the *Liberator*. The paper did not
confine its emphasis on differences *within* the black community to the United
States. The paper offered detailed analysis of the local political scene, particularly after 1933 when it became the *Harlem Liberator*, but it also offered extensive international coverage, which was particularly focused on West Indies,
Liberia, Angola, Ethiopia, South Africa and Central America. The headline of
the very first issue was 'Back the Haitian Mass Revolt,' and the paper followed
political developments in the colonised world very closely. Cyril Briggs penned
a series called 'The World Situation and the Negro' which ran over many weeks
from December 1931. George Padmore wrote a series of articles in 1933 on the
condition of black struggle worldwide, called 'Negro Liberation Struggle' and
in 1934 and 1935 a weekly column was devoted to 'Negro Struggles Abroad'.
In these reports the *Liberator* pointed to the conflicting class interests of the
race internationally, although the determining role of imperialism was never
neglected:

> The Liberian episode contains certain lessons for American Negro
> workers and *Liberator* readers. First it shows us that Negroes can be
> quite as vicious rulers under capitalism as white exploiters. The Vice
> President of Liberia was found to be up to his neck in the slavery busi-
> ness. Second we must always take the 'protests' of imperialist states-
> men with a large grain of salt. They are invariably hypocritical or are
> used to cover up underlying conflicts with other imperialist nations.
> And finally, we must see with increasing clearness that only the work-
> ers and poor farmers of the imperialist countries united with those of
> the colonial countries will put a stop to imperialist exploitation both at
> home and abroad.[62]

The *Liberator* was particularly concerned with placing, not just black
Americans, but the black world at the centre of anti-capitalist protest. The
solidarity with black people worldwide was premised on the basis that all
suffered the collective stigmatisation produced by white imperialism and
had the right to self-determination. This was not strictly a Pan-Africanist
vision, however, as it was only black *workers* who possessed the objective

---

61   *Liberator*, 8 August 1931, p. 7.
62   *Liberator*, 21 February 1931, p. 2.

class position to lead that fight. Black workers were the potential vanguard of anti-imperialist struggle at home and abroad. The *Liberator* proudly proclaimed that it was:

> the voice of the new leadership of the Negro race, the voice of the Negro industrial proletariat, whose experience in struggle and in the use of their collective power, together with a grasp of the scientific Marxian theory of working class struggle against imperialism, historically fits them for the hegemony of all Negro liberation movements as well as for an important role, as an integral part of the American working class in the struggles of the American proletariat for the overthrow of imperialism and the establishment of a workers and farmers government in this country.[63]

To be a consistent anti-racist was to be anti-capitalist, and as black and white workers needed to recognise each other as comrades, they were also urged to use that comradeship to make solidarity with other oppressed groups. And not just in America. Immediately following Hitler's rise to power, and two years before the Popular Front, a plethora of articles appeared comparing the situation of black Americans to that of German Jews, where even the discrimination suffered by the black middle class was cited:

> Negroes in this country suffer from discrimination. Our doctors and lawyers, writers and all professional and technical men have felt it as well as the masses. Our people are persecuted and lynched and the white rulers and authorities always say just as Hitler says 'There is a reason, they were guilty'. The Negro is guilty of being black – and the Jew is guilty of being a Jew.[64]

Significantly here, the paper acknowledges that racism forces black Americans into a common situation of oppression that the *Liberator* must recognise. This is a powerful instance of the paper's commitment to race. Yet this point is made in the context of *widening* the parameters of black political consciousness to include other oppressed groups. As part of an international capitalist system, racism was a worldwide phenomenon and black workers were urged to watch developments in Germany closely. In 1933 the paper warned 'What Negroes may expect of the developing fascist dictatorship in this country

---

63   *Liberator*, 29 March 1930, p. 2.
64   *Harlem Liberator*, 9 September 1933, p. 4.

is clearly indicated in the monstrous persecution of the Jewish minority by German fascism'.[65] The paper took a strong line on anti-Semitism and pointed to the dangerous consequences of the victory of Fascism for all who fell foul of ideals of racial superiority. Unsurprisingly, Communism alone was the force which could fight both anti-Semitism and racism as part of the world-wide struggle against capitalism:

> The *Harlem Liberator* owes a duty to the Negro masses to point out that only one political Party is waging a consistent struggle against the fascist reaction. That Party is waging a relentless struggle against the fascist attacks on the Jews and the German working class, and against the lynching and national oppression of Negroes in this country. That Party is the Communist Party of the United States. Negroes will do well to remember this at election time.[66]

Again, it was in black workers' *interests* to fight anti-Semitism, as it was in white workers' interests to be anti-racist. A point stressed by the paper in 1933:

> The white worker of America has been demoralized, degraded, defiled and prostituted in the process of Negro oppression and exploitation. Now their ruling class is driving them to that level of living to which it has for so long assigned the Negro masses. The resistance of the white workers can not be successful unless it is coupled with the struggles of and for the Negro people. The division of the oppressed is the main strength of the oppressor.[67]

Here, racism has infected the white working class, anti-racism is in their own interests, black liberation will also set them free. Communism was predicated on the unity of the entire working class; any division only strengthened the power of the ruling class. This was not a plea for abstract identification on the basis of injustice, but for political mobilisation on the basis of class interest and the furthering of the Communist cause.

The attacks on black moderates along with the international lens served to redefine the traditional racial boundaries of opposition. In the context of black nationalism and reformism any split within the race was counterproductive and served to disempower black Americans in the face of racism. If

---

65   *Harlem Liberator*, 20 May 1933, p. 4.
66   *Harlem Liberator*, 19 August 1933, p. 2.
67   *Harlem Liberator*, 18 November 1933, p. 2.

the establishment was antagonised it would close its ranks and refuse to give in to the most basic of reforms, but in the context of Communism, black workers gained the solidarity of the world working class in rejecting their leaders. Far from isolating themselves, they were relocated in a world-wide movement of solidarity, a world in which they occupied a privileged position as both exploited proletariat and oppressed minority. They became the vanguard in an international movement for black liberation.[68] As Theodore Draper expresses it, 'one did not merely belong to a national Party; one belonged to an international movement of which the Soviet Union was the single success and guiding star'.[69]

The fact that this movement was less an instrument for international socialism than for defending Soviet national interests becomes more significant during World War II, and will be discussed in Chapter Four. For Communists in the early 1930s the heady possibilities opened up by a Communist worldview were unbounded compared to the conciliatory politics of black moderates and the nationalism of Garveyism. Harry Haywood recalled how the Party's internationalism enabled them to extend their anti-racist message to the immigrant communities in the United States:

> T[hrough our militant working class policy, we were able to win workers of all nationalities to take up the special demands of Black people embodied in the Scottsboro defense. I'll never forget how the immigrant workers in the Needle Trades Union would sing 'Scottsboro Boys Shall Not Die' in their various Eastern European and Yiddish accents.[70]

---

68   The Comintern stressed the centrality of black Americans to the international struggle against imperialism, as evidenced in this key statement:

> The Negro question in the United States must be treated in its relation to the Negro questions and struggles in other parts of the world. The Negro race everywhere is an oppressed race. Whether it is a minority (USA, etc.) majority (South Africa) or inhabits a so-called independent state (Liberia etc.), the Negroes are oppressed by imperialism. Thus, a common tie of interest is established for the revolutionary struggle of race and national liberation from imperialist domination of the Negroes in various parts of the world. A strong Negro revolutionary movement in the USA will be able to influence and direct the revolutionary movement in all those parts of the world where the Negroes are oppressed by imperialism.

Degras 1956–1965, vol. 2, p. 555.

69   Draper 1987, p. 30.

70   Haywood 1978, p. 385.

This was not the advocation of a 'melting pot', but of a multi-cultural politics which retained the centrality of black struggle.

In many ways the *Liberator* challenges the most cherished myths about American Communism and black workers. The paper called for neither separation nor assimilation; the former represented the politics of defeat, the latter non-resistance. The Party's commitment to interracial class solidarity was never colour blind. The *Liberator* assured its readers that any successes in forging class unity were not to be confused with 'a Liberal intellectual gesture for racial equality'.[71] The terms of any interracial solidarity were explicitly defined.

2.3   The *Liberator* and Black Cultural Politics

> The white ruling class not only utilizes against us the instruments of culture at its disposal, it seeks to disarm the Negro people culturally as well as economically and politically. It has suppressed the revolutionary traditions of the Negro People. It has prostituted Negro Culture to suit its dictum of Negro inferiority, holding Negro Art to the level of black face clowning ... In all class societies, the dominating class rules by controlling the instruments of culture, along with economic and political power. To talk of pure and unbiased art under such circumstances is sheer rot and nonsense. Art is a weapon in the hands of the white ruling class. Art, can be and must be made a weapon in the hands of the toiling masses and the oppressed Negro People in their struggles for bread and freedom.[72]

The formulation of art as a 'weapon' was key to the *Liberator's* cultural politics. This was an area where the paper could articulate a working harmony of race and class and posit an ideal political subject. The concerted attempt to construct a working-class, 'Negro' culture was manifested in both negative reviews of black representation in mainstream culture and the extensive publication of poetry and short stories in the paper.

The *Liberator's* eclectic formal range of poetry and short stories set out to destroy distinctions between high and low art. Established black poets, with Langston Hughes as their vanguard, were published side by side with 'workers correspondence' and anonymous poems to create a cultural site where

---

71   *Liberator*, 5 April 1930, p. 2.

72   *Harlem Liberator*, 9 September 1933, p. 5.

dreams of interracial unity could be articulated. A 'worker-poet' from Arkansas declared in 1932, 'The pride of the "cracker" is on the wane/Many are moving into the "nigger" lane/... So lets go forward with the LSNR/To where there is no color bar'.[73] Sometimes aesthetically elevated and skilled, sometimes epigrammatic and hectoring, these poems stressed the liberating energies released by Communism and the imperative for black and white unity.

The poetry of the *Liberator* drew on a range of poetic styles, incorporating the traditions of resistance poetry coming out of slavery and abolition. Bill Morton's 'Black, White Go Marching On!' was published in July 1932. As part of the Communist presidential campaign of William Foster and black vice presidential candidate James Ford, readers were instructed that it was 'to be sung to the tune of John Brown's Body':

I

Our Party is the Party of the workers, black and white.
For the self-determination of the Negro Race we fight.
And we raise our scarlet banner in the face of bosses might
As our class goes marching on

Chorus:
Power, power, Ford and Foster!
Power, power, Ford and Foster!
Power, power, Ford and Foster!
Our class goes marching on!

II

We have graven on our banner that will never know retreat
The cry of starving labor as it lacks for bread and meat;
'You who rob us of our plenty, we shall work your sure defeat
As our class goes marching on'.

Chorus:
III

We are rising, rising in the cotton and the slum
We are organising labor for the workers rule to come.
In our millions we are shouting and no longer meek and dumb
Our class goes marching on!

---

73   *Liberator*, 16 January 1932, p. 3.

Chorus:
IV
Death to lynching and to lynchers is the slogan that we cry,
Free the Scottsboro boys from prison, we have vowed they shall not die!
Black and white we stand together and we hold our banners high
As our class goes marching on!

Chorus:
IV
Too long we've starved in patience while our children cried for bread,
While the grasping greed of bosses took a ghastly toll of dead,
Now we're backing Ford and Foster and we're voting voting RED
As our class goes marching on![74]

This poem is a radical revision of the famous abolitionist anthem of the Union army. Unlike the original *John Brown's Body*, which wrote out black history in a narrative of abolitionist self-sacrifice, here, the black and white working-class army are united by the specificities of racial injustice.[75] 'Our class' is unproblematic, it is the site where 'black and white' can 'stand together' as a powerful force against racism and as the avenging army of Communist retribution.

The poems of the *Liberator* stressed struggle at all cost, exhorting the reader to 'Revolt!,' 'Arise!,' 'March On!,' 'Unite!' Interracial unity was demanded as a prerequisite for liberation in verse more extensively and unambiguously than anywhere else in the paper, as in Victor Jerome's extensive poem 'To a Black Man':

> . . . We against them
> Fuse the fires
> you from the black breast
> I from the white.
> It's a war for the earth!
> Workmen fieldmen
> every hammer a gun
> every scythe a sword
> we against them![76]

---

74 'Black, White go Marching On!' by Bill Morton *Liberator*, 15 July 1932, p. 5.

75 For a reading of *John Brown's Body* as a representative of a martyrological vision see Wood 2003, p. 662.

76 'To a Black Man', by Victor Jerome, *Liberator*, 15 June 1932, p. 4 (the poem was published later that year in the *Daily Worker*: Solomon 1985, p. 251 n.39).

Again this poem, like *Black White Go Marching On*, works through appropriating and subverting popular tradition. Here, the biblical pacifist dictum of 'turning swords into ploughshares' is turned on its head via the imagery of the hammer and sickle. The white speaker of the poem overhears a black men tell his sons to 'Hate the white man!', to which he replies:

> And I a white man answer
> In the deeps of your being
> Let hate gather and rumble
> And rise

This validation and veneration of black rage is the basis from which to build interracial resistance to 'them'. The stress on interracial unity is predicated on the prior acknowledgement of race-conscious anger.

The poetry incorporated the slogans of marches and demonstrations into stanzas as a clarion call to fight for the red future. The poem 'Scottsboro' called on readers to 'Tighten your fists!/Gird your loins!/Prepare to fight for freedom!...Join the fighting ranks/To win or die!'[77] While Clyde Smyth proudly articulated the fusion between black and red identities:

> Now I am a Negro and a Red
> And that I be until I'm dead
> All of which I'm very proud
> And for their cause I'll cry out
> loud.[78]

In its stridency, this was a typical *Liberator* poem, although there were also less jargonistic attempts, such as an anonymous piece 'Stop fooling wit pray' in March 1932. This poem takes up a particular aspect of the black vernacular tradition, the spiritual as liberation theology:

> Sistern an' Brethern,
> Stop foolin' wi' pray:
> When black face is lifted
> Lawd turnin' 'way.

---

77   Scottsboro', by S. Van Veen, *Liberator*, 5 September 1931, p. 5.

78   'To the Boss who Fired Me', by Clyde Smyth, *Harlem Liberator*, 14 April 1934, p. 2.

… Your head 'tain no apple
For danglin' f'om a tree;
Your body no carcass
For barbecuin' on a spree.

Stand on your feet,
Club gripped 'tween your hands;
Spill their blood too,
Show 'em yours is a man's.[79]

Here, as elsewhere in the *Liberator*, the revolutionary potential of hate is constantly underlined, but in the poetry it is given sublime power, it is the motor of resistance and revenge which can mobilise black *and* white. In 'White Masters', an anonymous poem published in 1932, the furious poetic voice transforms the black slaves of the opening lines – 'you have lured us on to your pirate ships, Chained us, and beat us with scorpions and whips' – into a red army of 'wage slaves' by the final stanza.

But the day of reckoning draws near:
Out of the stupor kept year by year,
Rise hosts of Negroes and toil-blackened white,
Joining hands in a common fight.

In field and factory, mill and mine,
Wage-slaves are swinging into line.
Do you hear them marching, singing songs of hate?

TREMBLE, WHITE MASTERS! THE RED AVENGER
SHAKES YOUR GATE![80]

The ideal future is a Communist, interracial and godless synthesis of black, white and red epitomised in the final lines of 'Burnt Offering:'

Behold
Red flags streaming
Negro workers, White workers

---

79   'Stop fooling wit pray', by anon, *Liberator*, 18 March 1932, p. 7.
80   'White Masters', by anon, *Liberator*, 15 August 1932, p. 5.

Marching together
Without God
Without lynching.[81]

The *Liberator*'s cultural politics insisted that there was no revered space for 'high' art, even for black artists. In 'Home to Harlem Claude McKay' the poet asks 'How does it feel to be back in Harlem in 1934, And see all the red banners flying…and be out of it all?' This unusual poem incorporates, almost in its entirety, McKay's infamous 'If We Must Die' into its final stanza before adding its own, somewhat damning, concluding line:

Oh Kinsmen! We must meet the
    common foes;
Though far outnumbered let us
    show us brave,
And for their thousand blows
    Deal one death blow!
Then you betrayed us – And
    the poet is dead.[82]

Of all the Harlem Renaissance writers, McKay was one of the first to express the spirit of the 'New Negro'. 'If We Must Die' is one of seven poems by McKay in a two-page spread published in Max Eastman's radical newspaper *The Liberator* in July 1919. The reproduction of an 'improved' version of it in the *Harlem Liberator* as a reproach to McKay's repudiation of the Communist cause is doubly symbolic. There is no veneration of 'artists' in the paper, indeed the paper constantly called for its readership to contribute their own stories and poetry and envisioned itself as a forum for black workers to *creatively* articulate the impact of racism on their lives. Their ideal cultural subject was an activist *and* producer of art. The extent to which this was achieved was limited in comparison to a paper like *Southern Worker*, which was characterised by its extensive workers' correspondence, drawing attention to workers' experience of racist supremacy in the South.[83] Nevertheless with the onset of the Scottsboro case the *Liberator* carried a series of autobiographical articles detailing the impact of racism and poverty. These were usually the stories of the Scottsboro parents themselves, whose lives served as paradigms of the

---

81 'Burnt Offering', by Arthur Pense, *Harlem Liberator*, 18 November 1933, p. 4
82 *Harlem Liberator*, 21 April 1934, p. 8.
83 *Southern Worker* was openly a Party paper and published in the South from 1930–7.

black working-class activist.[84] In October 1931 the paper ran an autobiographical column which related the life 'so far' of a 'Negro worker born in Chatanooga in 1893' over 11 months entitled 'Experiences of a Negro worker'.

The paper produced extensive fictional narratives of individual oppression; Langston Hughes's story 'Party for White Folks' was published in October 1930. Hughes tells the story of two black children, Willie-Mae and Sandy, who are turned away from a Party at the local amusement park after being told at the gate 'Sorry...this party is for white kids'. Sandy gives his free ride coupons, lovingly cut out of the local paper by his aunt, to a puzzled white friend who 'stood dumbly for a moment wondering what to say to his brown friend, then went on in to the park:'

> 'It's yo' party, white chile!' a little tan-skin girl called after him, mimicking the way the man at the gate had talked. 'Whoa! Stay out! You's a nigger!' she said to Sandy.[85]

Hughes eloquent allegory about the psychological effects of racism is notable in the context of the *Liberator* in that it doesn't include explicit references to interracial unity, although it does posit black and white children as natural allies until the racism of the adult world divides them. The majority of published short stories in the paper were designed to illustrate the condition of the black worker and the terms for their liberation. These stories were often factional accounts of recent black struggles. 'We Stop A Lynching' by Charles Alexander relates the 'true story' of Paul Wilson, a World War I veteran and black Communist who organised protest meetings against lynchings in the South. The climax of this story is the example of an interracial crowd led by a black Communist turning on a would-be lynch mob:

> The defence corps and the crowd of 250 Negro and white workers transformed themselves into a solid group and closed in on the lynchers. The lynchers were unable to use their guns, and many were the tattoos beaten on their heads and faces by the iron fists of the workers. In a short time the battle was over and the lynchers had been repulsed.[86]

84 Mrs Janie Patterson tells of workers Life in Tennessee (16/5/31), Mother of Two Scottsboro Boys Tells Her Own Story (20/6/31), Mother of Scottsboro 14-yr Old Defendant tells Story' (8/8/31) Mrs Powell, Mother of Scottsboro's Youngest Victim, Tells Her Story (19/12/31), Mrs Montgomory Writes of Her Life (6/1/32).
85 'Party for White Folks', *Liberator*, 27 November 1930, p. 5.
86 *Liberator*, 1 September 1932, p. 5.

The 'iron fists of the workers' are more powerful than the weapons of the lynch mob. The story itself is framed around a photograph of the 'chain with which Laura wood, 65 year old share cropper, of Barbar's Junction, North Carolina, was lynched in 1930'. The photograph shows the chain shaped to spell out USA, creating an intentional implication in sharp focus. This detail again shows the formal ambition of the paper. Here the iconographic inheritance of slavery is re-invested to create a powerful contemporary visual satire.

Controversy surfaced around an archetypal story of awakening black consciousness, 'Pete', by Renala Gumbs, in August 1933. In this story a young black female Communist, Linda, convinces a black worker, Pete, to fight his oppression. He is shot by police, becoming a martyrological symbol to his previously apathetic workmates. Although Linda is black she speaks in a neutral dialect, patiently explaining to Pete that he 'must think about our conditions, how to better them and then ACT upon our thoughts'. Pete replies 'Dat's right. I always wanted to do something but I nebber knew what to do'.[87] This story works as polemic because of the bold formal experiment of mixing standard English with 'dialect'. William Fitzgerald, a loyal Party organiser and leading figure in the ILD, wrote to the paper expressing his discomfort at the use of dialect on the basis that it reinforced racist stereotypes and ridiculed black workers:

> The story gives an exposure of the denial of the Negro Worker the denial of even elemental training. But concretely there is no explanation or exposure of the ruling class, which forces the Negro worker to speak this way. Therefore we request that the language in this story be changed or that concrete clarification of the cause of some Negroes speaking this way be printed. Non-class-conscious white workers reading this story will not accept it in the manner we would like them to. They will take it in the usual way: that Negroes are ignorant and illiterate which will give them a feeling of superiority. On the other hand, it also tends to provoke the Negro people, after reading so much of the literature of the capitalist newspapers which only play up the backwardness of the Negro workers without showing its cause. We do not expect them to do so. But we consider the *Harlem Liberator* our paper and we hope these criticisms will be considered.[88]

The paper responded by explaining that the 'dialect used was true to life,' but also took seriously the criticisms of context and agreed that 'an explanatory

---

87   *Harlem Liberator*, 19 August 1933, p. 8.
88   *Harlem Liberator*, 7 October 1933, p. 5.

note' should have been published 'pointing out... the responsibility of the present social system for the illiteracy of a large number of Negro toilers'.[89] Both Fitzgerald's letter and the editors' response point to the sensitivities involved in representing fictional individual black workers in a context where the discourse was so racially charged. More significantly, the editors' response emphasises that the *Liberator* wanted its cultural products to be 'authentic' as well as doctrinal. They wanted to 'represent' as well 'instruct'.

The sensitivity to race and the political implications of linguistic registers was not confined to questions of fictional representation. In 1930 a piece entitled 'How not to Write Leaflets,' warned about the dangers of using obscurantist language when attempting to appeal to black workers. In 1935 the paper attacked 'white chauvinist' theories 'which claim that it is a "natural" or "racial" characteristic of the American Negro to use a different pronunciation from the American White': 'According to this fake doctrine, all Negroes say "Ah" for "are" and "sho" for "sure". All of this has been worked up into an elaborate theory of "Negro" dialect, which the "Amos and Andy" and other blackface comedians use to ridicule Negroes'.[90] In a prescient article about the significance of racial terminology, which ran over two issues, Cyril Briggs debated the desirability of changing the word 'Negro' to 'African American' or 'Ethiopian':

> The black man, because of his pigmentation, whether he be designated as Negro or Ethiopian, is outside the pale of civilisation, say the bourgeois 'race' theoreticians. He is incapable of progress, they declare, ignoring the historical fact that the Negro population of ancient Egypt, Ethiopia, etc., were the first to develop civilisation and the sciences... Not a change of name is required, but a sweeping, revolutionary change of the slave conditions imposed upon the Negro people by the white ruling class. Not by dropping the designation proudly carried into battle by Nat Turner, Toussaint L'Overture and other Negro revolutionary leaders can we achieve this end, but by carrying forward the fight for Negro liberation in the fearless spirit of these great leaders, and in the light of present conditions and the revolutionary traditions of the Negro masses.[91]

This insistence on activism as the most important arena for black liberation made within the wider context of racism is characteristic of the *Liberator*'s simultaneous recognition and reframing of 'cultural' issues.

---

89   Ibid.
90   *Negro Liberator*, 17 October 1935, p. 4.
91   *Negro Liberator*, 22 September 1934, p. 5.

The *Liberator* was far from blasé when it came to questions of cultural representation. Although the paper ceased publication before the heyday of the Popular Front, where the alliances between the CPUSA and left-wing intellectuals pushed cultural issues to the fore, it did anticipate some of the later developments. From furious indictments against Hollywood's presentation of African Americans, to proud assertions on the superiority of the black arts, the paper was increasingly concerned with the status of black culture. In an uncharacteristically passionate exhortation to young musicians to use spirituals in their work, Samuel Heyward proclaimed 'THE NEGRO SPIRITUAL is a music of a people, by a people and for a people. Therefore they shall ever linger and never perish from our hearts and memories'.[92] Elsewhere in the paper the spiritual was an act of cultural resistance:

> Bourgeois white 'liberals' have simpered over tea cups and gushed over the 'pathos' of Negro spirituals. Such people talk and write about the 'beauty' and the sadness of these 'sorrow' songs. They tell us that 'The Negro spirituals express so vividly the hopeful desire and longing of a poor oppressed people. How patient and forgiving the poor slaves were etc.' All of this is nonsense. The spirituals were not mere sentimental longings, for they expressed not only a desire for freedom, but were calls to action.[93]

Here, for the *Liberator*, the spiritual is at once a site of tradition, of popularity and of contest as they attempt to wrest it back from white liberals. The spiritual is a repository of resistance. In opposition to the white liberals, who can only imagine the spirituals as reflective and productive of the 'past,' the paper posits black culture as speaking to a now that is collective and desiring; generating an anger that is geared to the present. In its pointed and angry denunciation of liberal sentimentality around spirituals and its insistence on the *political* power of the spirituals as *art*, the *Liberator* articulates a nuanced theory of black art which is way ahead of its time.[94]

The paper constantly drew attention to the ways in which black artistic expression was suppressed by the white establishment and how African Americans were persistently demeaned and humiliated in Hollywood films. Periodically the *Liberator* review section, which was often little more than a listings page, cast a caustic eye over the week's film releases. The paper pointed

---

92   *Harlem Liberator*, 19 August 1933, p. 5.
93   *Harlem Liberator*, 20 January 1934, p. 5.
94   The political significance of the Spiritual is well articulated in Wood 2003, pp. 399–401.

to the humiliation black artists suffered in the film industry. 'In the Moving Picture as in every other field of artistic endeavour,' the paper reported in 1933, 'the Negro is the most exploited of all performers. He suffers more than any other minority group from all manner of ridicule in films and in the drama'.[95] Attention was drawn, not only to racist caricaturing, but also to revisionist histories of slavery and colonialism depicted in American films. The revival of *Birth of a Nation* in 1931 was greeted as a premeditated political act 'calculated to rouse the most intense Negro-baiting prejudices'.[96] *Sanders of the River* in 1935 was the object of trenchant criticism. The paper called for the film, whose star Paul Robeson had distanced himself from the movie, to be boycotted on the basis of its racist interpretation of British colonialism:

> The producers of the film have the nerve to create the disgraceful impression that the African Natives like the way the English robber barons exploit, brutalize and mercilessly terrorize them ... A picket line should be thrown around every theatre showing this picture. Protests should be sent to the theatre owners and managers.[97]

As well as protesting against the 'adulteration' of black culture, the *Liberator* was concerned with the 'goal of promoting a genuine Negro culture with a proletarian content' and urged readers to 'join one of the *Liberator* cultural groups and help promote Negro proletarian culture in this community'.[98] The New York run of the highly successful, Scottsboro-inspired, anti-racist play *Stevedore* was a major event, and the paper ran weekly competitions with tickets to the play as prizes, as well as serialising the text of the play over several weeks. As well as the *Liberator* theatre group, which was set up in July 1933, the paper organised drawing classes for 'Harlem kiddies,' a Liberator Band, and a 'Red Front Group' in Harlem – based on 'workers sports of all sorts with a semi-military formation and uniforms'.[99] The Liberator Chorus was set up in the summer of 1933 with an interest in 'proletarian songs of Negro origin'. Reporting on the first performance of the Chorus, the paper noted that 'they sang the chain gang classic "Water Boy", "Old Black Joe", "Dis Ole Hammer Killed John Henry", "Carry me back to Ole Virginny", and several requests'.[100] For 50 cents' admission, a patron

---

95   *Harlem Liberator*, 9 September 1933, p. 5.
96   *Liberator*, 28 March 1931, p. 5.
97   *Negro Liberator*, 15 July 1935, p. 5.
98   *Harlem Liberator*, 24 June 1933, p. 5.
99   *Harlem Liberator*, 24 June 1933, p. 3.
100 *Harlem Liberator*, 15 July 1934, p. 7.

of the '*Harlem Liberator* Entertainment and Dance' night would be treated to 'Prolet-songs' by Parker Watkins, reading of revolutionary prose by Alexander Moody, African songs and dancing by Asadata D'for and His Native Troupe, piano recital by Eugene Nigob and Jazz Johnson and his Rhythm Kings.[101]

At the core of the *Liberator*'s cultural politics is the assertion that black culture and black radical history is the preserve of those who comprehend the significance of black oppositional forms within American society. Any group can learn from the complicated experiences of another group, on the condition that they prove their willingness to fight racial discrimination in the context of class-based politics. The paper attempts to rearticulate black American identity in terms which prioritise the pivotal role of black culture and black history in the transformation of society as a whole. The *Liberator*'s insistence on the interracial character of anti-racist struggle points to a black political identity which is sourced in racial pride, but which equally made that pride the source for widening the parameters of political consciousness in Pan-African and internationalist directions. The paper sought to achieve a unity of purpose between the destiny of black Communists and the Euro-American working class, in the process of distancing itself from the historic alliances between black reformism and American liberalism. This process was by no means unproblematic; there is a tension in the *Liberator* between asserting racial pride whilst demanding interracial solidarity in a domestic context. The paper is constantly negotiating between its mode of address to black workers and its theoretical commitment to interracial politics. The cultural politics of the *Liberator* insisted on the promotion of a black culture which was 'authentic' whilst simultaneously reworking black cultural forms to include Communist sensibility.

The *Liberator* became bi-monthly in December 1934, and eventually suspended publication in the summer of 1935. Throughout its five-and-a-half years it had clumsily and eloquently expressed the political vision of a new black radical identity. The analysis of the paper given above is not intended to exaggerate its influence (readership numbers are difficult to estimate for a variety of reasons, but the paper never reached its target circulation of 25,000).[102] The significance of the newspaper lies in its confident modelling of the new

---

101   *Harlem Liberator*, 24 June 1933, p. 8.

102   The paper frequently promoted circulation drives, in order to widen the readership, but never published sales figures. The matter of circulation is complicated further by the fact that sale figures would not be a necessary indication of readership. Hosea Hudson points out that as many Southern black Communists were illiterate, one copy of the *Liberator* would often be read aloud to many comrades. See Painter 1979, p. 102.

African-American Communist, who could maintain race pride and international solidarity whilst retaining a heightened awareness of racism and a commitment to interracial class unity. In its pages some of the most persistent Cold
War and black nationalist myths about black / Communist relationships are
challenged. 'Blackness' is not abandoned for the purposes of *realpolitik*, it is
engaged with in the context of a political framework for understanding race
and class. Moreover, the paper embraced *any* black artistic art form available.
Its formal eclecticism celebrated the richness, diversity, subtlety and politicisation of black vernacular forms.

The paper is a unique, often neglected, historical testament which can be
made to open up a space for scholars to investigate the social relations and
power structures which gave rise to certain solidarities of race and class
in mid-century America. In terms of black 'hate,' working-class consciousness and historical racial awareness, its circulation of a black political identity, which resists both essentialism and accommodationism, offers a potent
model through which to read fictional representations of the CPUSA and black
subjectivity.

CHAPTER 3

Native Son: Ghetto Nightmares

3.1   'Poor Richard Wright': The Black Protest Novel[1]

The task of the preceding chapters has been to delineate the discursive models used by Communist activists to create a representational space in which race and class could coincide to produce a convincing model of black Communist agency. It is my intention here to place *Native Son* in relation to that discursive field. I am not suggesting that Communism in *Native Son* offers us an organic and untroubled mediation between race, class and liberation. Rather, the interest here is in how Wright utilises Communism as an ordering principle of black political consciousness, and its significance in the construction of a Northern urban black identity.

From the moment of its publication *Native Son* was greeted as a founding text of modern black American writing. Its unrelenting will to imagine a totalised black male subjectivity ensured that its critical reputation turned on its status as a seminal testament to black rage. This was the case even where the novel's reputation is most contested – in the critical reactions of James Baldwin and Ralph Ellison, both of whom construe the text as a damaged victim of the aesthetics of 'protest fiction'. Baldwin and Ellison charged the novel with being crude, simplistic and determinist. From different standpoints (though both were concerned with the limitations of protest literature *per se*) they assert that by creating Bigger out of the myths of white racism and cutting him off from any notion of community and tradition, Wright manufactured a reality which fitted his Communist politics more than the actual productive and complex lives of African Americans.[2] Ellison and Baldwin, as well as many contemporary critics, maintain that in *Native Son* the complexity of racial identity is simplified and sacrificed to a political ideology.[3] The rich traditions of folk culture are seen to be dismissed, literary form is wholly subordinate

---

1   Cruse 1967, p. 188.

2   'Everybody's Protest Novel', in Baldwin 1964, 'The World and the Jug', in Ellison 1964.

3   In recent times much work has been done in revisiting the site of 1930s CPUSA aesthetics and those debates do not need to be reiterated here. See Nelson 1989; Murphy 1991; Bloom 1992; Foley 1993.

to content and what results in formal terms is deemed a naturalist 'race and superstructure' text.[4]

The arguments about the status of *Native Son* as a protest novel are multi-layered, encompassing questions about the relationship between fiction and social reality, the function of literary texts, the limitations of propaganda, narrative authority and political didacticism and the fictional representation of race. Wright's work and life have often served as a paradigm for the failure of the experiment which attempted to meld Soviet Marxism and African-American writing. Writing only two years after the publication of *Native Son*, the cultural critic Alfred Kazin proclaimed unproblematically that Wright's politics undermined his craft:

> If he chose to write the story of Bigger Thomas as a grotesque crime story, it is because his own indignation and the sickness of the age combined to make him dependent on violence and shock, to astonish the reader by torrential scenes of cruelty, hunger, rape, murder and flight and then enlighten him by crude Stalinist homilies. Bigger Thomas 'found' himself in jail as Wright 'found' himself, after much personal suffering and confusion, in the Communist Party; what did it matter that Bigger's self discovery was mechanical and unconvincing, or that Wright – from the highest of motives – had written 'one of those books in which everything is undertaken with seriousness except the writing'.[5]

According to Kazin, crude, didactic, simplistic and sermonising tracts were the fruits of a Communist liaison with fiction. Ellison likewise famously lamented: 'How awful that Wright found the facile answers of Marxism before he learned to use literature as a means for discovering the forms of American Negro Humanity'.[6] This image of a deluded Richard Wright, his naivety hijacked by Marxism and manipulated by the CPUSA, is perhaps given greatest expression by Harold Cruse. In his influential *The Crisis of the Negro Intellectual* he places Communism as a direct adversary of African-American writing:

> Poor Richard Wright! He sincerely tried, but he never got much beyond that starting point that Marxism represented for him ... It will never be known whether or not Wright ever grasped the extent to which vulgar Marxism had rendered him incapable of seeing unique developments

---

4   Gates Jr. 1984, p. 292.
5   Kazin 1942, p. 387.
6   Ellison 1964, p. 120.

of American capitalism. Uncharted paths existed for the Negro creative intellectuals to explore, if only they could avoid being blinded by Communist Party propaganda.[7]

Indeed, Wright's own postscript to his Communist past deals severely with a Party culture portrayed as proscriptive and dogmatic. In his contribution to Robert Crossman's *The God That Failed* (1950), taken from his autobiography *American Hunger* (1944), Wright describes a Communist Party which ultimately frustrates his creative impulses. The Party here is one which distrusts writers, which is rigid in its conception of proletarian literature and which is dogmatically suspicious of expressions of individual creativity. *American Hunger* also describes Wright's engagement with the Communist-inspired John Reed club in Chicago. The John Reed clubs were committed to encouraging worker-writers and promoting proletarian literature. Following his exit from the CPUSA Wright's recollections of the Party's aesthetic practice in relation to race and writing are often contradictory. Of interest here is his attraction to the Party because of its commitment to black experience outside of the lens of bourgeois paternalism or, as he puts it, 'the lispings of the missionary:'

> But it seemed to me that here at last in the realm of revolutionary expression was where Negro experience could find a home, a functional value and role. Out of the magazines I read came a passionate call for the experiences of the disinherited, and there were none of the same lispings of the missionary in it. It did not say: 'Be like us and we will like you, maybe'. It said: 'If you possess enough courage to speak out what you are, you will find that you are not alone'. It urged life to believe in life.[8]

The argument here is not how or whether Wright's Party membership helped or hindered his writing. I do not want to fall into the trap of accepting a binary opposition between literature and politics, a trap which would generate only futile attempts to answer the equally futile question: would *Native Son* be a better or lesser text if written by a non-Communist Richard Wright? Nor do I want to set myself up as a champion of *Native Son* as an unduly discredited literary text. My task is to approach the novel as a text dependent on a particular model of black subjectivity, one inaugurated by both Communist discourses of black rage and Wright's particular rendering of African-American alienation.

---

7   Cruse 1967, p. 188.
8   Wright 1977, pp. 63–4.

Moreover, I argue that this model has been overlooked in the rush to epitomise Wright as a pitiable dupe of Communist aesthetics.[9]

In terms of African-American writing, protest literature is frequently posited as yet another example of the failure of an interracialism which constantly privileged the imperative for Soviet-based Marxist ideology over the experience and expression of black oppression.[10] There is an extensive body of work which details the impact of crude Stalinist cultural practice in the 1930s. It is beyond the scope of this chapter to detail the development of Communist aesthetics in the international Communist movement.[11] The complex history of the relationship between culture and politics in the early 1930s, however, should not be reduced to its Stalinist excesses. James F. Murphy has detailed the theoretical routes of the post-October positions on art and literature in Russia and their historical trajectories in the United States during the Depression in his comprehensive study *The Proletarian Moment*. Murphy makes an important distinction between proletarian literature and socialist realism in the 1930s:

> With the adoption of the new Soviet constitution in 1936, Stalin declared that Soviet workers could no longer be called proletarian since they were not exploited by capitalists. While the precise relations between proletarian literature and socialist realism remained undefined . . . in the mid-thirties, in practice the latter term was mainly confined to Soviet literature, while socialist-oriented works by writers in capitalist countries continued to be referred to as 'proletarian'.[12]

The distinction is particularly important in relation to *Native Son*, as the concept of proletarian literature was one which privileged the literary represen-

---

9   I am not suggesting that *Native Son* has *only* been read in this manner. Indeed since its
      publication a rich body of critical work on the novel has been produced. My point here is
      that in relation to Wright's *Communism* the seminal critiques of the novel (Baldwin and
      Ellison) retain their authority in relation to the politics of the text, particularly in the criti-
      cal reception of Book Three.

10   Perhaps the most authoritative and influential rendering of a Marxist aesthetic which
      constrained black expression and African-American letters is that of Harold Cruse. Cruse
      concentrates on the Harlem Renaissance, and in particular on the infamous relation-
      ship between Mike Gold and Claude McKay, see Cruse 1967, pp. 147–70. For a response to
      Cruse's characterisation of the relationship between Gold and McKay, see Maxwell 1999,
      pp. 97–104.

11   Kazin 1955; Pells 1973; Conney 1986; Wald 1987.

12   Murphy 1990, p. 104.

tation of socially determined working-class protagonists fighting a powerful establishment. As Michel Fabre recognises:

> The fact that Wright came of age, in a literary sense, under the aegis of the Communist Party and during the depression largely accounts for the special tenor of his naturalism... The novelists of the thirties seemed heir to new obligations, and were called upon to leave their ivory towers and become politically relevant. Authenticity, which had always been Wright's criterion, was rehabilitated to stand against artiness.[13]

Moreover, the concept of social determinism was not exclusive to Communists in the 1930s, it was the theoretical staple of the influential Chicago School sociologists, of which Wright was an enthusiastic supporter.[14] Debates about the status of art in the pursuit of a new society were not ones which emerged fully developed in the American Communist press in the 1930s. As well as the rich and multifarious debates around the *Proletkult* in post-revolutionary Russia, which engendered a formidable Marxist canon of literary criticism, America also had its own home-grown, if less erudite, Socialist cultural critics in the 1920s. Upton Sinclair's *Mammonart* (1925) insisted on the need for a partial, class-orientated art in which aesthetic considerations were subordinate to political allegiance. V.F. Calverton, editor of *Modern Quarterly*, argued in *The Newer Spirit* (1930) that literature could only be judged in 'strict sociological terms'.[15] The cultural critics around the CPUSA included the often overlooked Joseph Freeman as well as the caricatured Communist authorities on literature, Mike Gold and Granville Hicks.[16]

More significantly, Wright's own *Blueprint for Negro Writing* (1937) details the need for a Marxist aesthetic which is nuanced to the experiences of African Americans. This, much misread, text provides a rich investigation of the aesthetic and political problematics which face the politically committed writer. Wright insists that a Marxist vision 'restores to the writer his lost heritage, that is, his role as a creator of the world in which he lives, and as a creator of himself,' while also insisting on the complexities of the African-American experience. Wright summarises the function of the 'Negro' writer in the following terms:

---

13   Fabre in Bloom 1987, p. 43.
14   Smith 1988.
15   Calverton 1930, p. 123.
16   For a spirited defence of Mike Gold and Granville Hicks as literary critics see Foley 1993, pp. 3–44.

His vision need not be simple or rendered in primer-like terms; for the life of the Negro people is not simple. The presentation of their lives should be simple, yes; but all the complexity, the strangeness, the magic wonder of life that plays like a bright sheen over the most sordid existence should be there ... But anyone destitute of a theory about the meaning, structure and direction of modern society is a lost victim in a world he cannot understand or control. But even if Negro writers found themselves through some 'ism,' how would that influence their writing? Are they being called upon to 'preach'? To be 'salesmen'? To 'prostitute' their writing? Must they 'sully' themselves? Must they write 'propaganda'? No; it is a question of awareness, of consciousness; it is above all, a question of perspective.[17]

The concurrent centrality of *perspective* and *consciousness* in *Native Son* is not coincidental; *Native Son* was no raw naive Communist cry, but a sophisticated deliberate production of a literary model. Far from being a transparent allegory for the politics of the CPUSA, Wright constructs an opaque narrative in which the black antihero is objectified in a variety of discourses; where the 'success' of the Communist protagonists lies less in the expression of their politics than in their capacity to understand the legitimacy of Bigger's rage. It is the relationship between Bigger and the Party which Wright investigates and the capacity for an historically white organisation to comprehend and validate black rage.

Undoubtedly *Native Son* adheres to certain criteria of protest literature, though not as the caricatured blueprint of the genre as it is rendered in literary criticism.[18] It is remarkable that many literary-critical approaches to this novel as a 'race and superstructure' text, concentrate so narrowly on the political assertions of the novel itself, and in particular the speech of Max Boris. However, by concentrating on *how* those politics are rendered and more significantly the relationships that they engender, we can access a richer understanding of Communist representation in *Native Son*.

3.2   A Room of One's Own?: Bigger, Rage and Consciousness

When Bigger Thomas enters his accommodation in the Dalton household in Book One of *Native Son* there is already another presence there. The room was

---

17   Wright 1997, pp. 1384–5.
18   For a summary of literary-critical responses to protest literature see Foley 1993, pp. 129–69.

once the residence of his predecessor Green, the 'good Negro,' who had profited from the Daltons' patronage for a decade, attended night classes and gone on to 'better' things – working for the government. The walls in his vacated room are covered with a racially integrated gallery of posters – Jack Johnson, Joe Louis, Jack Dempsey, Henry Armstrong on one side and Jean Harlow, Ginger Rogers and Janet Gaynor on the other.[19] Boxers and Beauties: icons of twentieth-century celebrity and mass culture. But Green is the exemplar of an earlier age. This character has 'escaped' the black belt, and exists in the margins of the novel, but both Green's residual presence, and the modern cultural artefacts he has *left behind* in his wake, are significant in this novel about an urban mid-twentieth-century black America.

Green is literally a 'House Negro' who, although he has left the Daltons, remains a presence in the household of white-liberal sensibilities. Green is evoked as the exemplar who facilitates philanthropy. Bigger is not just occupying his old room; the Daltons are offering him Green's role, his history, his destiny. Because the Daltons can 'create' a Green, they cannot imagine a Bigger. The world of black hatred for them may exist in the sprawling black belt, but it cannot exist in their home. Patronage is the Daltons' hermetic defence against black anger and Green is the symbolic embodiment of their certitude in the racial uplift. Green haunts this text. We are invited to hypothesise the invisible Green – to put him where Bigger goes. Did Green go to Ernie's Shack with Jan and Mary? Did she encourage him to join a union? Did Jan attempt to recruit him to the Party? Did he refuse to lie for Mary? Was he the willing participant in Mrs Dalton's plans for him? How did he negotiate the racial codes for over a decade in this domestic microcosm of the hierarchies of race and class? The Dalton household reproduces in fervent detail the structures of racialised America. While Mr. Dalton's NAACP membership is a gesture to northern integration, his landlord status, in particular his ownership of the Thomas's house, evokes Southern plantocracy turned into capitalist real estate. Their money is both old (Mrs. Dalton) and new (Mr. Dalton). The material foundation of their wealth, hidden by their reforming zeal, is the poverty and exploitation of the Black Belt. Their paternalism is both token and demanding; Peggy tells Bigger that Green benefited from the classes that Mrs Dalton '*made* him go to'.[20] Bigger disrupts the racial equilibrium. In the racialised universe that Wright creates, Green is white philanthropy's comforting fiction. However, while he affirms the Daltons in their beneficent mission, his presence is restricted to kitchen conversation and old posters. Green is the Daltons' protégé, existing

---

19   Wright 1997, p. 98.
20   Wright 1997, p. 95 (my emphasis).

at the margins of the novel. He is renowned only for his obedience, his 'neatness' and his liking for posters. Green leaves nothing in his wake apart from his selection of cultural icons. He is the ideal accommodationist figure of race relations where black is absence and white intervention is received in silent gratitude. Green's legacy in the novel can be seen as a latter day take on the abolitionist society seal showing a kneeling black man imploringly announcing 'Am I not a Man and a Brother?' Peggy delivers his epitaph to Bigger, 'This was Green's room. He was always one for pictures. But he kept things neat and nice'.[21] Green is a tragic figure surrounded by images of forbidden white women and hyper-masculinised men living out a life of white-approved 'advancement' and leaving only his 'neatness' in his wake.

Bigger is not neat, he is not *rooted*, as Green is literally rooted in his room within the circumscribed space of the Daltons' house. Indeed Bigger's geographical and social space is problematic. He is neither of the North or the South (he has been in Chicago less than five years): he is a product of the Great Migration. He is no longer a child and not yet socialised into adult life. Bigger is emerging from the adolescent world of reform school, petty crime and gang identity. His acceptance of a chauffeur's job and his simultaneous rejection of the 'improvement' programme the Daltons have mapped out for him ('he was not going to any night school'),[22] remove him simultaneously from both the world of the *lumpenproletariat* and from the aspiring black middle class.

Native Son is concerned with nascent black *working-class* identity. The point is not that Bigger is poised on a journey of class-conscious resistance, but that he has entered a new topography which carries the potential for multiple positionalities within the lexicon of race and class. Unlike Green, whose identity is circumscribed and whose fixity as the model black protégé is ensured by his invisibility in the text, Bigger is *the process* of becoming. Wright situates his protagonist in a domestic setting rather than an industrial one and thereby creates a historically significant set of social relations in relation to race in America. Bigger begins his working life within the traditional circumscribed space of the white master, where Green is rendered mute and invisible. Bigger is oblivious to these particular white expectations. The rawness and rage he experiences in his short working life are in stark contrast to the abjection of the acclimatised black worker evoked in Green and exemplified in Bessie.

---

21   Wright 1997, p. 98.
22   Wright 1997, p. 95.

Bessie's characterisation in *Native Son* is, to put it mildly, problematic.[23] She is, however, a black worker and in the context of this chapter it is important to note her position as the only character of Bigger's acquaintance (apart from his mother), in paid employment. Bessie lives her life in the snatched moments of free time allocated to her by her employers:

> ... from her room to the kitchen of the white folks was the farthest she ever moved. She worked long hours, hard and hot hours seven days a week, with only Sunday afternoons off ... she had told him over and over again that she lived their lives when she was working in their homes, not her own.[24]

Bessie straddles two worlds, she lives her plantation life in the centre of Chicago, her only resistance against the world is booze and blues.[25] Her plaintive supplications to an unsympathetic Bigger take the form of a stylised complaint which details her hard working life. Bessie may present a pathetic figure to Bigger, but her protests against the pain and abuse of her life are the conscious expression of historical memory. According to Ellison, 'The blues is an impulse to keep the painful detail and episodes of a brutal existence alive in one's aching consciousness' – an interpretation validated by Bessie's limited but powerful insistence on articulating her oppression:[26]

> All I do is work, work like a dog! From morning till night. I ain't got no happiness, I ain't never had none ... Lord, don't let this happen to me! I ain't done nothing for this to come to me! I just work. I ain't had no happiness, no nothing. I just work. I'm black and I work and don't bother nobody.[27]

Bessie's painful articulation of her circumscribed life revolves around her work. Because Bigger is detached from Bessie's world – his working life lasts just twenty-four hours – he develops no tradition of resistance or accommodation. Bigger is such a powerful protagonist precisely because he stands in

---

23   Wright's depiction of women has generated a great deal of literary criticism. See in particular Keady 1995, pp. 43–9; France 1988, pp. 413–23; Harris 1990, pp. 63–84; Guttman 2001, pp. 169–193.

24   Wright 1997, p. 177.

25   See Watson's insightful essay analysing Bessie's blues motif in Bloom 1990, pp. 54–9.

26   Ellison 1964, p. 127.

27   Wright 1997, p. 219.

isolation from any structured adult world. He can hastily dismiss black folk-culture as servile and submissive: 'he did not want to sit on a bench and sing, or lie in a corner and sleep'.[28] His dissatisfaction and alienation are firmly located in the claustrophobic black ghetto of a sprawling city; his dismissal of black culture is sourced in a physical dislocation as well as an intellectual rejection.

It is Bigger's relationship to this *urban* landscape which dominates in the opening pages of the novel. A world where even the sky performs as an adver-tising hoarding, as the canvas of an aeroplane instructing the world to USE SPEED GASOLINE. Bigger's very modern sense of hopelessness is important and deliberate. His life is a succession of negating postures perilously balanced on a combination of fear and frustrated powerlessness.

It is precisely this context of rootlessness which provides a core, skeletal but viciously intense identity for Bigger. At one level Bigger is a kind of textual con-trol experiment, a metaphor for rage. As the archetypal black male rebel which Bigger became for a later generation of black activists, his criminality, his defi-ance, his transgressions are imbued with more revolutionary meaning: he is C.L.R. James's 'Negro in revolt'.[29] Eldridge Cleaver insists that Bigger was 'a man in violent, though inept, rebellion against the stifling, murderous, totalitarian white world. There was no trace in Bigger of a Martin Luther King type self-effacing love for his oppressors'.[30] Cleaver's reclamation of Bigger as a freedom fighter against both white supremacy and competing discourses of black liber-ation turns upon a very particular notion of a gendered black-radical identity, which is discussed in Chapter Five. What is significant here is that he is seen as a prototype for black rage. In *Killing Rage*, bell hooks underlines the political dimension of black rage, in ways which are particularly pertinent to this text:

> The black rage that white power wants to suppress is not the narcissistic whine of the black privileged classes, it is the rage of the downtrodden and oppressed that could be mobilized to mount militant resistance to white supremacy ... The rage of the oppressed is never the same as the rage of the privileged. One group can change their lot only by changing the system: the other hopes to be rewarded within the system.[31]

For hooks, as for the *Liberator* and for Wright, 'rage' is a political positioning, or rather, the expression of black rage threatens the boundaries of racist power

---

28   Wright 1997, p. 280.
29   James 1996, p. 56.
30   Cleaver 1970, p. 103.
31   Hooks 1995, p. 29.

structures and interracial class allegiances. As the embodiment of rage, then, Bigger is potentially revolutionary in terms of both class and race; he signifies multiple positions in the racial topography of the novel.

Bigger is skilled in negotiating the discursive codes of white supremacy. While he fears the vicious white policeman Britten, and the power he has to destroy him, Britten's open racism causes Bigger few problems. Britten, after all, is 'familiar to him'.[32] Bigger's consciousness of race as black corporeality, as object, ensures that he can perfectly play the part demanded of him by white racism.

Indeed Bigger's consciousness of the racial order is so heightened that any disruption within it causes chaos. Hence his virulent hatred for Mary and Jan when they insist on clumsily breaking the codes of racial discourse:

> He felt naked, transparent: he felt that this white man, having helped to put him down, having helped to deform him held him up now to look at him and be amused. At that moment he felt toward Mary and Jan, a dumb, cold inarticulate hate.[33]

Mary reads race as noble suffering, her voyeuristic interest in black poverty is concurrent with white shame:

> You know, Bigger, I've long wanted to go into those houses... and just *see* how your people live. You know what I mean? I've been to England, France, and Mexico, but I don't know how people live ten blocks from me. We know so *little* about each other. I just want to *see*. I want to *know* these people. Never in my life have I been inside a Negro home yet they *must* live like we live. They're *human*... There are twelve million of them... They live in our country... In the same city as us... her voice trailed off wistfully. There was silence.[34]

Although she addresses Bigger, she is not talking to him. Bigger is erased as he is evoked; he becomes 'you' 'them' and 'us'. The discursive practices of white people are instrumental signifiers for Bigger's behaviour and it is on this night when they are disturbed that the course of his life changes dramatically. He feels literally obliterated: 'He felt he had no physical existence at all right then; he was something he hated, the badge of shame which he knew was attached

---

32   Wright 1997, p. 202.

33   Wright 1997, p. 107.

34   Wright 1997, pp. 109–10.

to black skin. It was a shadowy region, a No Man's Land, the ground that separated the white world from the black that he stood upon'.[35]

Wright's employment of a trench warfare metaphor in this proto-Fanonian paradigm of black subjectivity is a critique of the objectifying lens of the liberal white gaze.

Significantly, the painful self-awareness Bigger feels among the Daltons, and the mortification he experiences with Jan and Mary, is nowhere apparent in his dealings with the Daltons' housekeeper Peggy. Bigger is unafraid of Peggy, at one stage he even imagines an alliance with Mr. Dalton against her if she mistreats him. He constantly forgets she is in the room, unthinkable in relation to the Daltons. Peggy may speak as one with her employers, 'Some people think *we* ought to have more servants than *we* do,'[36] but she occupies a very different social space in the cartography of race and class in the novel. After all, Bigger has told us a few pages earlier that, 'he felt that if he were a poor white and did not get his share of the money, then he would deserve to be kicked. Poor white people were stupid. It was the right white people who were smart and knew how to treat people'.[37]

Peggy's attempt to identify with Bigger on the basis of her Irishness does not engender the self-loathing that Jan's attempts at identification do. His fear of Peggy is always utilitarian, he fears she will make him do her share of the work, he fears she will find Mary's bones, he does not fear her as *white*. Class disrupts the racial monolith, and while this is of limited significance in the early section of the book, it does become important in relation to Max's courtroom speech, discussed below. There is no heroic transgression of the class/race divide in this novel, but there is a subtle gesturing towards a recognition of the role of class in structuring racial identity.

Bigger's negotiations with racist constructs of power are predicated through fictions of popular stereotypes of race and class that permeate the culture. In the text, there is no black 'community,' but rather an assortment of individuals caught in cycles of poverty and isolation. It is the interconnection between race, class, modernity and identity which Wright investigates.[38] The black ghetto is a squalid and alienating conglomeration of competing cultures. The billboard advertisements, the movie theatres, the churches, the omnipresent spectre of Buckley's pointing finger and, in short, the modern sterility of the

---

35   Wright 1997, p. 107.

36   Wright 1997, p. 95 (emphasis mine).

37   Wright 1997, p. 72.

38   See Gilroy 1993, Chapter 5, for a reading which sees modernity as dialectically related to the question of race in *Native Son*.

ghetto are a modernist apocalyptic vision. Bigger's brutalising isolation and fragmented consciousness are the result of physical and cultural decay. In a novel with such an obvious debt to naturalism both mass culture and the alienating lens of modernity occupy a central role.[39] This becomes more significant in Bigger's relationship to his crime *vis-à-vis* the later reports in the newspapers, but from the beginning of the novel his oppression is accentuated by his estrangement from the modernity that surrounds him. Images in the opening sequences of the novel underline this. The aeroplane that trails advertisements across the sky far above the ghetto, the long black car that speeds through and the cinematic magnified images of beautiful white women are all symbolic of a world of exclusion and dislocation. Before he visits the Daltons Bigger sees a movie with Jack and draws a prescient picture of what awaits him at the home of his new employers:

> Maybe Mr. Dalton was a millionaire. Maybe he had a daughter who was a hot kind of girl; maybe she spent lots of money; maybe she'd like to come to the South Side and see the sights sometimes. Or maybe she had a secret sweetheart and only he would know about it because he would have to drive her around; maybe she would give him money not to tell.[40]

This, of course, is a blueprint for what awaits him at the Daltons except that Mary doesn't give him money not to tell, she *trusts* him not to tell, and trusts him *because* he is black, because again she reads race in terms which confuse Bigger. His cinematic fantasies are predicated on a narrative of coherence and symmetry that is brutally contradicted by his fragmented identity. The Hollywood language for human emotion rests on an imagined universality and there is a chasm between the fantasy [movie] world and the reality of racial awareness which transforms desire and possibility into the humiliating self-cancellation he feels in Mary's company:

> He chewed his bacon and eggs while some remote part of his mind considered in amazement how different this rich girl was from the one he had seen in the movies. This woman he had watched on the screen had not seemed dangerous and his mind had been able to do with her as it liked, but this rich girl walked over everything, put herself in the way.[41]

---

39   For an detailed account of the roll of mass culture in the text see Pudaloff 1983, pp. 3–18; and Smethurst 2001, pp. 35–6.

40   Wright 1997, pp. 72–3.

41   Wright 1997, p. 94.

All the major protagonists in this novel are set against representations of their lives which proliferate in wider society. They are all introduced by pre-existing narratives of race, class and gender. The most obvious example is Bigger himself who comes to the Daltons with a report from relief which outlines his life. But Mary and Mr Dalton are the white millionaires of Hollywood movies and Jan and Max the dangerous Communists lampooned in the newspaper cartoons Bigger reads.

Most significantly, Bigger seems to be fascinated with the events of his own life *as a story*, admitting that after Mary's killing he doesn't want to flee as 'He was tensely eager to stay and see how it would all end, even if that end swallowed him up in blackness'.[42] This is a world of stories and information. The newspaper updates of Mary's disappearance are frequent and numerous, pictures of Bigger taken with the Daltons are published within two hours. He is literally running from the onslaught of information and the lurid constructions of race which determine his fate: 'He paused and reread the line, AUTHORITIES HINT SEX CRIME. Those words excluded him utterly from the world. To hint that he had committed a sex crime was to pronounce the death sentence'.[43]

Bigger is obsessed with stories about himself. In prison, once the despair has lifted and he decides to participate in the world again, the first thing he wants is a newspaper, 'he had not seen a newspaper in a long time. What were they saying now?'[44] He is constantly objectified in everybody else's narrative of identity. To the Daltons, he is a second Green, a grateful penitent poised on a self-improvement programme they have mapped out for him. To Mary, he is the embodiment of the noble ghetto. Jan casts him as a potential comrade purely because he is black. To Britten, he is first a Communist murderer and then a docile lackey. To the press, he is a ready-made 'beast'. All of them write him into narratives of race, class and gender which brutally annihilate his subjectivity and experience. After Mary's death, Bigger senses a liberation of no longer inhabiting the fictions of others, of having done what no-one suspects of him: 'had he not done what they thought he never could, the feeling of being always enclosed in the stifling embrace of the invisible force had gone from him'.[45]

Mr. Dalton is both figuratively and literally a figure who ensures that the black community remain housed in the Black Belt and kept in mental subjugation:

---

42   Wright 1997, p. 228.
43   Wright 1997, p. 282.
44   Wright 1997, p. 316.
45   Wright 1997, p. 188.

As long as he and his black folks did not go beyond certain limits, there was no need to fear that white force. But they feared it or not, each and every day of their lives and lived with it; even when words did not sound its name, they acknowledged its reality.[46]

Bigger goes beyond those 'limits' in the immediate aftermath of Mary's death. His sense of power is not illusionary, but it is limited and limiting. It is a violent reaction to his alienation, the adoption of another fiction while attempting to subvert it: 'act like other people thought you ought to act, yet do what you wanted'.[47] But in this text *subversion* is not the radical position it has become within the lexicon of particular variants of identity politics. Bigger is still defined by others, most pertinently and explicitly by the media. More importantly, he continues to define himself in terms of the fear and shame he believes he has exorcised. Because of his isolation Bigger continues to exist as an object determined by his environment, forced to act in direct response to the compulsion of events.

Ironically, Bessie's murder illustrates his utter powerlessness, the vicious reminder that Bigger's perceived transformation since Mary's death has not altered the fundamental hierarchies of his world. The target of his frustration and fear is still poor and black. Just as the proposed robbery of Blum ended in violence against Gus, Bigger's proposed extortion from the Daltons ends with a battered black female body flung down an air shaft.

There is little that is figurative in the power relations expressed in this text. Paul Gilroy argues that 'for Wright, violence coloured black social life as a whole. It was internalised and reproduced in the most intimate relationships'.[48] *Native Son* is not purely about the pathology of violence *reproduced* in interpersonal relationships, but rather about the power of violence, the necessity of violence, the messiness of violence as a prerequisite to a young black male enlightened consciousness. Though often quoted a-historically and arbitrarily in questions of postcolonial identity, Fanon's concept of revolutionary violence, articulated in 1961, is significant in this context: 'At the level of individuals, violence is a cleansing force. It frees the native from his inferiority complex and from his despair and inaction'.[49] This sentiment is given more concrete relevance to the United States by Chester Himes who asserted in 1970:

---

46   Wright 1997, p. 152.
47   Wright 1997, p. 151.
48   Gilroy 1993, p. 174.
49   Fanon 1990, p. 74.

> White people in America, it seems to me, are titillated by the problem of
> the black people, more than taking it seriously. I want to see them take it
> seriously, good and goddamn seriously, and the only way that I think to
> make them take it seriously is with violence.[50]

Through his insistence on the necessity of violence, Wright poses a challenge not only to the authority of racist mythology, but also to the limits of
reformism. In this novel liberalism is exposed as complicit with the system
of oppression which objectifies and ultimately kills Bigger. In the context of
CPUSA politics it is significant that the Daltons are members of the NAACP.
There is nothing subtle about Mr. Dalton's role as a segregationist in liberal
pose, his professed sympathies for black Americans are intricately bound up
with the continued exploitation of black families. That Wright chooses to
represent the NAACP through a character such as Dalton, places him firmly
within the paradigms of black Communist discourses of class evidenced in
the *Liberator*.

While Wright ensures that the politics of moderation are discredited, neither does *Native Son* contain any serious attempt to propose a black nationalist
solution (unlike Ellison's *Invisible Man, Native Son* does not engage with black
nationalism in any sustained manner): it is the commonality of poverty and
alienation which Bigger envisages in his cell, rather than skin colour alone.[51]
Wright's vision does not express itself in terms of reformism or separation. The
political resolution of the novel is neither Bigger's existential self-definition *nor*
Max's political abstractions – it is *both*, and therefore encapsulates Wright's
privileging of the dialectical relationship between black consciousness and
Marxist political ideology. It is the only ideology that can explain the world,
but race, as it is experienced in the United States, cannot be understood purely
at the level of abstraction. The black proletariat need to become their own
subject, to understand the significance of their hate and fear.

Bigger is not, as Henry Louis Gates Jr. suggests, a 'reacting protagonist voiceless to the last'.[52] Bigger locates a world outside of his subjective experience
which transforms his relationship to himself and society. He locates that possibility firstly in relation to Jan and Max and subsequently when, in his cell, he

---

50   Quoted Sallis 2000, p. 54.

51   This insistence on race as a social construct was retained by Wright, even after his defec-
      tion from the Communist Party. Writing in 1957, he stated, 'truly, you must know that the
      word Negro in America means something not racial or biological, but something purely
      social, something made in the United States'. Quoted in Wright 1964, p. 80.

52   Gates Jr. 1988, p. 106.

envisages a connection with other African Americans in the prison of the ghettos: 'and in that touch, response of recognition, there would be union, identity; there would be a supporting oneness, a wholeness which had been denied
him all his life'.[53] Bigger's consciousness of race and class is a consciousness of
exclusion, it is this redefining of the world he lives in that opens the possibility
for self-definition.

3.3   'Russian Folks': The Communist Party in *Native Son*

From the beginning of *Native Son*, Bigger is aware of Communism as something dangerous, threatening to the stability of the white world. At the movies
Jack tells him that Reds are a 'race of folks' from Russia:

> 'Reds sure don't like rich folks,' Jack said.
> 'They sure must don't', Bigger said. 'Every time you hear about one, he's
> trying to kill somebody or tear things up'.[54]

Skin colour is not the only colour which defines marginality and in the blunt,
sometimes laboured, colour symbolism of this novel, red and black are connected throughout the text. Put crudely, the white world offers Bigger only
exclusion and dispossession, the red world offers him the possibility of redemption. But, though both red and black signify marginality, there is no simple
equation between them.[55] It is the overt racism of Britten which attempts to
collapse difference and posit Communism in anti-Semitic discourse, to define
whiteness in relation to a Communist/Jewish/black other. This is illustrated in
his questioning of Peggy:

> 'When he talks, does he wave his hands around a lot, like he's been around
> a lot of Jews?' ... 'Did you ever hear 'im call anybody comrade' ... 'Does he
> pull off his cap when he comes in the house?' ... 'Has he ever sat down
> in you presence without being asked, like he was used to being around
> white people?' ... 'Does he speak first, or does he wait until he's spoken
> to?' ... 'Now listen Peggy. Think and try to remember if his voice goes

---

53   Wright 1997, p. 400.
54   Wright 1997, p. 71.
55   For an interesting discussion on the more multiple significations of 'red' in this novel see
      Wells 2010, pp. 879–81.

up when he talks, like Jews when they talk. Know what I mean? You see
Peggy, I'm trying to find out if he's been around Communists'.[56]

The novel itself, however, insists upon the difference between political scapegoating and racial oppression. Jan's politics ensure his arrest, but they also give
him the means to confront the police, which he does on more than one occa-
sion. Bigger's abjection in the prison cell is in stark contrast to Jan's refusal to
leave jail in order to prove the anti-Communist conspiracy. Bigger's oppression
is determined by his skin colour; he is, in Fanon's phrase, 'overdetermined from
without'.[57] Despite the novel's refusal to collapse the contradictions of racism
into a strict binary opposition, there is no escaping the power relations which
determine the course of Bigger's life; power relations which centre on race. The
master discourse *in* the novel is not Max's speech or Bigger's interiority, which
do not circulate in the public sphere. The master discourse is the newspaper
accounts of Bigger which construct 'race' within the paradigm of bestiality
and criminality. The media discourse of race is an unreconstructed treatise of
nineteenth-century pseudo-scientific racism:

> Though the Negro killer's body does not seem compactly built, he gives
> the impression of possessing abnormal physical strength. He is about
> five feet, nine inches tall and his skin is exceedingly black. His lower jaw
> protrudes obnoxiously, reminding one of a jungle beast ... His arms are
> long, hanging in a dangling fashion to his knees. It is easy to imagine how
> this man, in the grip of a brain numbing sex passion, overpowered little
> Mary Dalton ... All in all, he seems a beast utterly untouched by the soft-
> ening influences of modern civilisation. In speech and manner he lacks
> the charm of the average, harmless genial grinning southern darky so
> beloved by the American people.[58]

The official history of Bigger is the 'objective' and objectifying voice of pathological racism depicted by the press, literalised by Buckley and sanctioned
through Bigger's execution.

The tension in *Native Son*, which insists on the specificity of racial oppression yet suggests a unity of interest between African Americans and white
Communists is no way anomalous in the context of Marxist politics, even in
its Stalinised form in this period. As argued in Chapter One, by recognising the

---

56   Wright 1997, p. 231.
57   Fanon 1986, p. 116.
58   Wright 1997, p. 317.

specific nature of racial oppression, and linking its overthrow to the general exploitation of workers under capitalism, the CPUSA was armed on two fronts; against the divide and rule practice of the American capitalist class and against the class collaborationist policy of the moderate black organisations. In stressing Bigger's alienation as a black man, and relocating that experience, through Max's speech, into a broader context of capitalist exploitation, Wright is interrogating the dynamics of race and class within the paradigm of self-determination and working-class unity. Even before his dawning consciousness in Book Three, Bigger is conscious that red has more in common with black than white:

> Bigger knew the things that white folk hated to hear Negroes ask for: and he knew that these were the things the reds were always asking for. And he knew that white folks did not like to hear these things asked for even by the whites who fought for Negroes.[59]

In stressing that the white establishment resents the articulation of anti-racism from any quarter, a division is emphasised along *racist* rather than race lines. This point is crucial because Max's courtroom speech is not, as Baldwin and others suggest, simply that the black man is America's responsibility.[60] Beyond this, there is a convergence of interests between the American majority (the working class) and the black minority, it is a call for solidarity rather than 'responsibility'. There is little credence given in this novel to a concept of black unity against white, but rather of a political consciousness of race being the genesis for wider revolutionary consciousness.

Bigger's encounters are with Communists rather than Communism. Bigger never reads the pamphlets that Jan gives him. He never engages in political argument with Jan. He is no more aware of the politics of Communism at the end of the novel than he is at the start. After his arrest, Jan and Max are his vehicle for hope which engenders his own tremulous attempts at re-imagining his world. Criticism of Wright's Communism in *Native Son* tends to focus on Max's courtroom speech, a speech which Alfred Kazin is surely referring to when he charges the novel with containing 'crude Stalinist homilies'.[61] Max's Communist Party membership is ambiguous in the novel, he never names himself as a Communist, however I argue that it is not Bigger's relationship to Max which is key to Communist representation in the novel but his relationship to Jan.

---

59   Wright 1997, p. 235.
60   Baldwin 1964, p. 41.
61   Kazin 1942, p. 387.

Bigger's conversations with Jan are crucial. Both Mary's death and Bigger's fledgling self-awareness in the prison cell are precipitated (though in different ways) by his encounters with Jan. During the court case the hatred directed at Jan allows Bigger his first tremulous attempt at identification: 'He knew how Jan felt ... He was not the only object of hate here. What did the reds want that made the coroner hate Jan so?'[62]

Significantly, Bigger is not the only person who is transformed by their acquaintance, Jan is also destabilised by the events of the novel. When Jan visits Bigger in his cell, he is not the assured man whose confident assumptions had so disoriented Bigger at Ernie's Shack. Jan is now struggling for understanding, his speech is broken as he tries to articulate his altered worldview, to admit his own fear and ignorance.

> But there is something I just got to say ... You needn't talk to me unless you want to, Bigger. I think I know something of what you're feeling now. I'm not dumb, Bigger; I can understand, even if I didn't that night ... ' Jan paused, swallowed and lit a cigarette. 'Well you jarred me ... I see now. I was kind of blind'.[63]

Black and white worlds are not discrete and self-contained. There is no monocultural space in this novel. Even the Daltons, with their wealth and privilege, cannot escape the effects of racial discrimination, though, unlike Jan, the novel shows that they benefit materially from its continued practice. The terms of Jan's new offer of friendship to Bigger are paramount. Jan approaches Bigger, not on the grounds of charity or goodness as the preacher interprets, but on the basis of solidarity, the recognition of Bigger's 'right to hate'.[64] This extraordinary moment of potential solidarity in the novel is premised on a validation of black hate as legitimate and necessary. Jan's private assertion is qualitatively different from the public rights Max elucidates in his courtroom speech; it separates Jan from the rest of white society as Bigger experiences it. Jan chooses to ally himself with *Bigger's* right to hate, an act which has profound consequences for Bigger:

> Jan had spoken a declaration of friendship that would make other white men hate him: a particle of white rock had detached itself from that looming mountain of white hate and had rolled down the slope, stopping

---

62   Wright 1997, p. 362.
63   Wright 1997, p. 324.
64   Wright 1997, p. 325.

still at his feet. The word had become flesh. For the first time in his life a
white man became a human being to him; and the reality of Jan's humanity came in a stab of remorse.[65]

Jan's interventions on Bigger's behalf complicates the divide between black
and white worlds. While his earlier blundering attempts to 'include' Bigger
were experienced as the cruellest form of exclusion, Jan's willingness to associate himself with Bigger *against* white hostility is a radical alliance. This is a
concept which contemporary race theorists might construct as a sophisticated
undermining of the 'othering' which predicates the structures of racism.[66]

Jan, then, is the catalyst who enables Bigger's ambiguous rebirth, just as
Bigger shatters Jan's limited and surface race politics. Jan recognises Bigger's
motivation; it is Jan the Communist who affirms his hatred and fear, and in
doing so allies himself against white supremacy and white philanthropy. His
comprehension of the reality of African-American rage destabilises and deconstructs the paradigms of a liberal politics which is dependent on the white gaze
for its objectifying power. As with the discourses of black communist radicalism discussed in relation to the *Liberator*, there is a struggle here to wrest back
African-American agency from a philanthropic narrative which erases black
subjectivity.

Wright's representation of the Communist Party in *Native Son* is the antithesis of his later representation in his 1953 novel *The Outsider*.[67] In *Native Son*,
Communism is a humanist and flexible discourse of radical recognition.
Max's courtroom oration demands the extension of bourgeois democracy to
include African Americans while simultaneously exposing the violence upon
which that democracy rests. Max's speech is crucial for the critical reception
of Communism in *Native Son* and will be investigated for the remainder of this
chapter.

The trial of Bigger has dominated the critical legacy of *Native Son*. One of the
most interesting early criticisms of Max's speech comes from an unexpected

---

65   Wright 1997, p. 326.
66   'Racism – a true "total social phenomenon" – inscribes itself in practices (forms of vio-
      lence, contempt, intolerance, humiliation and exploitation), in discourses and represen-
      tations which are so many intellectual elaborations of the phantasm of prophylaxis or
      segregation (the need to purify the social body, to preserve "one's own" or "our" identity
      from all forms of mixing, interbreeding or invasion) and which are articulated around
      stigmata of otherness (name, skin colour, religious practices)'. Balibar and Wallerstein
      1991, pp. 17–18.
67   For a discussion of *The Outsider* see pp. 188–9.

quarter. On its publication, *Native Son* was generally received enthusiastically
by the American Left. Sam Sillen in *New Masses* claimed that the novel had its
'ultimate source in a revolutionary vision of life'. Sillen went on to proclaim it a
'philosophical novel, a creative affirmation of the will to live and to transform
life'.[68] However, leading African-American Communist Benjamin Davis Jr. was
less eager. He took particular exception to the character of Max, and it is worth
quoting him at some length:

> But Max represents the type of so-called legal defence which the
> Communist Party and the I.L.D. have been fighting, dating from
> Scottsboro. Some of his speech is mystical, unconvincing, and expresses
> the point of view held not by Communists but by those reformist betray-
> ers who are being displaced by the Communists. He accepts the idea
> that Negroes have a criminal psychology as the book erroneously tends
> to symbolise in Bigger. He does not challenge the false charge of rape
> against Bigger, though Bigger did not rape Mary, and though this is the
> eternal bourbon slander flung against Negroes. He does not deal with
> the heinous murder of Bessie, tending to accept the bourbon policy that
> crimes of Negroes against each other don't matter and are not cut from
> the same capitalist cloth . . . From Max's whole conduct the first business
> of the Communist Party or of the I.L.D. would have been to chuck him
> out of the case.[69]

Certainly in historical, factual terms even passing knowledge of ILD would
give full credence to Davis's somewhat pious and literal interpretation of Max's
speech. What is notable is how subsequent commentators on the book, few of
whom share Davis's outraged Communist sensibility, have approached Max's
defence as a self-contained section of the book, which contains the 'message'
of the novel.[70]

Clearly, seen in this way Max's speech is problematic in various ways: its
rhetorical nature, moralistic tone and the continuing objectification of Bigger.
There is also the fact that the speech labours an argument already eloquently
and emphatically expressed throughout the text. It is argued that Max re-writes
Bigger's life for the court within a Marxist polemic, which further alienates

---

68   Sillen 1940, *New Masses*, 5 March 1940.

69   Davis Jr. 1970, p. 76.

70   For example W. Lawrence Hogue collapses the character and author in Book Three: 'In
      the defense speech, Wright/Max poses a Marxist socio-political-economic explanation
      for Bigger's human situation'. Hogue 2009, p. 28.

Bigger.[71] Certainly the novel, in parts, demands this interpretation, as Bigger reflects that 'he had not understood the speech, but he had felt the meaning of some of it from the tone of Max's voice. Suddenly he felt that his life was not worth the effort that Max had made to save it'.[72]

If the content of Max's speech alone is a representation of Communist Party politics of race, then Davis is correct and Max is an anomalous type of Marxist. On first appearance, he is more the crusading liberal, seeking to redress the wrongs of a corrupt society, to avert catastrophe rather than confront the structures of racism. But Max's speech does not stand alone, unconnected thematically from the rest of the text. The speech needs to be read in relationship to the narrative as a whole. Even within the speech itself the earlier liberal gestures soon evaporate as Max deconstructs the American myth of 'Freedom'. He emphasises that the degree of freedom attained by Americans represents only a limited realisation of the objective of human emancipation. Echoing the earlier discursive battles with black moderates over 'freedom' in the pages of the *Liberator*, Max insists that in the United States such terms are merely formal abstractions because the socio-economic and racial inequalities still persist. Moreover he argues that Bigger's crime is sourced in slavery itself:

> It's the 'first wrong' – slavery – that is at the root of Bigger's crime. We must deal here with a dislocation of life involving millions of people, a dislocation so vast as to stagger the imagination; ... so old that we would try to view it as an order of nature and strive with uneasy conscience and false moral fervor to keep it so.[73]

Max relocates racist discourse from an individual prejudice, or the indiscriminate pathology of white society, to a function of class rule, an integral part of American capitalism. His speech includes the construction of an alternative history of America, one in which slavery underpins all of American life. It is a legacy which structures present day society:

> All of them – the mob and the mob masters; the wire pullers and the frightened; the leaders and their pet vassals – know and feel that their

---

71   See for example Brignano 1970, p. 78; Davis 1990, p. 17; Margoiles 1990, pp. 43–59; Gibson 1995, pp. 35–42.

72   Wright 1997, p. 438.

73   Wright 1997, p. 424.

lives are built upon a historical deed of wrong against many people, people from whose lives they have bled their leisure and their luxury.[74]

White society is not one great classless oppressor, but rather a society of competing interests, and Max explicitly aligns the interests of victimised black Americans with victimised political activists:

> The hunt for Bigger Thomas served as an excuse to terrorise the entire Negro population, to arrest hundreds of Communists, to raid labour union headquarters and workers' organisations.[75]

He also reiterates the Party line of the Black Belt thesis stating that Black Americans 'constitute a separate nation, stunted, stripped, and held captive *within* this nation'.[76]

But the most significant point is that Max's plea does not just fail, *it is rejected out of hand*. The judge does not even consider the case for the defence, his response to Max's argument is, 'court will adjourn for one hour'.[77] When it is placed in its narrative context, rather than read as a kind of pamphlet unconnected to the text, Max's thesis and its outright rejection by the court is a damning recognition that the American Dream is predicated on black exclusion. Max offers a version of history and society which is rejected and therefore placed outside official history. That Wright chooses a courtroom as Max's arena is not inconsequential, particularly in the context of the primacy of ILD activity in Communist Party practice in the 1930s.[78] More generally, as Michael Staub notes:

> Trials, like theatre, are full of speech. Both are performances of oral testimony … and both are, to a degree, ritualized activities, scripted according to certain cultural and social criteria and intended to create out of an enclosed space a version (and vision) of the world outside … As the trial proceeds, there is the interplay of voices competing for their version of historical truth. Yet once the final verdict is reached, these oral performances are assimilated into the written documentation, and the hierarchy of sources – with the written sources ranking above the oral ones – is

---

74   Wright 1997, p. 423.
75   Wright 1997, p. 422.
76   Wright 1997, p. 431. For a discussion of the Black Belt Thesis see chapter one pp. 17–19.
77   Wright 1997, p. 447.
78   See above pp. 34–44

re-established. Guilty or innocent: Once a final text has been decided and the memories of what was spoken become practically irrelevant, what remains are the court transcripts and the verdict. The political space that had been opened through speech is now closed again by writing.[79]

Staub's arguments are pertinent to this novel where the written word is invested with such significance. Bigger is fighting for a voice and is everywhere silenced by words written about him. Initially, it is not what Max says which inspires Bigger, it is the fact he allows Bigger to speak, and imagine the possibility of communicating with others:

> Many times, when alone after Max had left him, he wondered wistfully if there was not a set of words which he had in common with others, words which would evoke in others a sense of the same fire that smouldered in him.[80]

It is almost a *de facto* principle in the literary critical reception of this novel that Max's defence rests on the construction of a socio-political argument which is alien to Bigger's life and experience.[81] Again the speech needs to be read in conjunction with the rest of the narrative. Max's courtroom address is not rooted in abstract political propaganda, but in a meticulously constructed argument that relates intimately to Bigger's *own* account of events. At frequent points in the climactic courtroom speech Wright has Max talking *as*, almost quoting, Bigger:

> But under the stress of fear and flight, Bigger Thomas did not think of Bessie. He could not ... did he not love Bessie? Was she not his girl. Yes; she was his girl. He had to have a girl, so he had Bessie. But he did not love her.[82]

This directly corresponds to his earlier conversation with Bigger: 'Did you love her?' 'Naw. I was just scared. I wasn't in love with Bessie she was just my girl ... You have to have a girl, so I had Bessie. And I killed her'.[83] Far from

---

79   Staub 1994, pp. 22–3.
80   Wright 1997, p. 401.
81   This widespread interpretation of Max's defence is upheld in Gibson, in Butler 1995;
      Kresser-Cobb, 1978; De Arman 1978.
82   Wright 1997, p. 435.
83   Wright 1997, p. 390.

erasing Bigger from his speech, far from cancelling Bigger's voice, Max cites
Bigger's own testimony. He may be interpreting Bigger's life within a sociologi-
cal argument, but it is *Bigger's* life which forms the basis for his defence. When
Max tells the court:

> I know that it is the fashion these days for a defendant to say: 'Everything
> went blank to me'. But this boy does not say that. He says the opposite. He
> says he knew what he was doing but felt he *had* to do it. And he says he
> feels no sorrow for having done it.[84]

Again he is recalling his conversation with Bigger:

> M: Your mean you went blank?
> B: Naw; naw . . . I knew what I was doing, all right. But I couldn't help it.
> That's what I mean.[85]
> M: You say you hated her?
> B: Yeah; and I ain't sorry she's dead.[86]

Max structures his defence around his long conversation with Bigger. He uses
Bigger's answers to construct his argument. Throughout the speech Max constantly refers to Bigger's responses, the latter's quest for 'happiness' is evoked
in Max's questioning of the definition of happiness in the constitution. Max
returns repeatedly in his speech to Bigger's insistence that white society was
trying to kill him. When explaining Bigger's sense of liberation after Mary's
death: 'it was the first full act of his life . . . he accepted it because it made him
free'.[87] Max is relating to Bigger's earlier assertion, 'for a little while I was free,
I was doing something'.[88]

Max is not erasing Bigger's life in yet another alienating fiction. He is contra-
dicting the hegemonic rendering of race in America through a re-articulation
of Bigger's own experiences of racist objectification. The fact that Bigger does
not understand Max's address to the judge is not evidence of Max's failure.
Bigger is not his intended audience. Max's function in the novel is not to restate
Bigger's understanding of his crime, but to situate his actions within the lexicon of race politics in the US.

---

84   Wright 1997, p. 431.
85   Wright 1997, p. 389.
86   Wright 1997, p. 387.
87   Wright 1997, p. 430.
88   Wright 1997, p. 392.

For large parts of the novel Bigger is atomised and defeated. He is isolated from any feeling of self-determination and divorced from the system of power that determines his life. His consciousness is characterised by a lack of consciousness, by his conditioned *unconsciousness* of his own socio-historical and economic condition.[89]

Max's courtroom speech, then, is the representation of a political consciousness of race that takes Bigger's life out of the realm of pathological criminality and experiential self-hatred; moreover, it places Biggers actions within a coherent narrative of slavery and exploitation. *Native Son* considers such political consciousness of race as fundamental to challenging white supremacy but only in dialectical relationship to an experiential existential freedom. Bigger must also come to his own understanding of his fate. Baldwin' s proposition that *Native Son* is a plea or a warning to white society which demands that America admit its guilt and culpability in spawning this 'monster' is only half true.[90] The novel also addresses itself to how Bigger can emerge from the determining forces in his life: 'He stood up in the middle of the cell floor and tried to see himself in relation to other men, a thing he had always feared to try to do, so deeply stained was his own mind with the hate of others for him'.[91]

Bigger's self-realisation is painful and awkward. It is not a measured and resigned honourable statement, it is made in a 'frenzied anguish'. It is not what Max wants to hear, but Bigger insists he is heard, he has a desperate need to be heard:

> He summoned up his energies and lifted his head and struck out desperately, determined to rise from the grave, resolved to force upon Max the reality of his living.[92]

Wells argues that 'the 'terror' in Max's eyes is 'the terror that attends the realization that one's interpretive paradigms have failed, that one is finally at a loss'.[93] But does Max's horror at Bigger's narrative underline the unbridgeable gap between them or is it the silence of comprehension: the fact that one cannot transcend the brutal realities of oppression by imaginative repositioning within the paradigms allowed? Bigger's determination at the end of the

---

89   Lukács 1971, p. 52.
90   Baldwin 1964, p. 41.
91   Wright 1997, p. 398.
92   Wright 1997, p. 455.
93   Wells 2010, p. 893.

novel to remain defiant about his 'acts of creation',[94] emphasises that he has no point of redress in the system of power he inhabits. His only agency is in the re-appropriation of his actions. Only by doing this can he avoid being the 'victim' that Max's courtroom narrative has defines him as. Arguably Max does understand this, his is the silence, not of bewilderment, but of painful recognition. He has told Bigger earlier, 'oh, they'll hate me, yes... but I can take it. That's the difference. I'm a Jew and they hate me, but I know why and I can fight. But sometimes you can't win no matter how you fight; that is, you can't win if you haven't got time'.[95] The very fact that Bigger is hours from death and paralysed by frustration and the failure to communicate to Max what he feels, only underlies the importance of his self-avowal. Bigger persists, he articulates his frustration, he forces Max to deal with his reality.

Communism offers Bigger an alternative identity to those proffered by white society. In contrast to the scapegoating which surrounds the Bigger case and the emphasis on individual responsibility which underlies the entire legal system, Max defiantly disregards questions of evidence and morality and focuses instead on the historical and social landscape of racialised America. The fact that Bigger's *self-realisation* is different from Max's understanding of the political self, is not a critique of the latter. It is Wright's presentation of their *dialectical*, rather than symbiotic, relationship which opens up the possibility for Bigger's tremulous self-knowledge. Jan and Max are, to a degree, outsiders in this text. Their impact on Bigger's life is not based on *identification* with him; after all, this is what Jan attempts in his first disastrous meeting with Bigger. The role Wright ascribes to these characters and particularly to Max, is specifically a cerebral, abstract, scientific one. It is directly following his conversation with the white Jewish left-wing lawyer that Bigger allows himself the luxury of inclusion of imagining a world of black solidarity: 'and in that touch, response of recognition, there would be union, identity; there would be a supporting oneness, a wholeness which had been denied him all his life'.[96]

After the trial, for the first time in Bigger's life, he is no longer marked by a tangible conflict between what he says and what he thinks. From urging the robbery of Blums while plotting to avert it, talking to Mary and Jan while hating them, adopting poses for the Daltons, and bullying and using Bessie, Bigger has always been 'divided and pulled against himself'. Facing death, Bigger achieves a wholeness that he has lacked all his life and a clarity which is his

94   Wright 1997, p. 432.
95   Wright 1997, p. 396.
96   Wright 1997, pp. 399–400.

own: 'I ain't trying to forgive nobody and I ain't asking for nobody to forgive me. I ain't going to cry. They wouldn't let me live and I killed'.[97]

Ellison maintains that a major weakness of the novel is that 'in *Native Son* Wright began with the ideological proposition that what whites think of the Negro's reality is more important than what Negro's themselves know it to be'.[98] But in creating Bigger as the disaffected and voiceless agent of directionless anger, Wright is not adopting white history and myth in order to adapt it to black experience, he explodes it in a work of stark realism which attempts to negotiate a dialogue between political consciousness and racial oppression. Bigger's struggle is not a plea for understanding, nor is it a warning. His struggle is a fight for existence and self-expression against enslaving fictions and distortions. In *Native Son* there is no suggestion that the *experience* of 'blackness' is a prerequisite for fighting racism. Jan and Max may or may not automatically 'understand' Bigger but they certainly understand the power dynamic of racism and are involved in a struggle to end it. It is this *political* identification which is crucial. The novel points to the possibility of interracial political alliances recalling the successful mobilisations around Scottsboro and echoing the race conscious interracial solidarity of the *Liberator*. The symbolic force of class and race in ordering identity are simultaneous with actual social position and place among family, community and class.[99]

In *Native Son* it is the re-structuring of the self in relation to the social world which allows the possibility of emancipation from estranging concepts of selfhood. Blackness is confronted as a social and historical category rather than articulated as an inherent selfhood. Black subjectivity is a process rather than an essence. Wright does not suggest that the experience of racism is completely polymorphous, or that there is no common experience of oppression; but at this historical period when Northern African Americans were articulating a different experience of modernity and urbanisation, agency does not reside in ethnic particularity. It is precisely the question of political solidarity, the articulation of common interests, which allows for potential black political agency. That is the experience *Native Son* illuminates, and in doing so it speaks both from and to the discursive space of African-American Communism.

---

97   Wright 1997, p. 461.

98   Ellison 1964, p. 114.

99   'Racism does not stay still: it changes shape, size, contours, purpose, function – with changes in economy, the social structure, the system and above all the challenges, the resistances to that system'. Sivanandan 1983, p. 2.

PART 2

Betrayals and Defeat

∵

Introduction to Part 2

> The Marxist movement as represented by the Communist Party was so indissolubly linked with practically everything Negroes attempted to do, it was impossible not to find a Communist or two under the bed if one looked earnestly enough.[1]
>
> HAROLD CRUSE

The hostility directed towards the Communist Party in both *Lonely Crusade* and *Invisible Man* has traditionally been read through the paradigms of Cold War anti-Communism. Indeed, along with Richard Wright's 1953 novel *The Outsider*, these novels form a powerful cultural response to the perceived failure of Communism to comprehend the complexities of race and identity. However, these novels are informed by an anti-Communism, in part engendered by the wartime activities of the CPUSA, rather than by the anti-Communist discourse of the Cold War period. So while the hostility to Communism in the texts seems unambiguous, the *nature* of that hostility is best understood through an investigation of the *specific* character of the post-Depression CPUSA and its impact on black struggles.

This distinction is important as the oft-cited 'betrayal' of black workers by the American Communist Party – their self-serving adoption of black politics for dubious motives – which has characterised studies of this period until the recent past, is often presented as a tautological effect of Communism's inherent 'racism'. When placed in their historical context, the unquestionably damaging policies of the CPUSA in the 1940s are not evidence of a power hungry cabal intent on achieving political power on the backs of black Americans. We are presented, rather, with a chaotic tragedy of reckless political strategies which ensured the Party's isolation in the face of the sustained attacks of the McCarthyite era.[2]

Whilst I am not concerned with the extent to which biographical elements inflect *Lonely Crusade* or *Invisible Man*, both Himes and, to a greater extent, Ellison were drawn to Communist circles and both cited their empirical 'knowledge' of the movement in defending their representation of Communists in

---

1 Cruse 1968, p. 139.

2 According to many historians the disastrous effects of Comintern-led directives from the Hitler-Stalin Pact and throughout the War rendered the organisation incapable of withstanding the witch-hunts of the 1950s. For example see Isserman 1982, p. 169; and Naison 1985, p. 273.

their novels.[3] It is, therefore, pertinent to place their representations within a wider historical context in order to provide a useful paradigm for exploring the axis of anger and betrayal which characterises Post-War black fictional portrayals of the Communist Party. As in Part One of this book, my intention here is not to render a finite historical 'background' for the novels, but to focus thematically on specific historical events which can be made to illuminate the representations of the Communist Party in *Lonely Crusade* and *Invisible Man*.

Important here are the CPUSA activities during the Popular Front. The internationalism and pan-Africanism which characterised Third Period politics on questions of race in the United States was replaced during the Popular Front era by an *Americanisation* of the race question, which nevertheless positioned black culture as the cornerstone of 'American' life. Popular Front constructions of 'America' focused on black culture as pivotal to radical American cultural forms. Black culture was constructed as a privileged site, which could release the liberating elements of 'American' culture. This formulation forged an intrinsic relationship between race and nation, in which black indigenous culture could enrich a formative national culture. My focus in this section is not on the Americanisation of the CPUSA itself, but on the Party's attempt to Americanise blackness.

The cultural construction of black American identity privileged an interdependence between racial and national concerns which took on a different and precarious meaning with the onset of the Second World War. During the War the CPUSA's commitment to Americanisation took on an increasingly nationalist zeal, concentrating on defending the American *state*; a policy which transformed the Party's long-term relationship to, if not its immediate fortunes within, black communities. I will look at the contradictions inherent in a Communist 'patriotism' which saw the Party re-appropriate the 'Star Spangled Banner' as a revolutionary anthem. The 'respectability' the Party earned during the War lured Communists into a false sense of security *vis-à-vis* the American state, which was brutally ruptured at the onset of the Cold War. While both *Lonely Crusade* and *Invisible Man* are not rooted in McCarthyite anti-Communism, they (*Invisible Man* in particular) do decisively mark the breach between African-American writers and the Communist movement.

---

3 When questioned about *Lonely Crusade*, for example, Himes responded, 'I swear to God, my material for writing Lonely Crusade came from these experiences [Communist circles in LA]. I met these people'. Quoted in Sallis 2000, p. 79.

CHAPTER 4

'Communism is the Twentieth Century Americanism'

4.1   Popular Front: Remaking African-American Culture

I'm just an Irish, Negro, Jewish, Italian, French and English, Spanish, Russian, Chinese, Polish, Scotch, Hungarian, Litvak, Sweedish, Finnish, Canadian, Greek and Turk and Czech and double-check American.

'Ballad for Americans' (1939)[1]

1935 saw the disbandment of the League of Struggle for Negro Rights and the cessation of the *Negro Liberator*. The Seventh World Congress of the Comintern in that year discarded Third Period Communism in favour of broad-based alliances with liberals and left-wingers and the creation of a Popular Front against fascism and war.[2]

The effects of the shift in policy from the Third Period to the Popular Front were not uniform. While the move away from sectarianism ensured that Communists, on the East Coast in particular, were engaged in relatively successful broad-front campaigns which saw their ranks increase, in the Southern states the effects were more contradictory. In the South most 'liberals' were segregationists and the CPUSA's membership, which was almost exclusively black, rural and poor, began to decline.[3]

Overall, however, the Popular Front marked the Communist Party's period of greatest influence in American society. Socialists and Social Democrats – the 'social fascists' of the Third Period – were now wooed by Communists around the world into an alliance against fascism. Once again, Comintern directives were only half of the equation. The Party itself had already made overtures to black progressives in 1935 over the invasion of Ethiopia. As Harry Haywood recalled:

---

1   'Ballad for Americans' is most closely associated with Paul Robeson; it was written by the left-wing composer Earl Robinson. See Duberman 1989, pp. 235–37.

2   Barrett 2009, pp. 531–2.

3   Kelley 1990, pp. 119–37.

> Anticipating the call of the Seventh Congress, we Southside Communists seized the initiative to build a broad united front struggle against the growing threat of war and fascism. An emergency Southside conference was held on July 10, 1935, to plan a campaign to defend and support Ethiopia. The response was overwhelming. Over 1,100 delegates attended, representing all manner of Black community organizations: churches, lodges, clubs, Black nationalist groups and the Black YWCA, as well as a number of Italian anti-fascist groups.[4]

The political environment was then already conducive to the left-liberal alliance and was made more so by Roosevelt's attempt to build popular support for the New Deal. Indeed, by the late 1930s the CPUSA almost uncritically supported Roosevelt and the Democratic Party as it fought for political respectability, accepting 'a furtive role in coalition politics'.[5] By the end of the War it was the Communist's relationship with *America* rather than the Soviet state which prompted an angry Ralph Ellison to exclaim in 1945: 'If they want to play ball with the bourgeoisie, they needn't think that they can get away with it'.[6]

The Popular Front was not merely a rhetorical shift. In Europe, the class collaborationist policies engendered by Popular Front formations had devastating effects, particularly in France and Spain.[7] In the United States the wartime activities of the CPUSA mirrored its rhetoric in signalling a significant shift in political direction, in all aspects of its activities, including race. As Mark Naison details, the Popular Front Communist Party in Harlem did not neglect race, but it did direct its energies into winning over 'respectable' black organisations – often at the expense of grass roots local campaigns over housing and jobs, campaigns which had hitherto defined it as the champions of the black working class.[8]

The CPUSA did not create the environment in which they now operated. Michael Denning points to the significance of American populism *per se* in the period, a dynamic outside of the still relatively small Communist Party:

> The emergence of a populist rhetoric was not a retreat from revolution but a response to the growing power of the movement, and to the competing populist rhetorics of the time . . . The populist rhetoric of the

---

4   Haywood 1978, p. 448.
5   Kelley 1990, p. 177.
6   Quoted in Benston 1990, p. 204.
7   Torigian 1989, pp. 464–91; Carr and Deutscher 1984, pp. 83–6.
8   Naison 1985, pp. 279–84.

Popular Front social movement must be understood as a political and ideological response both to the social movements of the right and to the official populism of the New Deal.[9]

Popular Front rhetoric, however, as a 'political and ideological response' became deeply troubling, especially during the War, when the nuances and contradictions within Communist 'Americanism' were barely discernible from the official Patriotism of the war effort.

During the heyday of the Popular Front, however, the Communist Party's 'populism' was centred around the remaking of American culture which centred on difference as inclusion. The best of these radical impulses which informed Popular Front reclamations of 'America', is summed up by Rockwell Kent. Kent imagines American culture as 'like a tapestry, woven of brilliant colored threads, every one which can be distinguished and keep its own characteristics'.[10] This invocation of an America defined by differences was impressive and prescient, yet it was one defined by 'peoples' rather than classes. Although this was the 'Age of the CIO' and the heyday of industrial unionism, the discursive move away from the 'class' to the 'people' set a precedent in left-wing American politics (which had always been characterised by revolutionary syndicalism). This precedent was to transform the Party's relationship with black moderates.

The Popular Front marked a cessation in the hostilities which had characterised the relationship between the CPUSA and the black middle class, particularly in the arena of African-American culture. The early phase of Communist intervention in black struggle was predominantly one which emphasised the working-class character of black American life and the integration of black history into the history of international anti-capitalist struggle. With the onset of the Popular Front, the treatment of black culture expanded from a veneration of oppositional working-class forms, to an emphasis on recognising black American culture *per se*, as the standard bearer of radical American culture. African Americans were made to personify the tradition of struggle in America.[11]

In this context, where the relationship between Communists and 'progressives' was characterised by a camaraderie that was unimaginable in the early years of the decade, the Party's racial politics were radically transformed. The

---

9   Denning 1996, pp. 126, 128.
10   Quoted in Denning 1996, p. 132. Rockwell Kent was the President of the International Workers Order.
11   Foley 1993, p. 190.

despised black middle class of the Third Period became a vital ally in the struggle to build a broad-based alliance against the threat of fascism. The Party's
new found respect for black progressives and intellectuals was reciprocated in
the mid-1930s when a variety of Communist-inspired broad fronts were supported within the black community. By far the most important of these was
The National Negro Congress (NNC), which secured the allegiance of many
non-Communist black activists.

The NNC was set up in 1936 and important black leaders such as A. Philip
Randolph, Ralph Bunch and Adam Clayton Powell were among its founding
members. Clayton Powell could declare in 1945: 'There is no group in America,
including the Christian church, that practices racial brotherhood one-tenth
as much as the Communist Party'.[12] In correspondence with Wright, Ellison
recalled that his 'experience of the Congress was almost mystical in its
intensity'.[13] Churches, social clubs and civil organisations were approached
by the Party on a non-sectarian basis to work within and alongside the
National Negro Congress against fascism abroad and discrimination at home.
Representing over three million people, it was the pinnacle of the CPUSA's success in mobilising black American organisations.[14] The Congress had active
local chapters in more than 70 cities; it played an important role in recruiting black workers into the new CIO industrial unions and in some areas had
displaced the NAACP as the leading black community organisation by the late
1930s.[15]

However, unlike the NAACP, this broad organisation generally anchored
itself in the black working class, or more significantly the *American* black
working class. The emphasis on 'America' as a significant element in structuring Communist identity was a departure from Third Period formations of black
Communist identity which focused on internationalist class consciousness.
It still, however, placed African Americans at the centre of Communist Party
iconography. The early black Party radicals like Cyril Briggs and Richard
Moore had been Afro-Caribbean, yet by 1935 90 percent of black comrades
were Americans.[16] For the purposes of Americanising the Party, native-born
African-American art forms were seen as the cutting edge of radical American

---

12   Quoted in Marable 1986, p. 171.
13   Quoted in Denning 1996, p. 332.
14   The NNC's first conference was attended by over 800 delegates from over 550 organisa-
      tions. See Solomon 1998, p. 304; Kelley 1990, p. 124.
15   Isserman 1982, p. 21.
16   Solomon 1998, pp. 263–4.

culture, where American culture was configured as a battle of ideas over the very meaning of race, belonging and nationalism.[17]

The new inclusiveness of the Popular Front was a multicultural embracing of black culture as essential to American cultural life, yet it also entailed a retreat from the Third Period formulations of interracial class solidarity. Black culture was no longer valued because it was intrinsically anti-bourgeois, but because it was a vital part in the vibrant culture that was America, or rather the 'new' America.

The culture of the Popular Front was in part an attempt to reclaim American culture for the Left. As discussed in Chapter Three, the critical notion which assumes that 'protest' writing involved an aesthetic which emphasised *protest* at the expense of *writing*, is one which focuses on the 'bad' art of the 1930s as paradigmatic of the political art of the entire decade. The Popular Front, however, saw a convergence of native modernist writers, European émigrés and American working class intellectuals in an age of mass-consumerist culture. It included established writers radicalised by the Depression (most famously John Steinback) as well as left-wing activists who seized upon creative practices and theories from an established political position. It was a broad-based and multifarious movement that was, 'at different moments, a proletarian avant-garde, a movement culture, an aspect of state culture, and a part of mass culture itself'.[18]

Within this polymorphous matrix the concentration was less on Communist politics than on working-class American *experience*. In a 1935 anthology of proletarian literature one of the Party's leading cultural spokespersons, Joseph Freeman, reiterated that 'art, then, is not the same as action; it is not identical with science; it is distinct from Party program. It has its own special function, the grasp and transmission of experience'.[19]

The 'experience' of black workers and black intellectuals was transformed in the Popular Front era, both by the emergence of the Congress of Industrial Organisations (CIO) which prioritised the recruitment and retainment of black trade unionists and the radicalisation of the black middle class.[20] The mid-1930s saw a race-conscious black middle class embrace an internationalist and left-wing intellectual milieu, especially around the anti-fascist causes of Ethiopia and Spain.

---

17   Denning 1996, p. 129.
18   Denning 1996, pp. 60, 64.
19   Freeman 1935, p. 10.
20   Rabinowitz 2001, p. 112.

The new focus on black experience rather than exclusively on black protest saw the CPUSA develop an impressive, if uneven, approach to black culture. At the core, was a belief that the best of American culture was black culture. Mike Gold wrote in the *New Masses*: 'Negroes have given America all the truly native music it has thus far produced, and I believe that they can give us our first truly poetic theatre'.[21] Communist support of black art won the admiration of many black writers, intellectuals and performers, as Duberman recalls of Paul Robeson:

> Robeson was hardly alone among black artists in welcoming this uniquely respectful attitude toward black aesthetics. Here was an 'Americanism' that exemplified *real* respect for 'differentness' rather than attempting, as did official mainstream liberalism, to disparage and destroy ethnic variations under the guise of championing the superior virtue of the 'melting pot' – which in practice had tended to mean assimilation to the values of white middle-class protestants.[22]

The brief cultural survey given below is evidence of the powerful relationship that was formed between the CPUSA and black artists in this period. As well as championing the famous black musicians and actors of the day who explicitly allied themselves with the Left, the Party also instigated local initiatives which supported the establishment of black cultural forms. The Negro People's Theatre at Harlem's Lafayette Theatre was founded in 1935 and Orson Welles's adaptation of *Macbeth* was one of its first productions. Communist teachers, in particular, fought vigorously to incorporate black history into the curriculum, to introduce Negro History Week into the public schools, and to ensure that black students received equal opportunities in education. The *Daily Worker* sports editor spearheaded a campaign to persuade the Dodgers to hire their first black baseball players.[23] Celebrating the victory of Joe Louis in October 1935, *New Masses* declared:

> When Joe Louis knocked out Max Baer September 24, he touched off celebrations in every Negro community in the nation. Something of the same emotional release occurs whenever a Negro triumphs in competition with a white person.[24]

---

21   Quoted in Naison 1995, p. 207.
22   Duberman 1989, p. 250.
23   Starobin 1972, pp. 30–1.
24   North (ed.) 1969, p. 160.

Despite old-guard conservatism at the top of the Party, young Communists embraced Jazz and Swing as the epitome of radical American culture, and Communist journals and newspapers vigorously debated the merits of black American musical forms.[25] In 1939 *The Young Communist Review* argued that 'Swing is as American as Baseball and hot dogs'.[26] When *Gone With the Wind* was released in 1939 the Party launched a boycott against the film, picketing it in Harlem, and publishing a seven-part series in *The Daily Worker* which examined the role of the 'Negro in Hollywood films'.[27] When African-American Communist Ben Davis ran for New York City Council in 1943, he had the support of some of the leading Jazz figures of the day including Lena Horne, Duke Ellington, Count Basie, Ella Fitzgerald and Billie Holiday.[28]

This new emphasis on the significance of African-American culture was more than a token gesture to the important contribution of black artists and athletes; in Popular Front iconography the United States was presented as a 'nation of nations,' with the black nation at the forefront, articulating the best of the American tradition of struggle. The Popular Front saw a plethora of black cultural collaborations conceived as an alliance of left-looking black artists and CPUSA members. Ralph Ellison, for instance, founded the journal *Negro Quarterly* with celebrated black Communist Angelo Herndon in 1941. Though it only ran to four issues, the journal was an impressive eclectic mix of poetry, fiction, literary criticism and political theory. It included contributions from Ellison himself, Sterling Brown, Langston Hughes, Richard Wright and E. Franklin Frazier. Ellison also wrote reviews and articles for CP journals such as *The New Masses* and *Direction* in 1940 and 1941.[29]

On the West Coast, Chester Himes also came within the Party's orbit. He arrived in Los Angeles in 1940 with a list of contacts from Langston Hughes: 'most of them were connected with the Communist Party'.[30] Himes helped out in raising funds for Spanish Civil War veterans and in 1940 he wrote articles on the CIO for the Cleveland *Union Leader*.[31]

Claude McKay was not exaggerating when he wrote in 1940 that 'most of the Negro intellectuals' in Harlem were 'directly or indirectly hypnotised by

25   Naison 1985, pp. 211–213.
26   Naison 1985, p. 213.
27   Naison 1985, p. 299.
28   Denning 1996, p. 334.
29   Denning 1996, p. 331.
30   Himes interviewed in Williams amd Harris (eds.) 1970, p. 55.
31   Sallis 2000, p. 73.

the propaganda of the Popular Front'.[32] The apartment of Louise Thompson, a respected activist and black Party member in Harlem, was a celebrated space where black intellectuals and CP members discussed black culture and politics. Reminiscing about the times Richard Wright visited her home, Thompson recalled:

> we used to have discussions in our home with him, Paul Robeson, Langston [Hughes] and Jacques Romain, a Haitian poet we greatly admired ... We had jam sessions, long discussions ... Ralph Ellison used to be part of that scene as well. He used to be at my house almost every day.[33]

The Popular Front era then was one which moved away from the sectarianism of the early 1930s to initiate a rapprochement between black intellectuals and the Party. If the Party was not flooded by black artists wishing to join its ranks, it was joined by them on a variety of political and artistic platforms in a spirit of solidarity and mutual respect. More specifically, in terms of this study (and the chapter on *Invisible Man* in particular) the new formations around black *American* Communist identity generated a contradictory framework of allegiances for black radicals. The two opposing versions of America which structured the model of black identity in the *Liberator* set black cultural forms in a dialectical struggle with dominant American traditions. Now, black struggle was paradigmatic of 'America' itself. If 'American' interests were served by embracing black culture, were black interests served by defending America? The coming war would prove a gruelling test to the strength of the relationship between Communism and black artists forged in the Popular Front era.

4.2   Peace and War: Shifting Priorities

> The fight against Hitler and Hitlerism is the affair of every loyal and patriotic American.[34]

It was America's entry into the Second World War which heralded an uncharacteristic reticence to push black politics to the fore. From December 1941 onward the *Daily Worker*'s masthead slogan was 'National Unity for Victory over Nazi

---

32   Quoted in Naison 1995, p. 191.
33   Quoted in Naison 1995, p. 218.
34   Black Communist former vice-presidential candidate James W. Ford in 1941, quoted in Garfinkel 1959, p. 52.

Enslavement'. The politics of national unity had significant implications for fighting American racism. The concept of 'Americanisation' during the early Popular Front years was one which at least attempted to challenge the cultural and political institutions which had hitherto informed national identity. During the war the CPUSA made defence of the American state paramount; here 'Americanisation' had far more in common with old-style patriotism. In demanding that black Americans adhere to a set of loyalties in which black civil rights became secondary to American victory, the Party gambled its reputation on anti-racism. For the post-War black American novelists this was seen as a stark betrayal.

My argument here is that American Communism was not a 'God that failed' because the 'Communist Party could not accommodate race'.[35] The *anger* which accompanies the Party's representation in Himes, and even in Ellison, points to a bitter sense of treachery. Treachery and betrayal are in themselves a rejection of cynicism about the *ability* of Communism to fight racism; betrayal demands initial loyalty. I argue that this loyalty was, to some extent, 'betrayed' during the Second World War and an appreciation of the vitriol which accompanies Himes's and Ellison's representation of the Communist Party can be achieved by focusing on concrete aspects of CPUSA activity following the outbreak of War.

The disastrous effects of Soviet foreign policy become tangibly apparent in the late 1930s and early 1940s. Even the most nuanced historical accounts of how committed Party activists attempted to adapt and modify Comintern directives are necessarily overshadowed by the sheer impact of the Nazi-Soviet Pact in August 1939.[36] While this history need not be retold in detail here, it is nonetheless pertinent to sketch the political zigzags which, I argue, have been at the source of much of the suspicion which characterises black post-War fictional representations of the CPUSA.

On 22 August 1939, after four years of Popular Front work against fascism, Party members were greeted with the news that the Soviet Union had signed a non-aggression pact with Nazi Germany. The CPUSA General Secretary Earl Browder announced on 12 September that the impending war was now an

---

35   Peddie 2001, p. 119.
36   Robin Kelley argues that the effect of the Pact in Alabama was actually beneficial to the Party, as the racist nature of anti-Communism in the South meant the Communist-Liberal alliances which took off elsewhere never really emerged in Southern states. By abandoning Popular Front liberalism which had necessitated a dilution of radical racial politics, the Alabama organisation attracted a variety of committed activists during the 22-month lifespan of the Nazi-Soviet pact. See Kelley 1990, p. 191.

'imperialist war, in which both sides are equally guilty'. By 19 September the Party's national committee declared that 'this war cannot be supported by the workers. It is not a war against fascism'.[37] As McDermott and Agnew point out however 'no amount of theoretical sophistry could hide the fact that the Comintern had jumped to the discordant tune of Soviet foreign policy'.[38] The anti-fascist coalitions collapsed as the Party attempted to rally a new broad front against the War under the slogan 'The Yanks aren't coming'. It was met with anger and hostility. The *New Republic* accurately reported that 'fellow-travellers are dropping like ripe plums in a hurricane'.[39]

Former allies in the Popular Front now charged CPUSA members with being 'Communazis'. High profile organisations such as The League of American Writers were decimated; within a year one-eighth of its members and one-third of its officers had formally resigned, including Thomas Mann, Malcolm Cowley and W.H. Auden. Richard Wright was one of the few names to remain in the League. Though the Party lost few of its leading members, the prominent literary critic Granville Hicks resigned, stating: 'When the Party reverses itself overnight, and offers nothing but nonsense in explanation, who is likely to be influenced by a Communist's recommendations?'[40]

One of the few areas left relatively unscathed by the about-face was the CPUSA's black organisations, certainly in comparison to the Party's Jewish front groups which were devastated.[41] Although A. Phillip Randolph resigned from the National Negro Congress in fury and remained a committed anti-Communist for the rest of his life, the organisation survived the Pact. Logistics may have had a hand it this – Isserman suggests that the time lag between the Pact and the next NNC public function, which was not until April 1940, cushioned the blow.[42] Perhaps more significant, however, was the political rhetoric ushered in by the new Party line, a return to the anti-imperialist Pan-Africanism which had characterised the Third Period. The Party called on African Americans to step up the demand for equality at home and to boycott the Jim Crow army and the segregated war industries. As the War was now one of competing imperialists, the Party focused on the bloody history of British and French imperialism, a focus which struck a chord with many political

---

37   Quoted in Howe and Cosser 1962, p. 388.
38   McDermott and Agnew 1996, p. 198.
39   Isserman 1982, p. 37.
40   Lewy 1990, pp. 62–3.
41   For the impact of the Pact on Jewish Communists see Irving and Coser 1962, pp. 401–5; and Barrett 2009, pp. 542–3.
42   Isserman 1982, p. 39.

African Americans. Paul Robeson angrily told a reporter that Britain's democratic credentials were far from impressive as they had done nothing 'about giving India and Ireland and Africa a taste of democracy'.[43] Robeson was not alone in locating hypocrisy in the Allies' cause, and many black Americans failed to see a major distinction between German fascism, British imperialism and Jim Crowism at home.[44]

When Germany invaded Russia in June 1941 all talk of 'imperialist war' ceased. Fascism was again the main enemy and Party members 'responded as if German bombs were landing on their own homes'.[45] The *Daily Worker* declared in July 1941 that:

> Unconditional support for every measure and force and country that seeks to defeat Hitler is the only policy that will guarantee Hitler's defeat... no honest American, and certainly no Communist, will say that a limit should be set to the measures we should take to defend our country.[46]

The War saw the CPUSA turn back to its Popular Front stance of unity against fascism, only in a far looser capacity, using a political stance 'designed to include everyone and everything in between American Communism and J.P. Morgan'.[47] The Soviet Union was now an official ally of the United States and the Party's allegiance to the former informed its relationship to the latter. All struggles, including the black struggle, were secondary to the war effort.

While black membership of the Party did not dramatically decline during the war years, many black comrades, including Richard Wright, were thoroughly demoralised by what they saw as the betrayal of the CPUSA, the feeling that African Americans were, in Ellison's words, 'wartime expendable'.[48] In *Lonely Crusade*, Himes focuses on Communist *betrayal*, on the move away from black struggle precipitated by CPUSA political strategy during the War. Wright resigned from the Party in 1942 when the Party refused to support legal action against discrimination in the war industries. The Party had signed up to the no-strike pledge, which ensured that black workers who took industrial action in the extremely segregated war industries were effectively labelled as scabs.

---

43   Duberman 1989, p. 243.
44   Foner 1974, p. 278.
45   Isserman 1982, p. 103.
46   Isserman 1982, p. 113.
47   Torigian 1989, p. 412.
48   Ellison 1964, p. 89.

Ben Davis stated baldly: 'We cannot temporarily stop the war until all questions of discrimination are ironed out', going on to urge the 'Negro people to be ready to sacrifice'.[49] Another prominent black Communist, whilst insisting that the battle against discrimination should continue, stressed that 'it would be equally wrong to press these demands without regard to the main task of the destruction of Hitler, without which no serious fight for Negro rights is possible'.[50] This point became paramount as the Party insisted that the cause of African Americans was inextricably linked to the plight of European Jews and consequently to the war effort. Increasingly, the question of American interests became indistinguishable from those of black Americans, as *The Communist* in 1942 declared: 'The Negro people cannot be true to their own best interests without supporting the war'.[51]

This prioritisation of the national interest, at the expense of the 'Negro question,' was illustrated most clearly in the Party's refusal to support the March on Washington Movement.[52] The March on Washington Movement was set up by A. Phillip Randolph in early 1941 in order to secure a national fair employment practices code. The Party's initial reticence to get behind the organisation had been based on their opposition to the pro-war stance of Randolph during the duration of the Soviet-German Pact, when Randolph's support for 'Roosevelt and the white imperialists' made the proposed march suspect.[53] After the Soviet invasion in 1942 the proposed march was deemed by the Party to be an attack on the war effort.[54]

The March on Washington Movement proved to be a powerful pole of attraction for activists hostile to the Party. While the major black organisations and the black press rallied behind the slogan of the 'Double v' (victory over both Hitler and Jim Crow), the Party consistently refused to consider such a campaign to be anything other than a deviation from the war effort. If organised political protest was considered to be destructive of 'national unity' necessary to the war effort, spontaneous expressions of black anger were also suspect. When a race riot erupted in Detroit in 1943, the *Daily Worker* exclaimed, 'The

---

49   Foner 1974, p. 279.

50   James Ford quoted in Isserman 1982, p. 119.

51   Quoted in Garfinkel 1959, p. 42.

52   According to Isserman the M.O.W.M. was 'the most powerful nationally organized black protest movement to appear since the decline of the Garvey movement'. Isserman 1982, p. 118.

53   *Daily Worker*, 16 June 1941, quoted in Garfinkel 1959, p. 50.

54   Naison 1985, pp. 310–12; Starobin 1972, p. 132.

Enemy attacks in Detroit!'[55] The rioters were denounced as 'fifth columnists and pro-fascists'.[56]

Given the later allegations of 'racism' levelled at the CPUSA it is significant to note that it was not specifically black workers who had to 'sacrifice' for the sake of national unity. The Party didn't raise its voice against the 'relocation centres' that were set up for west-coast Japanese-Americans and Japanese-American Communists had to classify their own internment 'as a contribution to the anti-fascist cause'.[57] When the atomic bombs dropped on Hiroshima and Nagasaki, the CPUSA raised no objections. The Party also adopted a dangerously selective approach to civil liberties, when 29 Trotskyists were indicted under the Smith Act in 1941 there was barely a murmur of protest from the CPUSA, indeed, the *Daily Worker* could 'find no objection to the destruction of the fifth column in this country'.[58] The successful conviction of 18 of the Trotskyists set a dangerous precedent as the Smith Act served as the legal basis for the McCarthyite witch-hunts.

So the abandonment of fundamental Party principle was not confined to the Party's black politics. Class struggle itself was now seen as an anathema to being a good Communist. Earl Browder stated the Party's changed policy in the most explicit terms:

> We frankly declare that we are ready to co-operate in making capitalism work effectively in the post-war period ... We Communists are opposed to permitting an explosion of class conflict in our country when the war ends ... we are now extending the perspective of national unity for many years to come.[59]

At the 1944 Communist convention Browder instructed professional singers to be scattered through the audience so they could deliver 'the best rendition of "The Star Spangled Banner" ever performed by an amateur group'.[60] Despite the later charges of 'un-American activities,' the CPUSA's commitment to national

---

55 Isserman 1982, p. 168. Although as Isserman also points out, the CP played a very different role in the Harlem riot later that year when the *Daily Worker* pointed to the social problems which caused the riot rather than the 'pro-Nazi' nature of the rioters. See Isserman 1982, p. 169.

56 Foner 1974, p. 279.

57 Isserman 1982, p. 144.

58 Howe and Coser 1962, p. 418.

59 Quoted in Preis 1974, p. 221.

60 Browder quoted in Shannon 1959, p. 5.

unity was absolute. There was nothing insincere about the Party's commitment to the war effort. American Communists, many of them veterans from the Spanish Civil War, rushed to join the army. In total over 15,000 Party members served in the armed forces. American Communists were driven by 'what they believed was an authentic national purpose, to save America by moving it towards an alliance with Soviet Russia'.[61] Nothing, least of all class struggle or revolutionary socialism, would threaten the new alliance. Browder reaffirmed 'our war-time policy that we will not raise the issue of socialism in such a form and manner as to endanger or weaken that national unity'.[62] The 'alliance' was increasingly seen as permanent. Browder told the national committee in 1944 'capitalism and socialism have begun to find their way to peaceful coexistence and collaboration in the same world'.[63]

Bizarrely, the cause of the Soviet Union was now the cause of American capitalism. The shared interests of the CPUSA and the American war effort saw the Party in this period enjoy unparalleled popularity as their membership rocketed to between 75–85,000 members.[64] Nearly a quarter of the CIO memberships were in Communist-led unions.[65] In spring 1943 almost a third of new members were black, as opposed to one-tenth a few months previously. The cynicism that black Americans felt at the onset of the War had been replaced by a guarded optimism that the war against Nazism would open up the possibility of racial equality at home. The Party were at the forefront of characterising the conflict as a 'people's' war of 'national liberation'. The CPUSA was single-minded about the nature of the War as a fight against racial hatred for democracy and equality, and therefore appealed to many black Americans, despite the consequent deprioritisation of specific black demands.[66]

The CPUSA's *relative* inaction at pushing for black civil rights during the War was less a capitulation to racism than a retreat from their earlier vanguard position on race. However, by the end of the War, it became clear that the hopes invested in the belief that the fight against fascism would usher in change at home were brutally dashed. Thanks to the efforts of the March on Washington Movement, there existed a sizable and credible nationally organised anti-Communist black civil rights movement around A. Phillip Randolph, and a generation of black intellectuals and activists for whom the Party represented

---

61   Starobin 1972, p. 45.
62   Quoted in Isserman 1982, p. 188.
63   Ibid.
64   Shannon 1959, p. 3.
65   Ibid.
66   Howe and Coser 1962, p. 419; Isserman 1982, p. 167.

opportunism and deception. As Harry Haywood recalled, the war time line of the Party:

> continually pushed us into a position of tailing after Black reformist leadership. In the thirties, the Communist Party had often been looked upon as 'the Party of the Negro people'; in the forties however, our line led to repeated *betrayals* of the struggle.[67]

The Party did not completely abandon its struggle for black rights, but like all other areas of its work, it often limited its battles to those which benefited the war effort.[68] The attempt to abstract the CPUSA's strategy on racial issues from its general politics during this period must be done at the expense of the Party's history and its record in the 1930s. The proposition that Communist Party sold out black workers for reasons of opportunism and an underlying racism (best articulated by Record and Cruse) isolates the Party's racial policy from the tragic history of Stalinism in general. What the history of the 1930s and 1940s presents us with is a challenge, to examine the impact of multi-racial anti-racism on a generation of black activists.

For Himes, Ellison and Wright, the wartime activities of the Party amounted to a betrayal of black Communist supporters who had trusted the Party to prioritise black struggles. The dominant tone of *Lonely Crusade, Invisible Man* and Wright's *The Outsider* is bitter disillusionment with Communism. The aggressive political commitment and militant discipline, which had attracted these writers to the CPUSA while the Party was at the forefront of anti-racist struggle, were now seen as a threatening barrier to black liberation. Rather than dismissing the Party out of hand, Himes, Ellison and Wright called it to account. In 1942 Chester Himes argued in *Opportunity*:

> One of the unfortunate aspects of the Negro Americans' fight for freedom at home is the discovery that many organizations, humanitarian ideologists, and realistic political groups, Americans who have long been in the front ranks of the Negro Americans' slow march toward equality, are now deserting them, advocating that this fight be set aside until the greater fight for freedom is won.[69]

---

67   Haywood 1978, p. 534 (my emphasis).
68   As Marable points out, due to a consistent push on the labour front by the CP and CIO the number of black Americans in unions soared from barely 150,000 in 1935 to 1.25 million a decade later. See Marable 1986, p. 167.
69   Quoted in Himes 1975, p. 218.

Anger rather than cynicism was the immediate response to perceived Party betrayals. Ellison berated the Party leadership in 1945 in precisely the contradictory terms which mark post-War African-American fiction: 'I believe we should serve them notice that they are responsible to the Negro people at large even if they spit in the faces of their members and that they must either live up to their words or face a relentless fire of mature, informed criticism'.[70] Simultaneous to the anger expressed at Party betrayals is the idea that Communists '*must live up to their words*': this is an active call for Communist intervention in black politics, not the cynical resignation of anti-Communist scepticism.

Lonely Crusade and *Invisible Man* contain pointed and frequently hyperbolic criticism of Communist betrayal of black struggle and black life. These criticisms have often been de-historicised by literary critics placing of the novels within a generic anti-Communist paradigm. The chapters below re-visit the site of their hostility to Communism in the context of their contemporary relationship to the wartime activities of the CPUSA.

---

70   Quoted in Benston 1990, p. 204.

CHAPTER 5

Lonely Crusade: Union Dues

5.1 'History as Nightmare': The Critical Reception of *Lonely Crusade*

The American black is a new race of man; the only new race of man to come into being in modern time.[1]

This chapter investigates Communist Party representation in *Lonely Crusade*. On the surface this is a straightforward enough enterprise. The Communists in the novel occupy a variety of malevolent roles. They are a mixture of sexual degenerates, abstract theorists, calculating hypocrites or, at best, self-deluders. Himes presents a seemingly unambiguous portrait of an opportunist organisation which preys on black despair. The novel has been critically constructed as a straight anti-Communist text which highlights Himes's 'acid distrust' of the Communists.[2] However, Himes's portrayal of the Communist Party is more complicated than simple repudiation. Potent models of black male identity are circulated through his representation of the Communist Party. These models are central to the assertion of a black masculine identity which structures *Lonely Crusade*.

Himes is best known for his detective novels of the late 1950s and 1960s and their Harlem-based aesthetic of urban black cool.[3] In a reversal of Wright's literary trajectory, it is only in recent years that his 1947 novel *Lonely Crusade* has merited comprehensive critical attention. For the purposes of this study, *Lonely Crusade* is an essential text as a 1940s novel which centres on the politics of the Communist Party during the Second World War. Himes's early 'protest' novels are often considered as belonging to the 'Wright School'.[4] His first novel, *If He Hollers Let Him Go* (1943), along with *Lonely Crusade*, are seen as the literary heirs of *Native Son*. Yet, it would be a mistake to bracket *Native Son* and *Lonely Crusade* within the generic paradigm of black identity-construction. For all of their thematic similarity, both aesthetically and politically, these novels are

---

1 Himes 1973, p. 285.

2 Lee 1999, p. 69.

3 *A Rage in Harlem* (1957), *The Crazy Kill* (1959), *The Real Cool Killers* (1959), *The Big Gold Dream* (1960), *All Shot Up* (1960), *Cotton Comes to Harlem* (1965), *The Heat Is On* (1966), *Blind Man with a Pistol* (1969).

4 Lundquist 1976, p. 27.

as divergent as they are analogous. Himes's protagonist is a college-educated product of the American West Coast, socially and spatially a long way from Bigger Thomas. Historically, in the seven years between *Native Son* and *Lonely Crusade*, there was a shift in the relationship between the Communist Party and African-American workers. As discussed in the previous chapter, the Second World War saw the subordination of domestic politics to the defence of Mother Russia and many Party demands were effectively subsumed to the needs of the war effort.

The critical reception of *Lonely Crusade* is significant less as an act of literary contextualisation, than as a record of the transgressive nature of the text in 1940s America. Himes, who was devastated at the novel's reception, considered that the onslaught of negative reviews was an indication of the 'veracity' of the novel's confrontational treatment of sexual relations (especially interracial sex) black-Jewish relations and Communist treachery.[5] However, rather than restating Himes's claim that he pinpointed the 'truth' about American racial and sexual politics, the intention in this chapter is to interrogate the gendered racial identity within *Lonely Crusade*. Many of the novel's major themes prefigure seminal debates in black politics, particularly of the Black Power movement of the 1960s. The novel is a fascinating register of pre-Civil Rights discourses on black male identity. I am concerned with if, and how, those discourses relate to earlier models of black rage, articulated by the CPUSA.

Lonely Crusade was published in 1947 to mixed reviews. Although hated by the Communist Press and roundly criticised on stylistic grounds, the novel's reception was not as unconditionally negative as Himes later suggested: 'Of all the hurts which I had suffered before ... and which I have suffered since, the rejection of *Lonely Crusade* hurt me most'.[6] Although Arna Bontemps in the *New York Herald Tribune*, Arthur Burke in *Crisis*, and James Baldwin in *The New Leader* gave qualified, if not unreserved, praise for the book, Himes was not significantly overstating the general level of antagonism the novel provoked, particularly on the Left.[7] *The Daily Worker* published a cartoon with Himes carrying a white flag, and the critical reception led to personal appearances on radio and in bookstores to promote the book being cancelled.[8] *The New Masses* suggested: 'The issuance of this book ought to be met with more than passive anger, more than contempt. It should call for action. It should be buried deep

---

5 Himes 1973, p. 101.

6 For Himes's estimation of the critical response to the novel, see Himes 1973, pp. 100–2.

7 Sallis 2000, pp. 128–9.

8 Himes 1973, pp. 99–100.

beneath a rising mountain of protest, boycott and condemnation'.[9] The novel was criticised for its 'hate', its politics, its literary style, its anti-Semitism and, ironically for an 'anti-Communist' text, its crude protest polemics.

The following overview of the critical reception which greeted the book's publication locates the novel within the shifting dynamics of contemporary political debate.

While this novel provoked a variety of responses from Socialist, Communist, Liberal and Conservative critics, most of the reviews are marked by a negative recoil from the 'hate' in *Lonely Crusade*. The novel articulates post-War disillusionment with the Communist Party, but it also articulates black fury at exclusion. This finds expression in a militant reclamation of black manhood, a move which was read by some critics as a form of madness. *Ebony* magazine suggested that 'the character Lee Gordon is Psychotic, as is the author, Chester Himes,' and *Atlantic Monthly* held that 'hate runs through this book like a streak of yellow bile'. Similarly, the *Saturday Review of Literature* maintained that 'gall and wormwood have gone into this book, the bitterest we have come across in a long time'.[10] Many of the reviews see Lee Gordon as a hyperbolic symbol of Himes's 'bitterness'. One critic went so far as to see the character as a 'catalogue of the Negro's emotional distortions', whilst also claiming that the novel dealt with essentially 'universal' themes:

> Thus neurotic pattern is characteristic of our time and not of the Negro race alone. The victim is the classic modern hero; undefined pervasive fear, emotional and physical insecurity, sexual neurosis, the abnegation of beliefs, the loss of values, a general cynicism and brutality; these are universal disasters.[11]

Communist critics despised the novel. Black 'hate' had been constructed as a revolutionary position from which to build Communism in the *Liberator* and the early Comintern documents. Yet Himes's hatred was read as excessive and poorly expressed. Lloyd Brown in *New Masses* stated, 'I cannot recall ever having read a worse book on the Negro theme'.[12] Former president of the League of Struggle for Negro Rights Langston Hughes refused the publisher's invitation to write an endorsement of the novel as: 'Most of the people in it just do not

---

9   Quoted in Milliken 1976, p. 132.
10   Quoted in Milliken 1976, p. 100.
11   James Farrelly, *New Republic*, 6 October 1947, p. 30.
12   Sallis 2000, p. 127.

seem to me to have good sense or be in their right minds, they behave so badly, which makes it difficult to care very much what happens to any of them'.[13]

Communist reaction to the novel can be read as an indicator of how the Party had shifted its race politics during the War. The Communist Party that Himes distrusts is a Communist Party which now distrusts black hate. However, the Communist Party are not the only focus of the protagonist's 'hate' and the nature of Himes's particular articulation of anti-Communism is revealing.

Himes's anti-Communist invective is not the expression of frustration at the *inability* of Communists to comprehend black anger, but the expression of a sense of betrayal at their *refusal* to do so. It is essential to stress at this point that Himes's objection to Communism is not at all the same as the more general contention from Wilson Record in the 1950s through to Robert Young in the 1990s that Marxism *per se* is philosophically and historically alien to black experience and black struggle.[14]

African-American writers responded ambiguously to the novel. Ralph Ellison confessed to Richard Wright that he found *Lonely Crusade* 'dishonest' and 'false'.[15] James Baldwin, however, gave the text serious consideration in his 1947 review of the novel. Baldwin, who in *Notes of a Native Son* (1960) conducts a damning polemic on the negative and damaging legacy of Communism on black writers, barely mentions the Communist Party at all in his review of *Lonely Crusade*. Writing in the Socialist magazine, *The New Leader*, Baldwin found the novel had some merit but was 'written in what is probably the most uninteresting and awkward prose I have read in recent years'.[16] Baldwin was not alone in reacting to Himes's writing style. James Farrelly in *The New Republic* stated that 'for the most part the writing is inept', while a few years later Langston Hughes specifically alludes to *Lonely Crusade* in an article entitled 'How to Be a Bad Writer (in Ten Easy Lessons)':

If you are a Negro, try very hard to write with an eye dead on the white market – use modern stereotypes of older stereotypes – big burly Negroes, criminals, low-lifers, and prostitutes ... Put in a lot of profanity

---

13   Quoted in Rampersad 1988, p. 134.

14   For example Robert Gorman contends that Marxists in America 'always reduced concrete experiences of racial bigotry directly to capitalism ... When capitalist economic exploitation died, so would bigotry. Blacks, therefore, needed to mute or disregard entirely racial issues, and emphasize instead interracial working-class solidarity. They had to mobilize for socialism rather than against racism'. Gorman 1989, pp. 120–3.

15   Jackson 2000, p. 342.

16   Baldwin 1999, p. 3.

and . . . near pornography and you will be so modern you pre-date Pompeii in your lonely crusade towards the best seller lists.[17]

Ellison, Baldwin and Hughes find Himes's aesthetic values antithetical to their own modernist sensibilities. In his writing style Himes is somewhat out of his time and predicts the garishness of 1960s hip ultra-radicals such as Eldridge Cleaver and George Jackson. While Baldwin is sometimes horrified by Himes's writing style, 'some of the worst writing on this side of the Atlantic', he does not completely share Hughes's disdain for the novel.[18] Baldwin recognises both the ambitious thematic structure of the text and the palpable rage which underpins it, suggesting the novel 'is likely to have an importance out of all proportion to intrinsic merit'. He warns that after reading the book 'no white man ever again, should dare to turn his back on any Negro he feels that he has bought and conquered'.[19] Baldwin's review identifies Lee as a new prototype for the modern black American man:

> The minstrel man is gone and Uncle Tom is no longer to be trusted, even Bigger Thomas is becoming irrelevant. We are faced with a black man as many faceted as we ourselves are, as individual, with our ambivalences and insecurities and our struggles to be loved[20]

Baldwin identifies in *Lonely Crusade* a distinctly modern consciousness of race and exclusion and the articulation of black anger, which is seen less as a justifiable symptom of alienation and more as a radical expression of black integrity. The level of antagonism that greeted the novel's publication suggests that he was not alone in reacting to *Lonely Crusade* as the expression of new genre of black rage – the novel's much vaunted 'hate'. The tone of the novel was variously described as 'bitter,' and characterised by 'hurt pride'.[21] Arna Bontemps maintained that the novel was 'pushed along by a fury of excitement quite out of the ordinary' but suggested that: 'Certainly this is not exactly the mood in which to work for any kind of progress, and those who look to *Lonely Crusade* for a chart are likely to turn away sour'.[22] And James Farrelly contended that:

---

17 Farrelly, *New Republic*, 6 October 1947, p. 30; Langston Hughes quoted in Rampersad 1988, vol. 2, p. 207.

18 Baldwin 1999, p. 4.

19 Baldwin 1999, p. 3.

20 Baldwin 1999, p. 5.

21 Arthur Burke, *Crisis*, November 1947, quoted in Hughes 1967, p. 210.

22 Arna Bontemps, *New York Herald Tribune*, 7 September 1947, p. 8.

'The unsettling conclusion of this book is that equality is not enough for the Negro ... amnesties and privileges, no matter how generous won't annul this degradation'.[23]

Unlike *Native Son*, *Lonely Crusade* does not portray a targeted rage against a racist white ruling class which demands societal change. Himes offers a less focused attack. While Bigger Thomas is marked by unconscious fear, the educated, politically conscious and condescending protagonist of *Lonely Crusade* is marked by heightened, almost hyper, self-awareness. Lee Gordon's self-hatred is not a 'hate' which promises revolutionary change. But when it is set alongside Luther McGregor's violent revolutionary hatred and Lester McKinley's pervasive retributive hatred, Himes presents us with a sprawling political invective, which can be, paradoxically, radical in its posture and pro- foundly conservative in its politics.

This 'new' black anger that Baldwin identifies is informed by both a politi- cal pessimism and a revolutionary optimism. In *Lonely Crusade* it is the *duty* of the black American man to fight his oppression. The black man is alien- ated from this duty by his inability to function as a 'man' in American society. The targets for his anger are numerous: black women who reap the benefits of his oppression, white bosses who profit from his exploitation, Communists who manipulate him, white women who betray him, racist white workers who humiliate him and docile black workers who shame him. *Lonely Crusade* is perhaps the most gendered of the three novels discussed in this study. Himes's attempt to reclaim black masculinity from its debased rendering in American racism is neither a plea for integration nor a demand for recognition. It might rather be constructed as a frustrated anger and hatred which has a revolu- tionary potential, echoing both the *Liberator* and *Native Son*, but functioning within a more explicitly gendered field. It is tempting to read the novel as a blueprint for later discourses of black radicalism which place masculinity at the centre of racist debilitation of black life. As discussed below, the novel's racial/sexual dialectic bears significant parallels with Eldridge Cleaver's *Soul on Ice* (1970). *Lonely Crusade* is the expression of an embryonic 'modern' black masculine political identity, it looks forward to the powerful models of black male identity of the 1960s, but it is also informed by the 'hate' and anger which characterise mid-century Communist discourses of black identity.

In the ferocity of its scepticism *Lonely Crusade* is at core an intense indictment of American society. The negative critical reception of the novel acknowledges the sheer scope of its invective.

---

23   Farrelly, *New Republic*, 6 October 1947, p. 30.

5.2   'This Illusion of Manhood': Lee Gordon, Rage and Impotence

One might over-simplify our racial heritage sufficiently to observe, and
not at all flippantly, that its essentials would seem to be contained in the
tableau of a black man and white man facing each other and that the
route of our trouble is between their legs.[24]

The search for black male identity informs almost every paragraph of *Lonely
Crusade*, and Himes's fixation on this theme informs my reading of the novel.
When Communist Party representation is placed within the context of the
search for black *masculine* subjectivity which underpins Lee Gordon's 'crusade,'
a more complex picture emerges. Himes's obsession with the recuperation of
black 'manhood,' in a world where white racism has left the black man impo-
tent, imbues the Communist Party representation in this novel with a strange
dynamic. Communists, like women and Jews, offer Lee Gordon opportunities
to assert or negate his masculinity and it is therefore important to investigate
the nature of the male identity that is proffered in this novel. A male identity
that, on the surface, seems to reinforce rather than challenge traditional patriarchal values, but which is complicated by the dialectics of race.[25]

The question of black masculinity in the United States has produced an
extensive range of literature, especially in the past three decades. This chapter
is not an historical investigation of African-American masculinity or an intervention in the socio-political debates about race and gender in America.[26] Nor
is it my intention to investigate Chester Himes's autobiographical material on
sexuality or his writings on interracial relationships.[27] My central concern here
is with how masculinity functions in *Lonely Crusade* as an aspirational site of
personal and political agency. A traditional masculinity is denied to African-
American men in *Lonely Crusade*, but its inherent, albeit constantly deferred,
value as the location from which black men can assert both their 'humanity'
and their political agency is consistently reiterated.

Obviously, in this context, to overlook the racial and sexual topography of
American racism would be to render Himes's fixation with black manhood as

---

24   Baldwin 1999, p. 4.
25   For a discussion of the legacy of slavery and black masculinity see Wiegman 1995,
      pp. 85–6.
26   Blount and George Cunningham (eds.) 2000; Harper 1996; Hoch 1979; hooks 1992; Majors
      and Mancini Billson 1992; Marriot 2000; Wiegman 1995.
27   Himes 1972, p. 137.

a personal obsession rather than an American one during and since slavery.[28] The historically pathological fixation on the black male body as a site of menacing excess which has the power to infect both white female bodies and the white body politic has a disturbing history in the United States.[29] It is beyond the scope of this chapter to give an adequate, or even a truncated, account of the violence unleashed upon black bodies by white supremacist discourses and white supremacist practices.[30] Yet Himes's race rhetoric needs to be read against the grain of this pervasive white racist discourse.

Himes's narrative addresses itself to the questions of race, sexuality and resistance while drawing upon the most cogent myths of gendered racial stereotyping. In parts of this text Himes seemingly reiterates the most banal and offensive white-supremacist stereotypes. At times it is difficult to discern whether he is subverting the discourses of white supremacy or whether he is simply a flawed writer who is using recognisable tropes of race as a short-cut in character development. The characterisation of Luther McGregor is, on the surface, the most obvious example of this ambiguous replication of racist stereotypes. Yet I want to argue that Himes is seeking to destabilise dominant tropes of race through excess. Himes insists that his characters live on the boundaries of their historically conditioned identities and he deconstructs these identities, not through subversion, but through repetition. The Communist Party are key to these repetitions.

While this method can work to destabilise the dominance of white-supremacist discourse, Himes's unwavering focus on constructing alternative black male identity also ensures that black female identity is stabilised and domesticated. To illustrate this I want to focus initially on Lee Gordon's wife Ruth. Unlike Bessie in *Native Son*, whose abjection is sustained throughout the novel, Ruth Gordon is given consciousness, personality and limited power in *Lonely Crusade*. She is a crucial player in Lee's battle for self-determination. An initially complex and independent individual, Ruth is reduced to a passive cipher; from black harpy she moves to the position of a silenced black suppli-cant. The first chapter in the novel underlines the connection between racial fear, masculinity and impotence:

> Receiving no answer, he ran his hand over her breasts and stomach, sought caressingly the familiar tufted mound. But there was no passion

28   See Wiegman 1995, pp. 81–114.

29   Harper 1996, p. 9.

30   For a disturbing account of lynching and photography in this context see Marriott 2000, Chapter One.

in his actions – only an effort to find passion. During times such as this, when faced unavoidably with the consciousness of his fear, he felt a sense of depression that reduced him to sterility as if castrated by it.[31]

Lee's 'castration' by fear, and Himes's blunt literal portrayal of it, sets out the parameters of the novel's engagement with black agency as the recuperation of black manhood. Lee's self-disgust is displaced onto his wife's body and therefore compounded. Ruth's position, even in the first pages of the novel, is apparent, and here, black women's bodies are marked by black male impotence and fear. As the 'vessel of his impotency',[32] Ruth Gordon is a physical signifier of Lee's 'unmanliness:'

> [At first she] had not minded absorbing his brutality, allowing him to assert his manhood in this queer, perverted way, because all of the rest of the world denied it. But at so great a price, for it had given to her that beaten, whorish look of so many other Negro women who no doubt did the same. Even now, under the rigid discipline she applied to herself, she had not entirely lost it.[33]

Here, the black woman (Ruth) becomes the 'surrogate' for the black man's (Lee's) rage against white society. The sexual and domestic violence of the novel is, disturbingly, transformed into an almost benign signifier of black male dispossession:

> There had been the sublime joy when she [Ruth] had first learned that she could absorb his hurts – the great feminine feeling of self-immolation when he struck her, the sharp hurt running out of his arm into her body. Then came the slow knowledge that this was not enough – that what she could give him as a sponge for his brutality to rebuild his ego would never be enough.[34]

The metaphysics of female suffering in this passage are bizarre. Ruth's 'power' to be the instrument of Lee's rage is inappropriate because she is incapable of absorbing his pain. The fact that what she can give him 'is never enough' is sourced in *her* transgressions. As Lee's wife, she must re-learn her place in

---

31   Himes 1972, p. 5.
32   Himes 1972, p. 7.
33   Himes 1972, p. 5.
34   Himes 1972, p. 298.

the racial/sexual order, she must learn not only to submit to Lee but to also recognise that she has been the consistent ally of the racist onslaught on black masculinity. In this novel black women are rewarded by white society. Ruth's position at work, her self-belief, her relative solidity in the first half of the novel, are all arguably indications of her *privileged* position as a black woman in America, *vis-à-vis* the de-gendered and hated black man. Addison Gayle confirms Himes's sentiment in his reading of *Lonely Crusade*:

> Ruth receives largesses in terms of job and status, unattainable by Gordon. She is awarded the roles of provider, protector and sometimes authority figure. Not surprisingly, Gordon is forced first into panic, then into bitterness, and finally into committing acts of brutality.[35]

This conception of a male-dominated society in which black men are oppressed *as men* with the implicit assistance of black women (who are, at best, the unwitting vehicles for emasculation) has become depressingly familiar.[36] While the wider historical context of black male dispossession arising from slavery and beyond is an obvious context for reading gendered racial identities in this text, the novel is also the articulation of a particular and dominant, but not hegemonic, political positioning within African-American writing. Recently Robyn Wiegman has questioned traditional assumptions of black masculinity as *necessarily* a site of domination, while at the same time emphasising the exclusion of African-American women from black liberation discourse in the post-Second World War era.[37] Arguing against the political homogenisation of black male identities in the United States, bell hooks remarks pointedly that there are, and have always been, multifarious black masculine identities in the United States:

> Much is made, by social critics who want to further the notion that black men are symbolically castrated, of the fact that black women often found work in service jobs while black men were unemployed. The reality, however, was that in some homes it was problematic when a black woman worked and the man did not, or when she earned more than he, yet

---

35   Gayle 1975, p. 188.
36   As Manning Marable states in relation to the 1993 Million Man March, 'To construct a politics grounded in patriarchy, however "benevolent", is to denigrate the real struggles, responsibilities and interests of black women'. Marable 1996, pp. 144.
37   See Wiegman 1995, pp. 12–17.

in other homes, black men were quite content to construct alternative roles.[38]

In *Lonely Crusade* there is no 'alternative' role. Lee is thoroughly 'un manned' by his wife's job, as Ruth is simultaneously unable to fulfil her role as his wife. Black women in this novel become the instruments of white oppression of the black man. This is the conclusion Ruth must come to, not consciousness of her own oppression, but of how she has enabled Lee's. The narrative suggests that Ruth is less to be despised than pitied in this scenario, as she 'unwillingly becomes the tool of the forces arrayed against him'.[39] She is, however, instrumental in the process that robs her husband of his 'manhood,' or as Gayle puts it, her unwitting 'castration' of her husband.[40] Moreover, it is Ruth herself who articulates her own culpability in the destruction of her husband's claim to manhood:

> Society had put her in this place of advantage and she had accepted it, had accepted values. She had accepted the condescending smiles of her white employers whenever she referred to him, simultaneously indulging her and denying him any claim to achievement. Even the foreknowledge that in a predominantly masculine society the pattern for oppression would be masculine too did not inspire the rejection of the values, for these were what you lived by, black or white, or else they killed you.[41]

In the logic of the novel it is her privileges as a black woman which generate Lee's violence. It is her conscious collusion with her white bosses which strips away his dignity. Whilst this *could* be an articulation of the historical legacy of American racism's violent assault on the black family, Himes makes Ruth the guilty collaborator; it is *her* decisions which determine the nature of their relationship. In this monolithic world of race and power, in which black men are divested of subjectivity and authority, black women retain power which they choose to use against black men.

Lee's journey to consciousness is paralleled by Ruth's erasure in the novel. Her protestations of independence are revealed to be, just as Lee suspected, weapons with which to humiliate him. On his desertion she gives up her job without a second thought. Her articulate accounts of her attempt to negotiate

---

38   Hooks 1992, pp. 92–3.
39   Gayle 1975, p. 189.
40   Gayle 1975, pp. 188–9.
41   Himes 1972, p. 299.

race and gender in the workplace become the defence of a culpable assimi-lationist.[42] At the end of the novel she is chastened, submissive, 'wiser'. Lee learns to become a man, an independent self-aware agent in his own and other's destiny. Ruth, on the other hand, learns to become a wife, 'all I ever wanted, was just to love you, Lee'.[43] Ruth must learn to vindicate Lee's man-hood. This is not only what Lee demands of her, but the novel itself applauds her submission and the re-inscription of the gender hierarchy: 'Loving you has been life for me. The silly little job was unreality, only you were ever real'.[44]

While at one level Ruth Gordon symbolises the depressing notion that the black women's place is indeed 'prone,' there is another side to the sexual topog-raphy of the novel. As Lawrence Jackson notes: 'Himes was the first black male writer to treat seriously the relationship between a black husband and wife, the complex gender relationships of black lovers, and the peculiar attraction between white women and black men'.[45] The point is not, as has been sug-gested, that sex and love in this novel are *weapons* in a race war.[46] Rather, that the language of sexuality and gender cannot be abstracted from their com-plex rendering in the American racial landscape. Here, the Communist Party occupy particular space within the complex imbrications of race and gender – a point which becomes apparent in Lee's relationship with the young white Communist, Jackie Forks.

Initially, it is not desire that motivates Jackie's interest in Lee, but the politi-cal dictates of the Communist Party. It is only after her 'purge' from the Party, or rather, as Lee significantly calls it, her 'lynching', that she reads their rela-tionship in terms of race. In this scenario, which is a radical inversion of the iconography of American racism, a white girl is 'lynched' to protect the reputa-tion of a black man:

> Lee went sick at heart. In his lifetime he had seen many persons, mostly Negroes, victimised with cold-blooded premeditation. He, Lee Gordon,

---

42 Eileen Boris, offers a historical account of the behaviour expected of black American women in the workforce during the War: 'African American women had to engage in additional maintenance or survival labor, a form of self and community care work, to reproduce themselves as neater, pleasanter, more co-operative than their white counter-parts, to make whites feel more comfortable around them. They had to dress well and act respectable in public, whether engaging in the activities of everyday life or protesting discrimination'. Boris 1998, p. 96.

43 Himes 1972, p. 304.

44 Himes 1972, p. 342.

45 Jackson 2000, p. 243.

46 Sallis 2000, p. 147.

had been so victimized, not once or twice but many times ... But this was the first time he had seen a person *lynched*, and his reason found it intolerable and his heart unbearable.[47]

For the Party, Jackie must be vilified so Luther can continue. In a reversal of *Native Son*, a white girl is sacrificed to save a black chauffeur's reputation. Jackie is transformed from the modern anti-racist Communist activist into the outraged symbol of defiled white womanhood. She finds that her 'gentle white soul was utterly outraged that they would sacrifice her to save a nigger's reputation'.[48] Himes continues:

And as the seconds flowed like sand, her hatred for Negroes climbed like a blazing pyre. At first she hated three individual Negroes because of race, and then she hated the Negro race because of three individual Negroes. She hated their color, their souls, their minds, their character, their lips, teeth, eyes and hair – hated them with an attention to physiological detail she could not have ascertained had she made love to all the adult Negroes, male and female, in the world. In this pathological hatred, the Negro became the bugaboo of Southern legend, the beast of Klanist propaganda, a distorted, monstrous despicable object of her rage. And as her hatred rose, burning up all that was good within her, she became so much rife white flesh, of common value on the prostitution market, good only in America for getting some Negro lynched.[49]

In this extraordinary chapter the formerly radical anti-racist, Jackie, is brought to inhabit entirely her historical role of violated white female virtue. It is this submersion in the pathological fears and hatreds of white American society which enables her to emerge as a potential surrogate for Lee's 'manhood'. It is from her psychological position as the traditional enemy of black masculinity that she learns empathy with black men, who, like her, 'were always terribly hurt'. Gayle suggests that: 'The possession of Jackie, therefore equals possession of the American dream, and Gordon, torn between love and hate for his country, can only find salvation in this woman created in the image of a dream'.[50] But far from being the epitome of the American Dream, Jackie inhabits a quite different space in this novel. Throughout this text Himes ensures

---

47   Himes 1972, p. 263 (my emphasis.)
48   Himes 1972, p. 272.
49   Himes 1972, p. 273.
50   Gayle 1975, p. 189.

that his characters *inhabit* the extremities of their racial and sexual legacies/
stereotypes within American racism: the shuffling Jew, the bestial black man,
the emasculating black woman, the outraged yet desiring white woman. While
sometimes these positionings are uncomfortable and their meaning unclear,
Jackie's inscription into the legacies of gendered white supremacy points to
the imbrications of race and gender within American racism. Lee's relationship with Jackie is not simply the breaking of the great racist taboo, she is not
merely the forbidden white woman. By placing Jackie within the lexicon not
only of racist but of paranoid and obsessive white segregationist politics (she
attempts to fight her case along race lines within the Party), Himes is demys-
tifying a utopian dream of interracial sexual solidarity. At work here is a grim
declaration that the power of sexual/racial taboo is always below the surface
in American discourses of race, even amongst Communists. Just as Lee needs
to *learn* how to be a black man in America and Ruth must learn how she has
facilitated white America's assault on the black man in America, Jackie must
learn her place historically in the subjugation of the black man in America.

It is in this disordered space, where the racial/sexual mythology of protect-
ing white womanhood has been overturned, that Lee and Jackie attempt to
forge a relationship. James Sallis suggests that only by 'pitying her, by turning
her into a symbolic Negro, can Lee feel equal to Jackie'.[51] But although Jackie
eventually sees herself as a 'symbolic Negro', the novel sees her abjection in
terms of a *white* woman: betrayed Jackie flounders for an identity outside the
ruptured symbolism of her iconic status within racial mythology. Lee and
Jackie's utopian love affair, where 'the consciousness of race' can be 'covered
over for a time by the consciousness of truth',[52] cannot be sustained outside
the literal space of Jackie's bedroom and, eventually, not even there. As a white
woman, despised by her own race for her decision to love a black man, Jackie
increasingly sees herself as the white 'whore'. This is yet another positioning
within the racial/sexual lexicon which necessitates that the characters in this
novel inhabit a sexual space dictated by racial politics. Where Ruth invalidates
Lee through her historic role as collaborator, Jackie betrays him through the
utilisation of her racial privilege:

> This in the end became the greatest outrage – not so much what she
> had done, as that she would do it. It was this racial advantage all white
> women have over Negro men, to employ or not according to their whims.
> Outraged by the indignity that they should have this advantage; that in

51   Sallis 2000, p. 171.
52   Himes 1972, p. 209.

this predominantly masculine society the hammer of persecution over the male of the oppressed should be given to the female of the oppressors. It was this that completed his spiritual emasculation. First, Ruth, his own wife, could not see him as a man; and now Jackie, who could, would not.[53]

Lee here echoes the sentiments of the text. Even more specifically Jackie's feigned 'sisterhood' with Ruth suggests to Lee a female conspiracy to emasculate him. Jackie is better at caring for his wife's welfare than he is:

'I'm white, Lee – white! Can't you understand? I'm a white woman. And I could not hurt a Negro woman so'. For a long, emasculating moment, during which he suffered every degradation of his race, Lee Gordon stood looking at the whiteness of her face.[54]

For Himes, all positions lead to one unassailable truth, that it is black men who, through exclusion and debasement, are the ultimate victim of white patriarchal values. White society controls black men through women, by withholding traditional masculinity from black American men. While this alone is hardly the articulation of a new black masculine aesthetic, Himes's unwavering focus on female bodies, black and white, which must be wrestled back from male-dominated racist discourses to serve a form of black 'patriarchy' in the name of a (gendered) black liberation, points to later discourses of black identity. Huey Newton argued in 1967:

The White man is 'THE MAN', he got everything, and he knows everything, and a nigger ain't nothing... He is ineffectual both in and out of the home. He cannot provide for, or protect his family. He is invisible, a nonentity. Society will not acknowledge him as a man. He is a consumer and not a producer... He is dependent and he hates 'THE MAN': and he hates himself. Who is he? Is he a very old adolescent or is he the slave he used to be?[55]

This novel, written two decades before Eldridge Cleaver's *Soul on Ice* (1967), offers a prescient version of Cleaver's 'Supermasculine Menial' (Lee), 'Omnipotent Administrator' (Foster), 'Ultrafeminine' (Jackie) and 'Amazon'

---

53   Himes 1972, p. 310.
54   Himes 1972, p. 308.
55   http://www.mindfully.org/Reform/The-People-Newton15may67.htm

(Ruth).[56] Cleaver's controversial and esoteric text details how the torturous routes of desire, hatred and self-definition are enacted on racialised sexual bodies. The legacy of American racism can be read through the dialectical sexual relationships between black and white men and women, in a circular pattern of yearning and repulsion. Cleaver's male archetypes battle for supremacy over the body of the frigid white woman, whose sexuality is constrained by her iconic status. The black woman is deprived of masculine authority as the black man has been unmanned by the white man, who has in turn been feminised by the displacement of his corporeal masculinity onto the black man, whom he both envies and despises.[57]

In the associations between Luther and Mollie, Lee and Ruth, Lee and Jackie and Lee and Foster, these twisted relationships are played out. The point is not that Himes presents Cleaver with a blueprint, or that Cleaver's thesis is the formation of an ahistorical psychological 'truth': what *Lonely Crusade* presents us with is a literary enactment of post-War American psychosexual racial politics. In the novel it is not only that gender is racialised but race is also gendered. To be black means to be a Man. Again, this is hardly exclusive to Himes, as James Baldwin states it:

> *Negroes want to be treated like men*: a perfectly straightforward statement, containing only seven words. People who have mastered Kant, Hegel, Shakespeare, Marx, Freud and the Bible find this statement utterly impenetrable. The idea seems to threaten profound, barely conscious assumptions. A kind of panic paralyses their features, as though they found themselves trapped at the edge of a steep place.[58]

What is startling about Himes, unlike Baldwin, is that there is no critical engagement with the construction of 'man'. For Himes to be a man means to aspire painfully to the unreachable field of normative masculinity of the dominant culture. Obviously this places him in a different sexual and political space from that of Baldwin or even Cleaver. Cleaver maintains that 'manhood' is an ideological construct, that the denial of black masculinity is based on

---

56   Cleaver defines black masculinity through the repudiation of women and gay men. This is often deeply uncomfortable to read. Yet black masculinity at this historical juncture, and I would argue even more so for Himes, must assert what white masculinity can afford to leave silent. Michelle Wallace's *Black Macho and the Myth of the Superwoman* still remains a classic repudiation of black patriarchy.

57   Cleaver 1970, pp. 160–72.

58   Baldwin 1985, pp. 211–12.

'traditional patriarchal myths'.[59] The rage in this novel is not invested in gender formations, but the novel does interrogate the very racial mythology which underpins the legitimation of traditional masculinity. Jackie's whiteness forces Ruth into a vortex of self-hatred; Lee's blackness becomes Jackie's fetishized vehicle for self-definition; Jackie's persecution allows Lee to assume, however briefly, the traditional role of male protector which he is unable to fulfil with his wife. Throughout it all, Lee is attempting to attain his 'manhood'. It is in this context that Communist Party representation in *Lonely Crusade* can be usefully examined. How does a political organisation which is marked, in this text, by its interracial sexual relationships and powerful black masculine figures impact on Himes's attempt to find a stable empowering black male identity?

5.3   'Sure, I 'Longs to the Party. But I is a Nigger First': The Communist Party in *Lonely Crusade*

> In the spill of the light from the lamp on the window ledge, his dark face, topped by its mat of unkempt, kinky hair, contained an expression unearthly in its power to demonstrate his suffering as if, at some point in his twenty five years, his social-conscious protestations of hurt had leapt the bounds of amateur sincerity and had indeed become a thing of skill, of even professionalism, in the perfect symmetry of its tears.[60]

In Himes's short story *Into the Night* (1942), a black Communist, Calvin Scott, sits in a room in LA and attempts to explain black rage to two white Communists, Andy, a Jewish Southerner, and Carol, the daughter of a successful businessman. Andy is constantly overwhelmed by vestiges of racism which cause him 'aftermaths of shame which clogged him with a feeling of self betrayal'. Carol seeks to associate 'with blacks in their most intimate lives as if to prove by self-demonstration that black would not rub off'. Calvin's political persona is performative. This scenario where Communist circles consist of well-meaning Jews, zealously sexual white women and 'professional' black men is essentially the model of the Communist Party that Himes employs in *Lonely Crusade*. *Into The Night* is a satirical sketch of political stereotypes united by a coded language of political consensus which masks the personal/political fears which

---

59   Cleaver 1970, p. 170.
60   Himes 1975, p. 183.

haunt them. Theirs is a politics of avoidance. Himes here suggests that political radicalism is a game of self-delusion.

However, in marked contrast, Himes's non-fiction writing of the time is marked by a crusading polemic which insists on political mobilisation. In 1944 he declared:

> Martyrs are needed to create incidents. Incidents are needed to create revolutions. Revolutions are needed to create progress. These are the tactics devised by the peoples of the world who wanted freedom. No one has ever proved or denied that these are the best tactics to employ for the attainment of this end; it has been proved that these are the only tactics to bring about such attainment.[61]

The 'anti-Communist' Himes here calls for a black revolution in which Communists will play a leading role, a revolution that will 'bring about the overthrow of our present form of government and the creation of a Communistic state'.[62] These non-fiction writings are particularly important in understanding the denouement of *Lonely Crusade*, but they also inform the heavy-handed didacticism throughout the novel itself. There is a tension throughout *Lonely Crusade* between the political ideology of Communism and the political practices of the Communist Party, which creates an unusual dynamic in the text. I am concerned here to place the representation of Communists in the novel within the context of the recuperation of black male agency. The intention is not to suggest that Communist Party representation is other than hostile, but rather to investigate the nature of that representation. The power of the Communist machine in *Lonely Crusade* is almost omnipotent, and yet, principal Communists in the novel are conversely sympathetic or dynamic characters tenuously attempting to retain Marxist principles in the midst of destructive Communist tactics. Significantly, while Lee Gordon's antithetical relationship to Communism is maintained throughout the text, his redemption is, in part, predicated on his encounters with the Communist characters in the novel. It is essential to place this novel within its historical context, as Himes's negative representation of the Communist Party seems to confirm later Cold War anti-Communist discourses. Yet, many of Himes's criticisms of the Party are historically and politically contingent on Communist politics in the 1940s, and the models of black political identity which proliferate in the text echo Communist politics of the 1930s. The anti-Communist invective in

---

61   Himes 1975, p. 230.
62   Himes 1975, p. 232.

the novel is not informed by what was to become generic anti-Communist dogma in the 1950s and 1960s.[63]

The Communist Party in Lonely Crusade is corrupt, sexually degenerate, hypersensitive to race and ruthlessly utilitarian in its practice. However, whilst Himes's representation of the Communist Party is scathing, the sheer scale of his onslaught reveals a fascination with the Party as a powerful pole of attraction for black Americans. Far from being dismissed as insignificant to the struggle for black liberation, the Communist Party is engaged with at every level. Within the context of black masculinity, discussed above, Communists play a considerable role as both the emasculating co-opters of black manhood and the ideological-bearers of black self-determination.

Most significantly, although Communism is engaged with in Lonely Crusade, it is the Communist Party of the early 1940s that is being attacked in the novel, rather than Communism itself. Lonely Crusade consistently draws attention to its contemporary setting – the novel is published in 1947, set in the spring of 1943, spans 50 days, and the text makes numerous references to the policies of the CPUSA during the Second World War. Lee, Luther, Rosie, Bart and Jackie all reflect on the changed Party emphasis since America's entry into the War. That questions of race are now considered divisive, is underlined by the very first textual reference to the organisation, as Joe warns Lee:

> The Communists will be after you. Just be prepared. In case you don't know, this is how they'll work. They'll get somebody to make friends with you – either another colored man [Luther] or a white girl [Jackie]. Then they'll try – to recruit you. Anyway, they'll try to control you. But as long as they don't catch you agitating on discrimination, they'll help. *They got that unity crap going and they won't want you around agitating*. Now take their help. It can be good.[64]

Himes is at pains to create a historically specific and geographically rooted setting for his novel. This is Los Angeles during the War, a far cry from the racially hermetic world of Native Son:

> Niggers alongside nigger-haters. Jews bucking rivets for Jew-baiters. Native daughters lunching with Orientals. Lumped together in the war plants. Soldiers on the home-front nos. For this was a war-production city. The birthplace of the P-48. Womb of the Liberty Ship. Weak end of

---

63   See Cruse 1967, pp. 181–9.

64   Himes 1997, p. 24 (my emphasis.)

the armed forces. The bloated, hysterical frantic, rushing city that was Los Angeles in the Spring of 1943.[65]

The Communists of Himes's Los Angeles are omnipresent, they are present in Ruth and Lee's previous job as well as in his current one. Lee's distrust of Communists is founded upon his direct experience, specifically his experience of the vacillating positions on race engendered by the War. Initially head-hunted by the Communists to front an anti-discrimination committee during the Party's 'isolationist' period, his attempts to challenge racism at work are rebuffed when the War breaks out:

> After June 1941, when Germany attacked Russia [the anti-discrimination committee] was disbanded. The Committee to Aid Russia took its place. The ones who had led the fight against the discrimination of minorities in America now called for unity in an all-out effort to defeat Nazism. They urged that petty racial differences and factional fights be forgotten until the Soviet Union emerged victorious over Germany. Their isolationism had changed overnight to rabid interventionism.[66]

However, this oscillation does not initially engender anger, in fact, Lee 'was more bewildered than hurt' and 'in the end he and Ruth laughed about it'.[67] It is only when Ruth is targeted by Communists that he begins to see them as a threat. They become another target in his ongoing struggle to attain mastery in his domestic space:

> Shortly Ruth learned that the plant [where she worked] was owned by Jewish Communists. Most of the employees were Communists. They were organizing a union local when Ruth went to work, and she was elected to the executive board as a demonstration of unity ... Having no political convictions she was wooed by the Communists and included in all of their activities by day and by night. They gave her books, magazines, and other literature to read, and nights when her conscience kept her home she sat up reading it. Lee felt that the Communists were taking her away from him, and he began a slow, losing struggle for possession of her. It was then he studied Marxism to combat the Communists' arguments.[68]

---

65   Himes 1997, p. 133.
66   Himes 1997, pp. 43–4.
67   Himes 1997, p. 45.
68   Himes 1997, p. 48.

In fact, Lee becomes *obsessed* with Communists – he suspects everybody in the novel of being one at one time or another. He initially assumes Lester McKinley is a Communist because he has a white wife and continues to suspect him of being one right up to his last meeting with him. Lee also wrongly suspects union organisers Joe Ptak and Smitty of being possible Communists throughout the text. He assumes Mollie is a Party member, when in fact she is a barely tolerated fellow traveller who is around Party circles purely because of Luther. According to Smitty's secretary Sophia, 'they won't have her in the Party'.[69] Even Lee's encounters with minor characters like Elsworth make him question whether he is dealing with a Communist or not:

> 'If it's the truth, it's the truth' Elsworth replied. 'You can't escape the truth – you must go on from there'. If the man had been a Communist, Lee would have understood. For this was a Communist line. But Elsworth was not a Communist, Lee knew for he had refused at the beginning to join the union.[70]

Lee's obsession with the Communist Party in *Lonely Crusade* is fraught with contradictions. There are a variety of utterly opposed representations of the Party in the novel. Elsworth's 'truth' telling and Bart's lies, McKinley's interracial domestic harmony and Mollie's decadence, Joe's single-mindedness and Luther's role playing, are all read as evidence of some encounter with Communism. Communism, at times, becomes an overburdened signifier, the repository for all of Lee Gordon's fears and desires.

Lee's antipathy towards Communists is pathological and yet he spends more time with them – Luther, Jackie and Rosie – than anybody else in the text. More than just an anti-Communist, Lee is *shaped* by his encounters with Communism. His political consciousness is framed by his rejection of Communist theory and practice. The structure of the novel reflects this same impulse, where Communism is everywhere a source of attraction and repulsion.

Himes's depiction of the social and sexual politics of the Communist Party is coupled with an ideological debate on Marxism which is conducted through Lee's relationship with the kindly Jewish Communist, Abe Rosenberg [Rosie]. Lee and Rosie conduct detailed philosophical debates that frame the narrative in a strangely disjunctive fashion. This didacticism takes its most explicit form

---

69   Himes 1997, p. 93.
70   Himes 1997, pp. 61–2.

in the encounter between Lee and Rosie on the day before his death, where
Rosie attempts to convince Lee of the necessity of Communism:

> Listen, this is what I want to say to you: that matter is not a static sub-
> stance, but the infinity of change. And Communism but the present
> reflection of a movement of this change. Make no mistake about this,
> Lee. Time, and the profound progression of materialistic change, will
> make all men Communists – and then make them more. Within this
> movement, a tiny part of it, more symbolic than representative, more
> indicative than causative, is the socialist state of Russia and the small
> communistic movements throughout the world.[71]

Himes does not utilise Rosie's monologue for satiric purposes; after he has fin-
ished speaking Lee simply lies back 'admiring him'. Like their earlier verbal
sparrings about dialectics and historical determinism, these vignettes bear no
seeming relationship to the narrative. So while the Communist *Party* is lam-
basted, Communist Party *politics* are meticulously reproduced and engaged
with in a laborious fashion. This is a deeply political novel, informed by an
almost pious pride in its own theoretical understandings of Marxist philosophy. The novel goes to extraordinary lengths to display Himes's knowledge of
Communism. In this 'anti-Communist' text, although Lee constantly argues
against Party members, he never *wins* an argument. He is always silenced, he is
either browbeaten by bombastic Communists or, in the case of Rosie, forced to
concede in indulgent exasperation.

> 'You still haven't given me one really valid reason why the Negro should
> not be anti-Semitic'.
> 'Then I will give you one. Because the Negro has greater enemies than the
> Jew can ever be'.
> Now Lee laughed out loud. 'You always have the answer, Rosie'.[72]

The intellectual and humanitarian Rosie sacrifices his Party membership for
Lee, but never renounces his commitment to Communism. Rosie is the accept-
able face of Communism in *Lonely Crusade* but, significantly, he has no place
within the social world of the Party.[73] Primarily the Communist Party are

---

71 Himes 1997, p. 388.

72 Himes 1997, p. 164.

73 For a discussion of Himes's representation of Jewish stereotypes in *Lonely Crusade* see
    Wald 2003, pp. 143–4.

introduced through the black Party organiser, Luther McGregor, and the social milieu he inhabits. They are defined by excess; excessive sexuality, excessive drinking, and, in Luther's case, excessive 'blackness'.

The party Lee attends at Luther's house soon after they meet is a disordered and decadent scene where Lee is thoroughly disorientated by the way in which 'frantic people in defiant garb created the illusion of a costume ball'.[74] Communism and sex are unsubtly connected, as Lee is forced to witness Mollie and Luther at close quarters, 'a white woman in the last stages of debauchery and a green-lighted living-room on the Roman order'. In this decadent atmosphere Lee becomes increasingly disturbed. In one disconcerting passage Lee awakes from a drunken nap in a panic, seemingly fearing a sexual assault has taken place:

> He awoke to find himself stretched upon the bedroom couch, dressed except for coat and shoes. From the other room came the sound of many voices. Jumping to his feet, he fought down the impulse to escape through the window and began a frantic search for his coat and shoes, throwing aside the bedding and disarranging the room. He could not tell how long he had slept or what had happened during the interim, which was the thing that worried him. Finally finding the missing garments before his eyes, he fled to the bathroom where he sloshed cold water over his face until his sense of panic left. A swift, engulfing fear of self-abasement sobered him. He scoured his memory until he had provided himself with a fragile absolution. But it was with considerable aversion that he put on his coat and went hesitatingly into the living room.[75]

This sense of having his manhood violated is only heightened when, in a short but crucial encounter in the novel, he rejoins the Party. An old Jewish Communist drags Lee into a room to show him a photograph he carries around with him; Lee thinks it is a 'Negro ballet dancer' but it is in fact a picture of a lynching: 'Shock went through Lee like veins of gall. He struggled to his feet, fighting down the taste of nausea. "No!" he shouted. "No, goddamn it! You goddamn fool!" He was moving toward the door. It was like escaping'.[76]

Himes's clumsy imagery ('the Negro ballet dancer') can be read as evidence of his laboured literalism, which is less 'shocking' or transgressive than it is banal, especially in relation to the subject matter. Here, the ultimate violation of the black male body transformed into a souvenir, a keepsake for dubious

---

74   Himes 1997, p. 82.
75   Ibid.
76   Himes 1997, p. 91.

motives, betrays the wider assault on black masculinity that is so central to this novel. The Party threaten Lee's manhood by transforming him into a symbol of suffering through their objectification of black men as mutilated black bodies. The Party emerge as a parasitic fetter on black male subjectivity.

This scene bears a dialogical relationship to an earlier story of lynching, Lester McKinley's. Significantly Lester's narrative hardly mentions the details of what he witnessed: 'At the age of twelve he had lain in an ambush and seen a Negro lynched. And ever since he had felt the urge to kill white men'.[77] The core of his narrative is not *what* he saw, but how he told the story of what he saw to his psychoanalyst:

> He had related in a steady breathless flow how he visualized taking his pocket-knife and cutting a white man's throat, drawing the blade from beneath the ear in a clean, swift stroke underneath the chin. He saw himself stabbing the blade into the chest and lungs, cutting out the genitals – slashing the face until the white was obscured by blood. He had even studied advanced anatomy to learn more about the vital organs of the human body so that no knife stroke would be wasted. How deep within this homicidal mania, and seemingly unrelated was a desire to possess a delicate, fragile, sensitive, highly cultured blonde white woman, bred to centuries of aristocracy – not rape her, possess her . . . her whiteness to blend with his blackness in a symphony of sex, rejecting all that had come before and would come after.[78]

The assault, here, is displaced onto a white body, attesting to the horror of what he has witnessed, but refusing to revisit the violence on the black body and refusing the voyeurism of the racist gaze. As David Marriot points out in his work on lynching and photography:

> There are numerous images of black men, tortured and lynched; sometimes there are white faces with thin smiles, gawping up at them. Countless stories woven around the scene. There to frighten, to show black men their future, such images document the truth of lynching as both trauma and gala; a show *for* the white men, women and children before whom it is staged.[79]

---

77   Himes 1997, p. 69.
78   Ibid.
79   Marriott 2000, p. 5.

Lester's story subverts this scenario; a lynching story is retold to instil fear in the white man, to depict the violent killing of a white man for the love of a white woman. In witnessing Luther's knifing of a white policeman and briefly experiencing nihilistic love with Jackie, Lee fulfils Lester's desires and the re-writing of the lynching matrix. Lee watches a white man being killed in a blood bath by a black man for insulting a black woman (Luther's mother). The same black man has framed a white woman, who is 'lynched' on the orders of a black man (Bart), and then turns to another black man for protection. Only in the disordered realm of the sexual and racial topography of the Communist Party can this scenario emerge. The party at Luther's is an indication of this world turned upside down. The decadence, drunkenness, sexual licence, political posturing and transgressive racial politics appal Lee, but they also serve as an allegorical inversion of the racial and sexual traditions of 1940s America. While Lee may view it as a contemptible charade, it is precisely in this chaotic space that alternative sexual and racial positionings are enacted.

In the context of black masculinity that is at the centre of Lee's crusade, the Communist Party offers both opportunities for relative freedom and degrading self-cancellation. Unlike *Native Son*, representation of the Communist Party in *Lonely Crusade* includes black Communists, black Communists who maintain a strong sense of racial identity. Luther is perhaps the most forceful example of this, but even Bart, the ultimate apparatchik, retains a powerful awareness of his racial history. When Lee first meets Bart, the West Coast Chairman of the Party, 'he was amazed to find him so blatantly a worker and so black'.[80] Bart's divided consciousness, between his 'Protestant, puritanical, Negro inheritance' and his Communism, is both deep-seated and contingent.[81] As with Rosie, he makes a distinction between Marxism as a tool for understanding the world and the Communist tactics of the time. Alone in his office, 'when he no longer wanted to face the fact of his own inferiority in a bourgeois world but just wanted to be a nigger and forget about it',[82] Bart reflects on the recent history of the Party:

> And that severe division deep in his mind between right and wrong, vice and virtue, complicated his adherence to revolutionary tactics and made it extremely difficult for him to rationalize what had seemed at first to be political contradictions. He had found it hard to follow the Soviets in their pact with Nazi Germany, and harder still to follow the American

---

80   Himes 1997, p. 212.
81   Himes 1997, p. 258.
82   Ibid.

Communist Party line through its rejection of minority-group problems and into its coalition with capitalism.[83]

Bart's torturously mechanical Marxist analysis works side by side with his racial consciousness, his 'sixth sense'. Indeed, his elevated position in the Party is founded on this ability to role-play, to 'dissemble,' which he sees as his 'racial compensation in a nation where he had known but an inferior role'.[84] Bart, who is surrounded by 'sycophants,' is the only black man in the novel in a position of authority. Stoic, self-critical and ruthless, he is nowhere marked by the fear and hatred which characterises Lee, Lester and Luther. In a novel about black masculine identity and the necessity of self-sacrifice in the pursuit of higher ideals, his remote single-minded determination can be read as conversely admirable.

Lee is in no doubt about the opportunism of the Communist Party and he is repelled by it. Yet, he is also attracted to the Party, and particularly to Luther McGregor, who is perhaps the most dynamic embodiment of an alternative black male identity in this novel. Until late in the novel Luther's motivations and actions remain inscrutable and are subsumed within the multiple narratives of race, class and criminology that surround him. It is not only the decadent Mollie who fetishises his blackness; from his first appearance in *Lonely Crusade* Luther's black corporeality is underlined, often within the paradigm of racist tropes, as evidenced by Lee's first encounter with Luther:

Before him stood a man who normally looked dangerous. Fully as tall as Lee, his six-foot height was lost in the thickness of his torso and the width of muscular shoulders that sloped like an ape's, from which hung arms a good foot longer than the average man's. His weird long fingered hands of enormous size and grotesque shape, decked with several rings, hung placidly at his side, and his flat, splayed feet seemed comfortably planted in the mud. He wore a belted, light tan, camel's hair overcoat over a white, turtle-neck sweater, above which his flat featured African face seemed blacker than the usual connotation of the word. On his left cheek a puffed bluish scar, with ridges pronging off from it in spokes, was a memento of a pickaxe duel on a Southern chain gang; and the man who gave him the razor welt, obliquely parting his kinky hair, he always said

---

83   Ibid.
84   Himes 1997, p. 260.

was dead. He surveyed Lee without emotion through slanting eyes as yellow as muddy water.[85]

This description, which could have come straight out of one of the character vignettes in Thomas Dixon's *The Clansman*, is as disturbing as it is disconcerting.[86] Luther is characterised wholly in terms of racist stereotype.

The tropes used to produce Luther as the embodiment of black masculinity are tropes of an excessive or threatening physicality. These are so instantly recognisable as racist tropes and their reiteration is so systematic as to push the notion of a normative black masculinity into a position where it becomes strategic. Luther occupies this position in such a way as to enable both his own powerful agency and the text's formal capacity to exhibit the over-determination of black masculine identity. Both the text and criticism of the novel concentrate on Luther's menacing presence. According to one critic, Luther is 'grotesque' and 'venal'.[87] James Sallis describes Luther as the 'novel's real monster', who he argues 'seems cobbled together out of racial stereotypes, every boogie man story and irrational fear'.[88] Luther's black physicality, his almost *mythic* status as the personification of the black 'boogie man', is testimony to the transgressive impulses of the text. Luther *is* the threatening black man of fixated racial discourse. He *does* use white women sexually, kill white men and destroy the reputation of an 'innocent' white woman. Unlike Bigger Thomas, his actions are not the result of thwarted agency, but of a political consciousness of rage. Luther 'knows how to be a Negro and make it pay'.[89]

Luther, no less than Jackie, *occupies* his historical role in the racial/sexual topography of the United States. Yet Luther is also the definitive antihero of this text. He is known by everybody but to nobody. He does not just know how to be '*a* Negro'; he knows how to be everybody's 'Negro'. Black comrade, black

---

85   Himes 1997, p. 28.

86   Himes's constant references to Luther's 'muddy' or 'yellow' eyes are reminiscent of *The Clansman*'s Silas Lynch's 'dark yellowish eyes' (Himes 1997, p. 93) and his description of Luther is evocative of Gus Caeser:

> He had the short heavy-set neck of the lower order of animals. His skin was coal black, his lips so thick they curled both ways up and down with crooked blood marks across them. His nose was flat and its enormous nostrils seemed in perpetual dilation. The sinister bead eyes, with brown splotches in their whites, were set wide apart and gleamed apelike under his scant brows.

Dixon 1905, p. 216.

87   Rosen 1999, p. 223.

88   Sallis 2000, p. 146.

89   Himes 1997, p. 328.

brawn, black brother, 'Uncle Tom,' Luther can play all these roles. More than just a chameleon-like performer, Luther owns his blackness as a creative art form. As a literary character Luther suffers, as Stephen Millikin suggests, from a 'gigantism' where 'everything about him is outsized like a figure out of folklore, from his affections to his hatreds'.[90] There is nothing subtle about the characterisation of Luther, who emerges fully-formed from the mythology, not only of American racism, but of the Western tradition. This is nowhere more apparent than in his relationship with his girlfriend Mollie, who is instrumental in introducing Luther to Lee: 'Then she cooed: "come to me, my intellectual Caliban, my strong, black apostle with the pygmy brain; come to me and make love to me, my dark, designing commissar"'.[91]

The fusion here of literary, religious, anthropological, and political tropes in the service of a racialised sexual discourse underlines Luther's status as a mythic figure. Mollie's grotesque and overblown fixation on Luther's racial/cultural body is conceived within a sexual context, where black equals maleness and black maleness is a site of excess which overwhelms its immediate environment. Luther's very body stands in opposition to 'culture' and 'civilisation':

> Kicking the sofa to one side, Luther crossed the room and stacked Sibelius's First Symphony on the record player. Against the symphonic music, he was grotesque, with his long, black, muscle roped arms swinging from the white, T-shirted, convex slope of his shoulders like an ape's.[92]

His ritualised form of masculinity stands in opposition to Lee's anguished presence in the text. Luther is nothing if not an active conscious agent in his own survival. Though Lee distrusts Luther, he is also somewhat in awe of him, of his *Communist* abilities:

> But against his will he had to admire the Communists for the job they had done on Luther. They had taught him poise, restraint, the skill of adjustment, how to tome a parry, the art of interviewing, and the value of retaining and restating and persisting in a contention, no matter how distasteful it had become to everyone, until it wore all opposition down. And they had taught him the subtle trick that was the trade-mark of the Communist – confusing the opposition with a disconcerting question, then holding forth the Marxist answer in all its pristine logic. All such

---

90   Milliken 1976, p. 187.
91   Himes 1997, p. 80.
92   Himes 1997, p. 79.

insidious techniques of coercion were considered dangerous in the knowledge of the oppressed. The gall and the effrontery no doubt had been Luther's own, Lee conjectured, but he could see the fine hand of the Communists in the manner in which Luther now employed them.[93]

Communism facilitates Luther's dynamic masculinity, a masculinity that Lee is drawn to. He finds Luther's company 'comforting' and leans on him 'for emotional support'.[94] Ralph Reckley suggests in a dubious argument that Luther, along with Lester McKinley, represents Lee's 'repressed' selves:

> If we conceive of Lee as representing the Ego, the balance between the two extremes, and Luther as the Id, and Lester as the Super Ego, we might conclude that when racial pressures affect us at the primal level we could react violently as Luther McKinley did. When they affect us at the level of the higher self we could attempt to control our aggression, but in so doing we could become psychotic as Lester McKinley did. When they affect us on the level of the Ego, we could become like Lee, spiritually and physically emasculated.[95]

However, such a reading limits the radical space that Luther occupies in the novel. Far from being Lee's 'opposing self' or the personification of pure instinct, Luther inhabits the role of the black thug in the service of a particular social and political self-positioning. Luther's violence is far from unconscious, it is methodical and disciplined. His presence as the exaggerated epitome of black hyper-masculinity, nursing a murderous hatred for all whites, is startling. Significantly, when Luther is given a voice by Himes, it is a three-page monologue, an outstanding manifesto to black rage:

> Look, man, do you call it murder when you kill a man in this war?... In this goddam world they's all kinds of wars always going on and people is getting kilt in all of them. They's the races fighting 'gainst each other. And they's the classes cutting each other's throats. And they's every mother's son fighting for hisself, just to keep living. And they's the nigger at the bottom of it all, being fit by everybody and kilt by everybody. And they's me down there at the bottom. I gotta fight everybody... But I knows how

---

to be a nigger and make it pay. If I can't make it pay one way I makes it pay the other. 'Cause if the white folks wants some nigger, let 'em pay for us.[96]

While Luther's monologue confirms Lee's deep held belief that Communists use unwitting African Americans, he also describes how the shrewd black man can utilise the Communists in his own self-preservation. Luther tells Lee, 'Sure, I 'longs to the Party. But I is a nigger first'.[97] Again, it is the Party's *recent* politics which anger Luther:

> yesterday wasn't nothing too good for a nigger in the Party. Goddamn, all you'd a-thought the Party was for was just to bow down and worship at the nigger's feets. Today they want something else. They done sold the nigger out.[98]

Luther sees a symbiotic relationship between himself and the Party, they have a *need* for each other. Unlike Bart, he does not suffer from a 'severe division' between his black self and his Communist self. The Party recognise the significance of his 'simple antagonism toward authority and his deep vicious hatred of white people'.[99]

Luther eventually inspires an appalled awe in Lee, who is literally speechless in the aftermath of Luther's soliloquy to black vengeance, ' "well – yes", Lee Gordon said, and arose and left the house'.[100] But the effects of Luther's speech on Lee dominate the final section of the novel, as he constantly evokes Luther's theory of the 'nigger' in his own struggle to become a 'Negro'.

> The white people had always said a nigger didn't have a soul, and Luther proved them right. Yes maybe Luther was the only right one after all. For he, Lee Gordon, felt more like the murderer for having seen it done than did Luther who had done it. Being a murderer to Luther was just being a nigger after all, since being a nigger was being anything.[101]

Luther's speech is essential to Lee's crusade, it forces him to realise that he is always the object of the racist gaze, that the very idea of the racial uplift

---

96   Himes 1997, pp. 332–3.
97   Himes 1997, p. 332.
98   Himes 1997, p. 333.
99   Himes 1997, p. 259.
100   Himes 1997, p. 334.
101   Himes 1997, p. 335.

is a myth: 'It's the truth, Jackie. And you may as well face the truth. I'm a nig-ger... Face it Jackie! Face it! Goddammit, I had to face it'.[102] This stands in stark contrast to the young Lee's promise 'that he would make white people give him more consideration than they had given his father'.[103] The fact that Luther shoots a white policeman in the pay of a white employer is particularly symbolic. Lee's patrons were both his father's employers and the same white policemen who shot his father. His college education was thus paid for by the blood of his father disguised as white patronage. Luther has an altogether dif-ferent approach to white investment:

> I been taking dough from Foster and being a nigger for him. Now I done killed his stooge and tooken all the money. And what's he gonna do to me. Nothing!... He gonna know I done it but he ain't gonna say one word. Cause if he do I is gonna tell everybody I been taking his money to double cross the union.[104]

Luther's killing of a white policeman is not like Lester's pathological, but unre-alised, murder fantasies. It is not *the* culmination of black anger striking out, it is a spontaneous expression of black rage, almost impersonal. After the act he concentrates on the practicalities of covering it up:

> And finally the murderous intent went from Luther's muddy eyes and in its place came urgency. Hurried but not hasty, Luther began to move, his actions as calculated as an automaton.[105]

Although horrified by the violence, Lee is also 'charmed by the menace' in Luther's 'muddy eyes'. Luther is unbounded by social convention: as the embodiment of a streetwise, politically conscious black man who can kill a white figure of authority in the spur of the moment, he offers a potent model of strong, urban black masculinity. Like Bigger, Luther's 'hate' is validated and accommodated by the Communist Party, though obviously here in more ambiguous terms, as the Communists in this novel recognise black hate, but also need to control it, in the interests of national unity.

---

102 Himes 1997, p. 338.
103 Himes 1997, p. 35.
104 Himes 1997, p. 333.
105 Himes 1997, p. 324.

Luther's version of black manhood, the revolutionary anger and sublime dialectic of hatred, is rejected by Lee but its effect on him remains a significant element in his struggle to exorcise his 'shame':

> Being a Negro was a cause – yes. Thus far Luther had been right. But it was never a justification – never – which was what Luther had found out in the end. Because being a Negro was, first of all, a fact. A Negro is a Negro, as a pine tree is a pine tree and a bulldog is a bulldog – a Negro is a Negro as he is an American – because he was born a Negro. He had no cause for apology or shame.[106]

Explicitly the 'shame' that Lee Gordon has felt is the shame of being less than a 'man,' and, in the final pages of the novel, the experiences of Lee's 50-day crusade become concentrated in one definitive act; to martyr himself by marching toward armed police lines holding aloft the union banner:

> He pushed with all of his might into the chest of the deputy in his path, saw him fall away. Ducking beneath the blackjack of another, he was through the line. Out of the corner of his vision he saw the gun of Walter come levelling down on him. And from the parking lot he heard a worker cry: 'Don't shoot that boy!' He reached Joe Ptak, snatched the union banner, and holding it high above his head, began marching down the street.[107]

That the misanthropic Lee decides to become a union martyr has struck many critics as implausible, misguided or idealistic. Stephen Milliken describes it as the 'novel's rather melodramatic denouement', Addison Gayle suggests that 'the incident serves to underline the inability of the protagonist to comprehend the world in which he is fated to live,' while James Lundquist sees the act as 'an existential solution'.[108]

The first, if somewhat prosaic, point about Lee's sacrifice is that Lee is already doomed, the police are waiting to take him away. Also Lee has been transformed by the events of the book, transformed by his fraught relationship with Communism. While Lee rejects the manipulative and self-serving Communist Party, his final act is a moment of interracial working-class solidarity. The man who sacrifices himself at the end of the novel is not the same man who finds black workers so repugnant and inferior at the novel's beginning.

---

106   Himes 1997, p. 367.
107   Himes 1997, p. 406.
108   Milliken 1976, p. 99; Gayle 1975, p. 188; Lundquist 1976, p. 67.

Rosie's earnest polemics, Smitty's selfless faith in him, Luther's rage, and Joe's bravery transform Lee's political consciousness. It is his *political* consciousness which is instrumental in his decision to commit himself to a single act of martyrdom, as are the friendships he has made:

> Thoughts flashed like sheet lightning through the turmoil of his brain – Joe Ptak, lying there unconscious in the sun, who had done the best he could for the thing in which he most believed – the disappointment in Rosie's eyes – the hurt in the face of big, bluff Smitty, the only white gentile he had ever known to be his friend (was his faith in human nature to be lost?) – and Ruth! – 'All I ever wanted was just to love you, Lee'. A thin flame came alight in his mind, burning ever brighter. Words spun through his thoughts: 'When the occasion calls for it –' Not tomorrow or an hour hence. But now! *For the time was running out.*[109]

Communists, real and imagined, are a powerful factor in Lee Gordon's decision to act. At core, Lee's sacrifice is the moment of his 'manhood'. It is the farewell speech of the white Southern officer to the black soldiers that Jackie read to him that he calls to mind. This speech has a significant impact on Lee and he recalls it throughout the novel:

> The lines kept running through his thoughts: '... only remind you in the midst of these problems of race that seem so serious now ... that we must not forget the human race, to which we all belong and which is the major problem after all ... and most important of all – *men*. No one can ask more than that you acquit yourselves like men'. Well – yes, Lee Gordon thought, Lieutenant Colonel Noel F. Parrish, a white Southern officer. The white Southerners had always known it. And always been first to deny it.[110]

In the context of American racism, where the Southern fixation on black masculinity and white womanhood is the justification for lynch law, Lee's constant evocation of a Southern white lieutenant's speech to a squadron of black soldiers is unusual, to say the least. As Stephen J. Rosen points out, 'it was by courageously fighting for the unjust cause of slavery that Southern army officers established their iconic masculinity in American culture'.[111] However

---

109   Himes 1997, pp. 405–6.

110   Himes 1997, p. 131.

111   Rosen 1999, p. 233.

Lee Gordon is not challenging traditional masculinity, rather, he is *reclaiming* it. Himes's non-fiction wartime writings are instructive here:

> At this point Negro martyrs are needed. The martyr to create the incident which will mobilize the forces of justice and carry us forward from the pivot of change to a way of existence wherein every one is free. It is obvious that we can not stay here; we've got to go somewhere. If we can not of our own accord go forward, we will against our will be pushed backward.[112]

Lee becomes the symbolic embodiment of the active black male subject, sacrificing himself for a greater good. More than just a sacrificial victim, he is a soldier and, as a restitutive act, it is appropriate that the words of a white Southerner spur him on. By taking the banner from Joe and marching towards the police lines as a symbol of the wartime black worker, Lee is exorcising the shame and fear that characterised his life since he was expelled from school for spying on white girls. Throughout the text the Southern officer's, words have been a reproach:

> The Line that etched itself of Lee Gordon's mind and crucified him to his seat was '... that you, as Negroes, have not been particularly encouraged to be heroic in the past'. In this nation rooted in heroism, built on heroism; where this one virtue runs through the pages of its history like a living flame, where its people worship heroism before they do their God! It was a hurting thing to hear a white man's admission that this exalting and redeeming virtue had been denied a people because of race.[113]

Now, those words become a call to arms, not in the service of American patriotism abroad, but of the struggle of black men on the homefront. This novel attempts to work through the legacies of American racism: it does so by forcing its characters to occupy their archetypal roles and attempts to rupture those roles through excess. Lee's final act can be seen as the ultimate break with the past. Wanted for the murder of a white man, on the evidence of a white woman, Lee simply refuses to be remembered as either black murderer or black victim:

> He looked back at Ruth and saw the agitation in her face, the worry and concern. And he could not help thinking of what it would do to her – the degradation and dishonor, a woman scorned in the eyes of the world

---

112   Himes 1975, p. 233.
113   Himes 1997, p. 107.

because her husband had been convicted of a murder – the grief inside of her, the protest and the fear, and the knowledge of his innocence she would have to carry – not just for a day, but for all the days of her life.[114]

Where Bigger Thomas in his isolated cell imagines for the first time other black lives and a burgeoning sense of solidarity, Lee Gordon, among the solidarity of his union members, imagines for the first time a sense of individual destiny. His decision to martyr himself for the workers of Comstock Aircraft Corporation is his decision to re-forge the legacy of the black American man. Remembered not as a murderer, or as a victim, but as a hero.

Crucially, it is the War and wartime activities of the Communists that frame the narrative of *Lonely Crusade*. To abstract the novel from its historical milieu and posit it as a straight anti-Communist text is to transform the potent invective which underlies the narrative into hysterical red-baiting. This pre-McCarthyite novel is not an attack on Communism as a trans-historic barrier to black liberation. The novel is informed by the failures of the American Communist Party to prioritise black struggles during the War. Corrupt and ruthless as they are, the multiracial Party in *Lonely Crusade* are not the white middle-class intellectuals of anti-Communist mythology. It is the abandonment of black struggle rather than the adoption of it which is most severely attacked. This is a novel of betrayal, a betrayal rooted not in inherent racism but in historically specific political opportunism. *Lonely Crusade* offers us an intriguing portrait of black political identity in the pre-civil rights era, where Communism is a ubiquitous and ambiguous presence in the structuring of black male agency.

---

114   Himes 1997, p. 405.

Invisible Man: Un-American Activities

6.1 'Beautiful Absurdity': Ellison, Responsibility and Identity

I have no desire to write propaganda[1]

According to one critic, Chester Himes based Elsworth – a minor character in *Lonely Crusade* – on Ralph Ellison:[2] ' "I'm not trying to be like white people", Elsworth said. "I'm seeking the truth about myself and my heritage, and I don't give a damn what it proves" '.[3] Ellison's own literary legacy surpasses his walk-on part in Himes's story. In terms of both critical legacy and contemporary reception, *Lonely Crusade* and *Invisible Man* could hardly be more different. Intellectually, aesthetically and theoretically these novels share an awkward literary space. *Lonely Crusade*'s blunt literalism stands in stark contrast to Ellison's esoteric and multi-layered text. One of the only things that unites them is the, somewhat predictable, acerbic reception they received from the Communist press. In his 1952 review of *Invisible Man* in *Masses & Mainstream*, Lloyd Brown explicitly connected the two novelists, along with the now traitorous ex-Party member, Richard Wright:

> Ellison is also a disciple of the Richard Wright-Chester Himes school and shares with these writers their bitter alienation from the Negro people, their hatred and contempt of the Negro working masses, their renegade's malice – and their servility to the masters. Cut off from the surging mainstream of Negro life and struggle and creativity, they stagnate in Paris, wander in *Lonely Crusade*s or spit out at the world from a hole in the ground.[4]

The *Daily Worker* asserted of *Invisible Man*:

> Written in a vein of middle class snobbishness – even contempt – towards the Negro people, Ellison's work manipulates his nameless hero for 439

---

1 Ellison 1964, p. 17.
2 Jackson 2000, p. 335.
3 Himes 1997, p. 61.
4 Quoted in Reilly (ed.), 1970, p. 99.

pages through a maze of corruption, brutality, anticommunism slanders, sex perversion and the sundry inhumanities upon which a dying social system feeds.[5]

Despite Communist outrage, however, *Invisible Man* was almost universally well received and has, over time, built a reputation as one of the most venerated American novels of the post-War period. The temporal space of the novel is somewhat and justly disputed. According to Leslie Fielder, the novel had 'bypassed all formulas of protest', while Noel Schraufnagel insisted that the 'publication of *Invisible Man* is the climax of the revolt against the Wrightian protest novel'.[6] However, Paula Rabinowitz has maintained that '*Invisible Man* is a 1930s novel even if it didn't appear until 1952', and Michael Denning has argued that *Invisible Man* is 'one of the major novels of the proletarian movement' which 'did not appear until well after the proletarian movement was pronounced dead'.[7]

In terms of Communist Party representation, the historical milieu which the novel inhabits is ambiguous. *Invisible Man* is very much a Depression novel in terms of its thematic concerns and the repertoire of black political discourses on which it draws. *Invisible Man*'s brand of anti-Communism, however, echoes the emerging anti-Communist discourse which informs Cold War histories of the period.[8] Beyond the novel's thematic concerns, which locate it as both a pre- and post-War text, I also argue that *Invisible Man*'s temporal contradiction centres on two further elements. Firstly, there is Ellison's commitment to the moral responsibility which characterised the great nineteenth-century American novel. Secondly, there is the modernist sensibility which he believes is necessary to delineate black American experience, responsibility and identity. Ellison's dual commitment to the autonomy of art and the moral role of the artist accounts for (but does not resolve) the narratorial contradictions which structure *Invisible Man*. I will also place Ellison's brand of anti-Communism within its historical context. Ellison's antipathy to Communism, when combined with his utilisation of key Communist models of black identity, makes his anti-Communism more complicated than mere repudiation.

Often cited as the weakest section of the novel, the section on the Brotherhood produces Communism as the stereotype of political extremism – it consists of

---

5   Abner N. Berry, in the *Daily Worker*, 1 June 1952, quoted in Benston (ed.) 1990, p. 108.
6   Fielder 1967, p. 493; Schraufnagel 1973, p. 78.
7   Rabinowitz 2001, p. 232; Denning 1996, p. 228.
8   See Chapter Four for a discussion of the historical roots of this hostility.

the abstract dictums of middle-class whites, shot through with paranoia and self-validating dogma. Critics as far apart as Saul Bellow and Irving Howe have questioned the veracity of the presentation of the Brotherhood. Bellow didn't think that 'the hero's experiences in the Communist Party are as original in conception as other parts of the book. In his review of *Invisible Man*, Irving Howe insisted that the Brotherhood section 'did not ring true' and that Ellison made 'his Stalinist figures so vicious and stupid that one cannot understand how they could ever have attracted him or any other Negro'.[9]

Where Wright presents Communism as hope, and Himes presents Communism as betrayal, Ellison seemingly presents us with a full-blown political and theoretical parody. The self-conscious literariness and stylistic complexity which structures the rest of the novel are often notably absent in the chapters dealing with Communism. Yet the Brotherhood section of the novel is pivotal to the dynamics of the narrative. As the co-opters of black political agency, the Brotherhood is central to the rupturing of the racialised social identity which preoccupies this text from the scene in the Battle Royal to the Harlem riot.

The textual analysis of *Invisible Man* which follows, as with *Native Son* and *Lonely Crusade*, places Ellison's representation of the Communist Party within its cultural and historical moment. It also necessitates an engagement with the question of responsibility which, I argue, is central to Ellison's conception of an active modernist black subject. The focus here is on Ellison's earlier theoretical writings, particularly his 1944 essay 'Twentieth Century Fiction', and by focusing on *Invisible Man*'s mode of address I aim to investigate how the relationship between identity and responsibility is configured in the novel. Ellison's commitment to realising the former through a critical engagement with the latter ensures that Communism has a particular role in this novel. Moreover this mode of address acknowledges and challenges the universalist 'I' of classic realism. Although the novel seems preoccupied with the alienating effects of Communism on the formation of black subjectivity, the early chapters of the book are the site of a bitterly satiric critique of the black middle class. Ellison's characterisation of Bledsoe as a self-interested collaborator on the edges of white society is suggestive of earlier Communist constructions of the black bourgeoisie.

Both the dominant critical interpretations of *Invisible Man* and Ellison's own polemics against the limits of protest writing have ensured the novel's status as a definitive anti-Communist text. *Invisible Man*, however is not simply an aesthetic assault upon the protest novel as form, or rather its modern-

---

9 Bellow 1952, p. 609; Howe in Reilly 1970, p. 101.

ist aesthetic does not speak for itself in this regard. This is a deeply political novel with a *moral* commitment to social change. This commitment is realised *through* writing and the re-appropriation of American identity.

Ellison's assault on the concept of a fixed social identity is somewhat contradicted by *Invisible Man*'s mode of address. In relation to those narratives of identity (organised textually through the discourses of class and race) which would lock the self into a predetermined story, the novel itself acts as metadiscourse. Who are the readers whom the novel 'speaks for?'[10]

Questions about American identity and the power of 'art' are key to Ellison's oeuvre. Ellison was deeply aware of the necessary ironies involved in approaching these questions and came at them from different perspectives in his theoretical writings. Ellison's later essays, particularly his infamous argument with Irving Howe about the role of black literature, argue the necessity of separating 'art' and 'politics'. Yet much of his non-fiction writing in the 1940s and early 1950s displays a serious engagement with the relationship between literature, social protest and the moral role of the artist. *Invisible Man* would seem to incorporate both emphases; the necessity of the autonomy of art *and* the moral responsibility of the artist to society.

Ellison's 1946 essay 'Twentieth Century Fiction and the Black Mask of Humanity' insists that both the power and function of literature is dependent on the reception of literature. The meaning of the literary work is not self-contained but is rather a negotiation with the readership. In short, Ellison argues that literature has a social function which is determined by the political and cultural environment in which it operates. He asserts that realism cheats readers, not because it is prosaic or sullied by its relationship with politics, but rather, he argues that realism's 'presentation of sheer fact' negates the possibilities of portraying more radical visions of how the world could be different.[11] That Ellison sets up a nuanced and articulate defence of his own craft is hardly surprising, what *is* significant is how seriously Ellison takes the political and social responsibilities of the novelist. This seriousness is not limited to one essay, again and again in the 1940s and early 1950s Ellison insists that the artist's responsibility to political and ethical concerns is as important as his aesthetic practice:

> What has been missing from so much experimental writing has been the passionate will to dominate reality as well as the laws of art. This will is the true source of the experimental attitude... Our task then is always

---

10   Ellison 1965, p. 469.

11   Ellison 1964, pp. 24–45. The essay was first published in 1953; it was written in 1946.

to challenge the apparent forms of reality – that is, the fixed manners
and values of the few, and to struggle with it until it reveals its mad, vari-
implicated chaos, its false faces, and on until it surrenders its insights, its
truth.[12]

This is a far cry from Ellison's exhortation to Irving Howe in 1963 that 'I can
only ask that my fiction be judged as art; if it fails, it fails aesthetically, not
because I did or did not fight some ideological battle'.[13] That Ellison became
a more conservative thinker and more hostile to his own former Communist
sympathies as he got older is scarcely news, but we cannot let Ellison's later
positions retrospectively deny the startlingly different emphasis of his earlier
critical work. Just how ideological his early writings are is surprising when one
takes into account his status as the iconic modernist writer who severed the
links with the rigid and 'crude' protest novels of the 1940s.[14]

Ellison's early essays contain a heightened political awareness of the relationship between the writer and society. Always polemical and frequently
informed by Marxist aesthetic theory of the 1930s, these writings attempt
to delineate a particularly American aesthetic which is both inherently
radical and socially aware.[15] This is particularly apparent in his discussion of
nineteenth-century American literature. Ellison insists that twentieth-century
fiction can no longer express the democratic ideal in realist modes, but he
does so while paying homage to that ideal and to the great nineteenth-century
American novelists:

> The difference in terms of perspective of belief is that Melville's belief
> could still find a public object. Whatever else his works were 'about' they
> also managed to be about democracy. But by our day the democratic
> dream had become too shaky a structure to support the furious pressures
> of the artist's doubt.[16]

---

12   Ellison 1964, pp. 105–6.

13   Ellison 1964, pp. 136–7.

14   For a coherent overview of Ellison's early political radicalism see Michel Fabre in Benston
      1990, pp. 199–216.

15   As well as a more general similarity between Ellison's defence of Modernist techniques
      and Brecht's attack on Lukács, thematically and rhetorically there is a continuity between
      Ellison's critical practice and Wright's *Blueprint for Negro Writing* as well as the work of
      fellow Communist Joseph Freeman. See Freeman 1935, pp. 9–28.

16   Ellison 1964, p. 40.

Ellison contends that it is precisely the ethical commitment to a democratic aesthetic of Melville and Twain that the modern writer needs to maintain. Twain's genius is located in his ethical drive to represent a *social* reality in his constitution of his readership:

> The other thing to be said is that while it is unlikely that American writing will ever retrace the way to the nineteenth century, it might be worth while to point out that for all its technical experimentation it is nevertheless an ethical instrument, and as such it might well exercise some choice in the kind of ethic it prefers to support. The artist is no freer than the society in which he lives, and in the United States the writers who stereotype or ignore the Negro and other minorities in the final analysis stereotype and distort their own humanity. Mark Twain knew that in *his* America humanity masked its face with blackness.[17]

The complex of tensions apparent here make this essay key for any study of *Invisible Man*. Those tensions which insist that modernism is the only form capable of speaking to twentieth-century fragmentariness, yet simultaneously to the commitment of the universalising ambition encoded deep into the form and moral code of realism. Ellison has a tense commitment to the political imperative he sees as necessary for the novelist yet he also continues to believe that the novel, if it is to be art, must be politically independent.[18] Additionally Ellison believes in the necessity of including hitherto marginalised voices in fiction, yet simultaneously believing the novel is a space which should encompass all, which should be the space of that universal 'We'.[19] As a novelist, Ellison's voice is constantly shifting between the classic novel's narrative address (universal humanity) and the fragmentation of this address when confronted with questions of black subjectivity which must constantly struggle to maintain dominance in such a rubric.

---

17   Ellison 1964, p. 44.

18   See discussion of protest fiction in Chapter Three.

19   Joseph Slaughter argues that the novel genre and universal human rights are 'mutually enabling fictions': that each projects an image of the 'human personality that ratifies the other's idealistic visions of the proper relations between the individual and society'. And moreover that the discourse of universality 'becomes available for appropriation and transformative rearticulation of the egalitarian imaginary by historically marginalised subjects (e.g. women and members of racial, religious, sexual and class minorities) not comprehended practically within its original enabling fiction'. Slaughter 2007, pp. 4–6.

Ellison's commitment – to both modernist technique and the nineteenth-century moral tradition, to a political role for the artist and yet to the necessity of political independence of the artist, to the necessity of marginalised voices and yet the imperative of non-minority art – creates a contradictory critical practice, which, can be traced in *Invisible Man* itself. Ultimately, the purpose of the narrative is to represent the protagonist's attempt to reclaim a subjectivity whose authority is unrecognised. This task is mediated through stories, memory, decision and particularly, through responsibility.

To achieve coherence, the protagonist of *Invisible Man* needs to relocate 'responsibility' from the vast impersonal machine of American race relations back to the individual. The individual, however, is marked by his disengagement with social models of identity and concurrent commitment to a deconstructed model of social responsibility. The protagonist is wrestling with 'false' models of responsibility: Washingtonian, Capitalist, Marxist and Black Nationalist, which work to erase the subjectivity of the African-American individual. This concentration on personal responsibility is a re-appropriation of black agency, but it is also analogous with the founding myths of American identity.

In *Invisible Man* Ellison steadily demystifies the patterns of American racism through the prism of archetypal racial mythologies, yet, after this war of negative possibility is waged, we are left with an awkwardly banal conclusion. In order to emerge from underground the protagonist must not only take responsibility for a life that has been portrayed as a series of distorting racial projections, he must transform that life, through art, into a narrative of a specifically *American* possibility. My point here is not to reduce this intricate novel to a monologic conservatism, not least because the novel itself painstakingly reconstructs the 'American' narrative to recognise the African-American claim of authority upon that narrative. A complex world is evoked where the narrator places himself within the competing claims of responsibility which would ensure his abjection.

For the purposes of this chapter – which attempts to maintain a central focus on how the Communist Party is represented – it is significant that Ellison's attempt to achieve an ideal discursive identity by rejecting fixed social identities is accomplished through an appeal to common (American) humanity. He makes this appeal explicit in his non-fictional writing of the 1940s: 'A people must define itself, and minorities have the responsibility of having their ideals and images recognized as part of the composite image which is that of the still forming American people'.[20]

That the Communist Party is portrayed as alien to this incomplete yet unifying form of identity is particularly significant in the early 1950s, a period in

———
20   Ellison 1964, p. 44.

which the concept of Communism as foreign and alien has a particular resonance. The most enduring criticism of the impact of Communism on black life and literature emerged in the 1960s when both Harold Cruse's *The Crisis of The Negro Intellectual* (1967) and Baldwin's *Notes of a Native Son* (1964) condemned Communism as a malign appropriator of black experience – a view which has dominated this history until the recent past. However, the anti-Communist paradigms which inform these writings emerged in the early 1950s, which saw the publication of Wright's *The Outsider* (1953), Richard Crossman's *The God that Failed* (1951) and Wilson Record's *The Negro and the Communist Party* (1951). Like Ellison, Record focuses in particular on the inability of the Communist Party to recognise the basic 'patriotic' nature of black Americans.[21] Record insists that 'in the Communist's mind, Party ends came in the course of time to be inseparable from the ends which Negroes should seek'.[22] In all of these texts Communists are radical outsiders in black-face, who manipulate black agency for their own shadowy motives. *Invisible Man*'s construction of the Communist Party in the early 1950s enforces this sentiment.[23]

Ellison is not 'red baiting,' but he is keen to construct a particular relationship with the reader, a relationship which eventually represents Communists as the most insidious threat to a tremulous common identity. This relationship between the narrator and the reader, one constructed through the novel's mode of address, has been significantly engaged with in critical work on *Invisible Man*.[24] I am interested here in how Ellison constitutes his reading public. The opening paragraphs of the prologue detail a series of displacements which alienate the acts of seeing and of being seen:

> I am an Invisible Man. No, I am not a spook like those who haunted Edgar Allan Poe; nor am I one of your Hollywood movie ectoplasms. I am a man of substance, of flesh and bone, fibre and liquids – and I might even be said to possess a mind. I am invisible, understand, simply because people refuse to see me. Like the bodiless heads you see sometimes in circus

---

21   Record 1951, p. 293.

22   Record 1951, p. 296.

23   For an illuminating account of how Ellison's drafts of *Invisible Man* chart the development of his anti-communism, as opposed to the text being structured by anti-communism, see Foley 2003, pp. 163–82.

24   For a particularly insightful account of the narrative voice in *Invisible Man* see Fabre 1985, pp. 535–43.

side-shows, it is as though I have been surrounded by mirrors of hard distorting glass.[25]

The reader must be reminded of the various social structures which mediate the act of looking. Invisibility must be re-appropriated from its rendering in literature (Poe), cinematic culture (Hollywood), and racist projection. At one level, this textual work is simply preparing us for the main narrative trajectory, namely, the impossibility of subjective value in the context of a variety of mediating forms which centre on the axis of race and representation. However, there is a stability of address in both the prologue and epilogue which is interesting, less for what it tells us about the text's assumed reader, than for what it tells us about the agreed value on which the claim to common humanity rests – the concept of responsibility which haunts the text:

> I am one of the most irresponsible beings that ever lived. Irresponsibility is part of my invisibility; any way you face it, it is a denial. But to whom can I be responsible, and why should I be, when you refuse to see me? And wait till I reveal how truly irresponsible I am. Responsibility rests on recognition, and recognition is a form of agreement. Take the man whom I almost killed: who was responsible for that near murder – I? I don't think so, and I refuse it. I won't buy it. You can't give it to me. *He* bumped me, *he* insulted *me*. Shouldn't he, for his own personal safety, have recognized my hysteria, my 'danger potential'? He, let us say, was lost in a dream world. But didn't *he* control that dream world – which alas, is only too real! – and didn't *he* rule me out of it? And if he had yelled for a police man, wouldn't *I* have been taken for the offending one?[26]

Here, responsibility is directly dislocated from the individual to society in a pretty straightforward manner. But the protagonist then assumes responsibility as a kind of *contract* with the reader, a reciprocal gesture of good will which necessitates that we hear his story:

> Yes, yes, yes! Let me agree with you, I was the irresponsible one; for I should have used my knife to protect the higher interests of society. Some day that kind of foolishness will cause us tragic trouble. All dreamers and sleepwalkers must pay the price, and even the invisible victim is responsible for the fate of all. But I shirked that responsibility; I became too

---

25   Ellison 1965, p. 7.
26   Ellison 1965, p. 16.

snarled in the incompatible notions that buzzed within my brain. I was a coward ... But what did *I* do to be so blue? Bear with me.

The opening pages of the book, therefore, set up a call and response narrative, the assumed reader is evoked as an absent critic who calls upon the narrator to account for himself, to take responsibility for his actions, while the narrator promises to undertake that responsibility on condition that the reader hear his story. As Michel Fabre points out, the narrator/narratee relationship is 'built essentially on persuasive rhetoric'.[27]

This relationship is key to comprehending the nature of Communist Party representation in the novel. What is it that the narrator is trying to *persuade* us about the Brotherhood? Why does the Brotherhood dominate the second half of the novel? Why, in a novel about the deceptions which attend dominant narratives of the racial self, does Ellison spend so much time on the Brotherhood? There is a seeming structural imbalance between the often (uncharacteristically) crudely drawn caricatures of the Brotherhood and the dominant role it plays in the text. These questions cannot be addressed by abstracting the Brotherhood section from the rest of the novel; the protagonist's earlier experiences, particularly as a student, are especially instructive in examining how the Communist Party is represented in this novel.

Though racism is portrayed as monolithic in this novel, it is not static: the narrator encounters a variety of different racisms – the brutal and biological racism of the South, fixated on miscegenation, incest and narratives of savagery and humiliation; the economic racism of the North, which allows the African Americans at the boarding house to adopt the garb of the white entrepreneur while denying them access to the professions; the racism of Norton, which thrives on imagined colonial benevolence, and that of Jack, which pretends colour blindness in order to ignore the reality of racist oppression. Racism is produced by the novel as a multiple hegemonic process. Hence, 'blackness' is not a self-contained ontology for this text, but is rather a social category of identification, a positioning through stories told about you and stories you tell about yourself.[28] As Ellison articulates it in a 1945 essay, 'Negro sensibility is socially and historically conditioned'.[29] In *Invisible Man* black identity is a site of competition, where the narrator is brought into conflict with a variety of fixed social identities which struggle for supremacy. For my purposes, in

27   Fabre 1985, p. 537.
28   Hall 2000, pp. 144–53.
29   Ellison 1964, p. 98.

relation to Ellison's deconstruction of concepts of 'responsibility,' by far the most important of these competing narratives early in the text is that of Bledsoe.

As a student, the narrator is part of the 'privileged' oppressed, on the edges of white respectability. He tries to emulate the values of white 'patronage,' but is defeated because that philanthropy does not recognise his claim on it. Norton's 'benevolence' insists on black performativity in which the reality of African-American lives must never infringe on the narrative of the racial uplift. At the college the students must act according to the exemplar archetype of industrious, responsible aspiring black intelligentsia. They must learn to scorn all blacks who do not or cannot accept the Washingtonian path of assimilation and compliance. Ignorant of the politics of accommodation and deference as performance, the protagonist is oblivious to the complexities of conforming to this illusion. The dark comedy of the early chapters emphasises the potential dangers that accompany the narrator's lack of self-awareness. As Bledsoe informs the Invisible Man, being black in the South requires more than mere obedience, it involves a complicated process of deception and self-abasement, of understanding the psyche of racism and emulating the unspoken expectations of white benevolence. Bledsoe knows all about power and manipulation:

> These white folk have newspapers, magazines, radios, spokesmen to get their ideas across. If they want to tell the world a lie, they can tell it so well that it becomes the truth; and if I tell them that you're lying, they'll tell the world even if you prove you're telling the truth. Because that's the kind of lie they want to hear.[30]

Bledsoe is the sole authority within the microcosmic world of the campus and even beyond its boundaries. His power is not illusory (he expels the narrator of his own volition, he ensures the offending veterans leave town): he has come to a compromise with the system which benefits him. He retains a tight control over his world so that nothing can disrupt the fragile symbiosis between white benevolence and black deference which facilitates his authority:

> and I'll tell you something your sociology teachers are afraid to tell you' he said 'if it weren't for men like me running schools like this there's be no South. Nor North either. No, and there'd be no country – not as it is today.[31]

---

30 Ellison 1965, p. 120.
31 Ellison 1965, p. 119.

Bledsoe's position in society, his identity and his social standing are wholly dependent on the maintenance of racial inequality. Despite the fact that Bledsoe is affected by racism, in this novel there is no commonality of interests purely on the basis of skin colour. Bledsoe and Brother Tarp could never be part of the same struggle. Bledsoe is the personification of the black bourgeoisie and will retain his relative privilege at any cost. Through his representation of Bledsoe, a representation which throws Bledsoe into a dialectical relationship with the naivety of the Invisible Man, Ellison echoes the critique of black accommodationism produced, not only by Communists but by many African Americans on the Left. However the novel's construction of Blesdoe as a venal and strategic mouthpiece for segregation also recalls that discursive struggle visible in the *Liberator*'s desire to wrest authority from the black bourgeoisie.[32] Here, Ellison is competing for a model of black identity through the parodic representation of a monstrous self-serving black bourgeois prototype. Blesdoe's meaning in the larger economy of subject positions generated by the novel is vociferous and unambiguous. It is not thrift and educational success which Southern whites reward, but adherence to a strict racial code. To succeed on the terms of Southern racism is to carve out a space for individual authority within the parameters of racist domination and guard it against all which could threaten it. The myth of the racial uplift is that it can be achieved by 'social responsibility'; this novel suggests that it relies on the abdication of the social and is responsible only to the dictates of paternal racist hegemony. As Bledsoe brutally states it:

> I didn't make it, and I know that I can't change it. But I've made my place in it, and I'll have every Negro in the country hanging on tree limbs by morning if it means staying where I am.[33]

Bledsoe threatens the very *life* of African Americans who threaten the precarious balance of deference and performative servility which is necessary to his authority. This critique, in which class differences within the African-American population obliterate any basis for racial solidarity is best understood through the lens of Third Period Communist discourses on the African-American bourgeoisie.[34] At the same time Ellison, here, is brutally disentangling 'responsibility' from those practises which affirm and reproduce racial authority.

---

32   See pp. 49–52 above.

33   Ellison 1965, p. 120.

34   I am grateful to Paul Heideman for this observation in an earlier draft of this chapter.

The narrator rejects this class-based notion of 'responsibility' and assimilation only when he has been betrayed. He does not chose exteriority, it is forced upon him, and marginality is not easily a stable oppositional space. In fact, the Invisible Man is horrified at his expulsion, he accepts the responsibility for the Norton incident rather than risk eternal banishment from Bledsoe's world:

> Somehow I convinced myself I had violated the code and thus would have to submit to punishment. Dr. Bledsoe is right, I told myself, he's right; the school and what it stands for have to be protected.[35]

His exclusion only strengthens his resolve to become Bledsoe's protégé, but by disturbing the strict codes of Washingtonian 'social responsibility' the Invisible Man has ensured his exile from Bledsoe's world. A point which is emphasised by his encounter with the customers at the Golden Day, the pitiful consequences of the failed black bourgeoisie. The Golden Day veteran ensures he can no longer misrecognise the function of benevolence, even if he refuses to reject it:

> 'You see' he said, turning to Mr Norton, 'he has eyes and ears and a good distended African nose, but he fails to understand the simple facts of life. Understand. Understand. He registers with his senses but short-circuits his brain. He takes it in but he doesn't digest it. Already he is – well bless my soul! Behold! A walking zombie! Already he's learned to repress not only his emotions but his humanity. He's invisible, a walking personification of the Negative, the most perfect achievement of your dreams sir! The mechanical man'.[36]

The early versions of selfhood that the Invisible Man is offered revolve around the axis of race *and* class. He is not offered abstract identities so much as strict social roles premised on debased notions of 'responsibility' which facilitate the continuance of social divides and racist stereotypes. By the time he joins the Brotherhood, the protagonist's experience of Bledsoe and the Golden Day veterans has ensured that he is no longer a naive self-deceiver, but rather a strategic one. Ellison has insisted that 'responsibility' is now a site of conflict, and this insistence is mobilised through a vicious and powerful satiric representation of the black bourgeoisie which is indebted to earlier Communist discursive polemics.

---

35   Ellison 1965, p. 123.
36   Ellison 1965, p. 81.

6.2 'Riding Race Again': The Communist Party in *Invisible Man*

Thus on the moral level I propose that we view the whole of American life as a drama acted out upon the body of a Negro giant, who, lying trussed up like Gulliver, forms the stage and the scene upon which and within which the action unfolds.[37]

In Mary Rambo's apartment, the morning following his introduction to the Brotherhood, the narrator notices a coin box, 'a cast iron figure of a very black, red-lipped and wide mouthed Negro'.[38] After smashing it accidentally, the Invisible Man stuffs its 'jagged fragments' into his briefcase, but he is incapable of disposing of it. Neighbours castigate him for adding to their garbage, and his attempt to simply drop it is foiled when a passer-by returns it to him. He is stuck with it. When the narrator joins the Brotherhood he drinks to 'history' but, crucially, his entrance into the Brotherhood necessitates his severance from his past, unsubtly signified in this inability to destroy Mary's coin box. It is 'history' and historical meaning which structures Ellison's fictional representation of the Communist Party.

Initially the Invisible Man does not join the Brotherhood because he is convinced of their politics, but rather because he is flattered. He is offered paid employment and the organisation allows him the opportunity to use his hitherto debased skills of oration. From the beginning the whites in the Brotherhood are represented in a peculiar fashion. Whilst the vicious racists of the Battle Royal are presented as the grotesque epitome of segregation, and Mr. Norton as the deluded fantasist of Northern philanthropy, the Brotherhood is marked by ambiguity; the class pretensions of its members are in contradiction to their plush surroundings: 'I noticed a clip of blazing diamonds on her dress... how could they have such an expensive place, I wondered... I was struck by the contrast between the richness of the room and their rather poor clothing'.[39] This ambiguity is more than Ellison's knowing gesture towards the dilettantism of wealthy white radicals. Throughout the text the Brotherhood conceals not only the source of its wealth, its motives and its 'master' plan, but it is, at core, mysterious, outside of its epistemological function as the co-opters of radical black political identity. It has no historical roots, no personal histories (except for Tarp, discussed below); even its central base, which is outside Harlem in 'a strange

---

37   'Twentieth Century Fiction and the Black Mask of Humanity', in Ellison 1964, p. 28.
38   Ellison 1965, p. 258.
39   Ellison 1965, pp. 243–4.

part of the city,' suggests that the Brotherhood is enigmatic / other, as Invisible Man comments: 'I could see the word *Chthonian* on the storm awning'.[40] The protagonist joins a Communist organisation, indeed works full time for them, and yet there is little presentation of Communist *politics*, they are subsumed in the oft-cited 'science' of the Brotherhood.

There are a few references to contemporary Communist tactics. Brother Jack explicitly refers to the imperatives of the Popular Front: ' "You see", Brother Jack said with a grin, "we've always avoided these leaders, but the moment we start to advance on a broad front, sectarianism becomes a burden to be cast off" '.[41] Brother Hambro echoes this when he stresses that 'we are making temporary alliances with other political groups'.[42] But, unlike Himes, whose antipathy to Communism was dominated by recent Party betrayals, Ellison's interest lies in revealing the theoretical limitations of their worldview, their obsession with 'history' more than engaging with the specifics of their day-to-day political manoeuvrings. Ellison constructs Communism as the epitome of a cold scientific schema. The politics of the Brotherhood are left obscure. The narrator's indoctrination with Brother Hambro is omitted, and except for phrases like 'history,' 'science' and 'brotherhood of man,' there is little detail of exactly what nature of political doctrine they ascribe to. For the protagonist, the Brotherhood provides a safe space, a retreat from the blatant hostility of American racism, but its prohibitive identity politics – identity as discipline and erasure of personal history – is a threat to black political agency.

Such an analysis of Communism in terms of how it demolishes black subjectivity is not unique to Ellison. Wright's *The Outsider* (1953), published soon after *Invisible Man*, lambasts the Communist Party in similar terms:

> Above all he loathed the Communist attempt to destroy human subjectivity; for him, his subjectivity was the essence of his life, and for him to deny it was as impossible as it would have been for him to deny himself the right to live.[43]

40   Ellison 1965, p. 243.
41   Ellison 1965, p. 294.
42   Ellison 1965, p. 404.
43   Wright 1993, p. 197. Wright's attack on the Communist Party in *The Outsider* also empha-sises how removed the Communists are from the experiential elements of black life. Stressing that the Party consists of 'White men of cold, sharp minds who sat in dim offices and who ran things, the intellectuals'. Wright 1993, p. 234.

The Outsider is a passionate attack on Communism, which is seen as yet another objectifying and self-serving movement that seeks to erase black subjectivity for base and opportunistic motives. As the antithesis of *Native Son's* Bigger Thomas, *The Outsider's* Cross Damon is acutely aware of the mechanisms of power. He possesses an almost omniscient insight into the social and racial codes that dictate his environment. Like Bigger, Cross also murders; like Bigger, he turns these killings into acts of *creation*. Unlike Bigger, however, Cross is not lashing out in fear and hatred, he is reacting to the dictates of his conscience and his intellectual scepticism. Bigger kills out of fear, Cross kills out of disgust. The Communist activists of *Native Son* are sincere and well meaning, in the *Outsider* they are malignant.[44] Wright's antipathy to Communism in *The Outsider* is framed in terms which are familiar to readers of *Invisible Man*.

Like Wright, Ellison is concerned with the limitations of abstract determinism and the dynamics of any institution which attempts to speak on behalf of the 'Negro,' while distancing themselves from African-American life. The members of the Brotherhood are formalists, more anxious about strict adherence to Party discipline than relating to black workers but, more importantly, they possess a worldview which rejects the significance of lived experience. This is most obviously manifested in Jack's reaction to the protagonist's first speech for the Party where the Invisible Man's references to his personal experiences are cut short: 'And suddenly Brother Jack was beside me, pretending to adjust the microphone. "Careful now", he whispered. "Don't end your usefulness before you've begun".'[45]

More than a mere political strategy, this exclusion of lived experience is essential to the Brotherhood world vision:

I was dominated by the all embracing idea of Brotherhood. The organisation had given the world a new shape, and me a vital role. We recognised no loose ends, everything could be controlled by our science. Life was all

---

44 The Communists in *Native Son* are nowhere marked by the obnoxious disingenuousness that characterise them in the later fiction. This disjunction between the two representations is usually explained in biographical terms; *Native Son* is posited as the somewhat crude sociological protest novel of a black Communist imprisoned in the straitjacket of thirties socialist realism. The *Outsider* serves as the failed existential experiment of the disillusioned anti-Communist. While there is some truth to this proposition, overall it is a limiting one, presuming an aesthetic and philosophical development which directly parallels the biographical details of Wright's life. There is a strain of existential thought in all of Wright's work, and though he broke definitively with Communism, Wright retained a Marxian worldview throughout his life.

45 Ellison 1965, p. 279.

pattern and discipline; and the beauty of discipline is when it works. And it was working very well.[46]

As the protagonist becomes more involved with the Brotherhood, he becomes completely removed from the reality of black lives and internalises the dictum that 'politically, individuals were without meaning'.[47] It is only after Tod Clifton's death that he *sees* Harlem for the first time; up to this point his membership of the Brotherhood has rendered its inhabitants *invisible*. His realisation that the chaotic diversity of black urban life cannot be contained by the scientific dogma of the Brotherhood marks the beginning of his disenchantment with the organisation: 'For they were men outside of historical time, they were untouched, they didn't believe in Brotherhood, no doubt had never heard of it; or perhaps like Clifton would mysteriously have rejected its mysteries; men of transition whose faces were immobile'.[48]

Here, not only is consciousness of self a condition for historical action, it remains to some degree outside of history. It is certainly outside the Brotherhood's notion of history. Their 'history' is, in fact, an artificial structure which cushions 'man' from the chaotic heterogeneity which characterises real experience. Again, this is something Wright emphasises in the 1950s. In *American Hunger* he writes:

> The Communists, I felt, had oversimplified the experience of those whom they sought to lead. In their efforts to recruit masses, they had missed the meaning of the lives of the masses, and conceived the people in too abstract a manner.[49]

In *Invisible Man*, history, as an abstract positivism, becomes merely a stage. The Brotherhood conceives of history as a linear background in its onward march to the future. Ellison is concerned with revealing as illusory the deployment of concepts like 'responsibility' and 'history'. As with Bledsoe's self-serving notion of 'social responsibility,' the Brotherhood's depersonalised notion of 'history' is viciously satirised. To the Brotherhood, 'history' is a control experiment in which the outcome is already predetermined, and only those elements which guarantee that end result are beneficial to its political programme. Therefore, 'real' Harlemites, in all their zoot-suiting, yam eating, blues singing, justice

---

46   Ellison 1965, p. 308.
47   Ellison 1965, p. 359.
48   Ellison 1965, p. 355.
49   Wright 1977, p. 66.

seeking, beer drinking, number playing ways, are outside their understanding, and outside this version of history. Harlemites are disposable canon fodder to be used in a strategy of *realpolitik* which abhors the actuality of black traditions and communities.

For the Brotherhood, political awareness means negating the individual in favour of an abstract and unified collective agent. In comparison to Blesdoe's self-serving compromise with Southern racism, the Brotherhood's stress on theoretical solidarity holds a certain charm for the Invisible Man. But, following Tod Clifton's death, the protagonist begins to see the citizens of Harlem in contradistinction to the Brotherhood's vision of the 'people':

> For the boys speak a jived-up transitional language full of country glamour, think transitional thoughts, though perhaps they dream the same old ancient dreams. They were men out of time – unless they found Brotherhood. Men out of time who would soon be gone and forgotten... But who knew (and now I began to tremble so violently I had to lean against a refuse can) – who knew but that they were the saviours, the true leaders, the bearers of something precious? The stewards of something uncomfortable, burdensome, which they hated because, living outside the realm of history, there was no one to applaud their value and they themselves failed to understand it.[50]

The protagonist's awakening to the alterity of black life and possibilities that reside in the streets of Harlem echoes Ellison's 1943 editorial for the Communist *Negro Quarterly*:

> Much in Negro life remains a mystery; perhaps the zoot suit conceals profoundly political meanings; perhaps the symmetrical frenzy of the Lindy-hop conceals clues to great potential power – if only Negro leaders would solve this riddle... The problem is psychological: it will be solved only by a Negro leadership that is aware of the psychological attitude and incipient forms of action which the black masses reveal in their emotion-charged myths symbols and wartime folklore.[51]

Without overstating the case, it seems pertinent that the stress on positive heterogeneity, which is seen as the essence of Ellison's anti-Communism in 1952, is present also in the position he held a decade earlier, while he was not

---

50   Ellison 1965, p. 355.
51   Cited in O'Meally 1980, p. 55.

only a Communist sympathiser but writing in a Communist publication. The point is not that Ellison's politics remained static, but that the Communist Party of the mid-1930s provided a space in which questions about the nature of 'Negro life' were debated. By the early 1950s these questions were seen as antithetical to Communist politics. The interpretation of the activities of the CPUSA during the War, Ellison's own move away from Communism, and the emergence of anti-Communist hegemony in the US altered the meta-narrative of the Communist's engagement with black communities. Altered it to the extent that the same sentiments that defined Communist approaches to black life and culture can now be mobilised to castigate them. Significantly, in this respect, however, Ellison does not suggest the Brotherhood is racist. Throughout the Brotherhood section of the novel Ellison is articulating a mistrust, but it is one based not on any suspicion of Communism's inherent racism as it is on an antipathy to political expediency and suspect philosophical doctrine. The Brotherhood's blindness is not restricted to colour blindness. Brother Jack relates to the working class, in general, as a malleable resource: 'very well, so now hear this: We do not shape our policies to the mistaken and infantile notions of the man in the street. Our job is not to ask them what they think but to tell them'.[52]

The Brotherhood does not simply misrecognise or fear the heterogeneity of black life; it negates it. 'The People' can be spoken *for* as an abstract phenomenon, but there is never any attempt to speak *to* them. This is more than a question of political expediency and manipulation: the Brotherhood is *alien* to Harlem, its members are not of the place, they do not even know the place. It is significant that the protagonist can find a home in the Brotherhood only when he severs his links with all that he knows. He must become *unblack*, losing all traces of his body and history except as a physical signifier. His new persona is not, as he first imagines, one that is 'broader than race', but is one that negates the reality of race.[53] More specifically, the Invisible Man must also become *un-American*, the model of identity proffered by the Brotherhood removes him from his sense of unbelonging in America. Brother Westrum's suggestion that the Brotherhood needs a banner reminds the protagonist that 'there was always that sense in me of being apart when the flag went by. It had been a reminder, until I found the Brotherhood, that *my* star was not yet there'.[54]

Ultimately, for the narrator, that sense of unbelonging should not be escaped from. Unbelonging is central to the constitution of the modern African-

---

52   Ellison 1965, p. 380.
53   Ellison 1965, p. 285.
54   Ellison 1965, p. 318.

American subject for Ellison. It is not only that the Brotherhood demands too high a price in order to avoid the anxieties of displaced identity, those anxieties are central to representing the 'truth' of African-American existence.

The Brotherhood's indifference to the reality of Harlem is illustrative of the fact that they are antithetical to the narrative of America that Ellison is proposing, a narrative of America as a heterogeneous ideal. They are marginal to American life, not through subjugation, but through choice – unlike in *Native Son* and even *Lonely Crusade*, *Invisible Man* contains no suggestion that Communists are themselves subject to political harassment or pose a threat to the dominant culture. In a novel which confronts the complicity between African-American life and modern American identity, an organisation which seeks to place itself outside lived American experience is perhaps the most dangerous threat to black self-definition.

The Brotherhood is *alien* to American culture. Even the vicious racists of the battle royal are symbolic of an American reality; but, by being colour blind in a nation obsessed with race, the Brotherhood exposes itself as foreign. In the infamous scene where Jack's eye pops out, Jack's uncharacteristic anger leads him to begin 'spluttering and lapsing into a *foreign* language'.[55] Jack is either not American or owes his allegiance somewhere else. Two decades after the publication of *Invisible Man*, Ellison still stressed that the Communists were an anathema to domestic American life:

> They fostered the myth that Communism was twentieth century Americanism, but to be a twentieth century American meant, in their thinking, that you had to be more Russian than American and less Negro than either. That's how they lost the Negroes.[56]

As discussed in Chapter Four, the wartime activities of the CPUSA were perceived as a watering down of the Party's previous commitment to race politics – when the imperatives of Soviet foreign policy seemed to dictate even the most local struggle. In *Invisible Man*, however, the Soviet Union is not mentioned. Ellison's critique is less locally and contingently focused.

It is not just Party tactics which are condemned, but the danger is posed by an organisation which reduces lived experience to a theoretical abstraction. The Brotherhood approach Harlem from an outside, a 'history' which its members imagine to be paramount, so that all beyond it (self, personal history, responsibility) becomes invisible, without significance. Ellison's Brotherhood,

---

55   Ellison 1965, p. 380 (my emphasis.)
56   Ellison quoted in 1976 in Benston 1990, p. 88.

which is incapable of even understanding the world it is attempting to transform, is a marked shift from Himes's contention that Communism has sold out African Americans. Here, the Brotherhood feeds off black marginality in America, but does so from a space which is radically alien to the concept of responsibility that unites both narrator and reader in the text.

The 'contract' between narrator and narratee initiated in the prologue is one which centres on the acceptance of personal responsibility; the Brotherhood is therefore doubly marked out by the text as alien to both black and American experience. This whole notion of personal responsibility is an anathema to Jack who derides the protagonist by referring to him as 'Brother Personal Responsibility'.[57] In one of the many 'meetings' the Party call to discipline the Invisible Man, meetings which are conducted as purges, the narrator is labelled as a 'petty individualist'.[58] Directly alluding to Brother Jack in the epilogue, the narrator pleads 'let man keep his many parts and you'll have no tyrant states'.[59]

Many commentators have attempted to collapse the historical and cultural specificity in *Invisible Man* into a parable for modern alienated 'man'.[60] But it is perhaps in the Brotherhood section of the novel that Ellison most explicitly invites the reader to ally themselves as American individuals against the common threat of Communist uniformity. The blinding conformity of the Brotherhood and its world vision is *Anti*-American, as the protagonist reminds us: 'America is woven of many strands; I would recognise them and let it so remain'.[61] This is *one* of the 'Americas' deployed by the text, an idealised site of difference and individuality. As with 'responsibility,' Ellison is competing for meaning against a series of 'false' Americas – the most powerful of these being the viciously segregated America exemplified in the Battle Royale scene. 'America' emerges out of the conflict between the competing claims upon its authority. But the Brotherhood is outside of this dialectic, it does not represent a competing version of America. Initially, the Brotherhood offers an *escape* from the racism of American life. It offers a safe haven, it gives a 'pattern to the chaos' to existence, and therein lies its charm for the naive protagonist. But, for Ellison, the Brotherhood's collective 'we' denotes exclusion.

---

57 Ellison 1965, p. 382.
58 Ellison 1965, p. 324.
59 Ellison 1965, p. 465.
60 Saul Bellow's review is the most pertinent example of this when he asserts that 'Mr. Ellison has not adopted a minority tone. If he had done so, he would have failed to establish a true middle-of-consciousness for everyone'. Bellow 1952, p. 609.
61 Ellison 1965, p. 465.

However, the Brotherhood does offer a site for the articulation of solidarity among African Americans that is promised elsewhere in the novel but never delivered. Crucially, the Brotherhood is the first place where the narrator associates with other African Americans on equal terms – with both Brother Clifton and Brother Tarp. The representation of a political party which only consisted of ineffectual hacks, like Westrum and Tobit, would scarcely move beyond the overstated satire of the committee men, whose very thoughts are constrained by blind adherence to the obscure theoreticians who govern the Brotherhood's every move. But the Brotherhood is also home to Tod Clifton, the youth leader who embodies the proud hope for a multi-racial future society, and Brother Tarp, who signifies the historic struggle of Southern black Americans.

With the exception of Brother Tarp, Tod is the only sympathetically drawn member of the Brotherhood. Free of the dry, competitive jealousy that characterises the other Brothers, his beauty, intelligence and driven idealism is stressed from the outset. Though he in no way resembles Himes's Luther McGregor, he does share his somewhat mythic status:

> Then the young man was moving with an easy Negro stride out of the shadow into the light, and I saw that he was very black and very handsome, and as he advanced mid-distance into the room, that he possessed the chiselled, black marble features sometimes found on statues in northern museums and alive in southern towns ... I saw the broad, taut span of his knuckles upon the dark grain of the wood, the muscular, sweatered arms, the curving line of the chest rising to the easy pulsing of his throat, to the square, smooth chin.[62]

Even Ras sees Tod's innate leadership qualities, his primordial status as a leader for his people. As throughout the narrative the Invisible Man has already been in thrall to a variety of objectifying identities, it is *Tod's* membership of the Brotherhood rather than the protagonist's that denotes Ellison's recognition of the powerful attraction of Communism. Despite the narratorial antagonism to the Brotherhood, the politics of the Brotherhood are somewhat successful; it does mobilise African Americans in Harlem in sizeable numbers. Initially, in the Brotherhood the narrator finds a home, a voice of protest against the racism of a society which abuses him; paradoxically, even his politicisation eventually facilitates the critical distance he needs to discover their true nature. Furthermore, black nationalism, in the person of Ras, offers no political strategy for dismantling the institutions of racism. Communism and black

---

62   Ellison 1965, p. 293.

nationalism are simply alternative social and political identities, neither have any inherent connection with the inhabitants of Harlem. The Invisible Man's narrative is a process which insists that he interrogates rather than accept projected identities; whether those identities are black, white or red. For Ellison, the politics of self-realisation cannot be obtained within organised politics. Ellison's antagonism to fixed and unifying narratives of the self as a political subject can be related to the modernist release of subjectivity from realist constraints. However, this conception of a fluid self, invested with an epistemology of discontinuity and heterogeneity, is complicated by Ellison's stress on personal responsibility. The Brotherhood is 'other' precisely because it disallows both selfhood and personal responsibility.

The damaging consequences of the Brotherhood's otherness, as much as their megalomania, are demonstrated in the fate of Tod Clifton. Tod is trapped between the scientific 'objectivity' of the Brotherhood and the emotionally charged rhetoric of Ras. He cannot bridge the gap between the two totalising narratives of class and race. He is the victim not merely of racial manipulation by the Brotherhood, but of the structural limitations of racial polarisation. By eventually plunging outside the 'history' of the Brotherhood, he is not *liberated* from an alienating identity, he is cast adrift. Tod is left with knowledge of his powerlessness. Beyond their laboured symbolism, the puppet 'sambo' dolls that Tod sells on the street after his defection from the Party also signify the tragedy of a complex black identity smothered and distorted by the limitations of the binary oppositions which govern racial identity. Clifton can accept neither Ras's mythic African past, nor the Brotherhood's myopic transnational future. He seeks to define himself without the metanarratives of class and black nationalism and is left with the performativity of race as objectifying spectacle. He becomes a peddler of American racist artefacts. The still 'deluded' protagonist cannot comprehend Tod's actions:

> Why should a man deliberately plunge outside history and peddle an obscenity, my mind went on abstractedly. Why should he choose to disarm himself, give up his voice and leave the only organization offering him a chance to 'define' himself? . . . Why did he choose to plunge into nothingness, into the void of faceless faces, of soundless voices lying outside history?[63]

Although it is precisely this refusal of definition that the protagonist himself eventually chooses, Tod is unable to complete the imaginative transgression

---

63   Ellison 1965, p. 353.

that is essential for Ellison's concept of subjective identity. Rather than withdraw from society to create himself through art, through the retelling of old stories to form a new narrative, Tod becomes a victim of the oldest narrative – killed by the state while 'yessing' them with his racist artefacts. Even his status as a symbol of black martyrdom after his death is punctured as it is revealed that the riots which follow his death are as much the result of Brotherhood machinations as they are of an explosion of black anger. Tod's death facilitates the protagonist's rebirth, but as a prototype for a black politically-conscious working-class activist he is scarcely relevant to the text.

In this novel there can be no black leadership until there is self-knowledge, and even then that knowledge is not necessarily for utilisation in a political struggle. Clifton's demise and murder, Rinehart's chameleon existence and Ras's frantic nationalism, disrupt any Manichean construction of 'race' in opposition to racist discourses: there is no one way to be black. Ellison is not negotiating the politics of duality, but rupturing those politics in a culture which inscribes blackness wholly in relation to whiteness. Ellison's insistence on the hetrogeneic experience of race is undoubtedly concerned with de-essentialising racial identity. However, it is less a sustained polemic on the political concept of a black 'essence' than an assertion of existential individuality; a 'consciousness of existence' which is 'determined in part by the long-term constraints and possibilities experienced in specific life situations'.[64] Combined with this existentialist vision is Ellison's commitment to ensure that the historical legacy of American racism is woven into modern black consciousness. Mostly, as with the Trueblood incident, this commitment produces a challenging and articulate acknowledgement of the centrality of black cultural expression to the emergence of a new black consciousness. It is less successful when Ellison attempts to integrate the experience of conscious *political* resistance to a fragmented construction of black subjectivity. A point illustrated by the representation of Brother Tarp.

Somewhat disconcertingly, Brother Tarp simply disappears from the novel; when the dream of the Brotherhood implodes he vanishes from the text. This is significant beyond the narrational implications – that Tarp has exhausted his 'usefulness' to the Brotherhood. As a character, Tarp is identified with Frederick Douglass, he is defined by his commitment to struggle, by his refusal to be a 'yes' man. He symbolises not only rebellion, but the historical memory of the act of rebellion. As he tells the narrator when he gives him the link from his old chain gang chain:

---

64   Paget in Gordon (ed.) 1997, p. 15.

'I'd like to pass it on to you, son. There' he said, handing it to me. 'Funny thing to give somebody, but I think it's got a heap of signifying wrapped up in it and it might just help you remember what we're really fighting against. I don't think of it in terms of more than two words, yes and no; but it signifies a heap more'.[65]

In passing on his chain link Brother Tarp articulates a concept of resistance which is not about the eradication of history. Within the abstract political arena of the Brotherhood Tarp is 'real,' he has struggled and attained a measure of freedom and political consciousness; Tarp does not give the narrator advice on how to act in the world, he does not elucidate on the nature of his imprisonment or the story of his escape, his story retains all the elements of a scriptural release from bondage. It forges a bond between the narrator and the idea of struggle. After their encounter the Invisible Man declares confidently: 'here in the Brotherhood was the one place in the country where we were free and given the greatest encouragement to use our abilities'.[66]

Many commentators have grouped Tarp with other 'folk' characters in the novel – the Golden Day vet, Dupre, Wheatstraw and particularly Mary Rambo – characters who serve to anchor the protagonist to his cultural past.[67] Like Mary, Tarp is therefore critically important but also somewhat anachronistic. Tarp is venerated in the novel, he remains in the text as a symbol (the leg chain), but his defining moment of simply saying 'no' or rather '*hell* no!' is no longer an option in the Invisible Man's radically destabilised and contradictory world.[68] As with the Grandfather's 'yes,' Tarp's 'no' belongs to a different era. Tarp's significance becomes sublimated within the wider mobilisation of memory which is essential to the novel.

Whilst the novel emphasises that it is essential that the memory of resistance is maintained, memories in the text do not function to construct alternative histories, or to function as political incentives, but to conceive a modernist black identity. Memory emerges as a kind of anti-history which breaks down structural barriers to self-knowledge. African-American experience cannot be represented in its entirety, its totality cannot be grasped. The continuity between past and present can only be realised in fragments of redeemed memory, when history is no longer perceived as a litany of events connected to the

---

65   Ellison 1965, p. 313.
66   Ellison 1965, p. 314.
67   O'Meally 1980, p. 88; Blake 1979, p. 130.
68   Ellison 1965, p. 312.

present by causal progression: 'Beware of those who speak of the *spiral* of history; they are preparing a boomerang'.[69]

Invisible Man creates a chaotic continuum which ruptures teleological narratives to allow for the possibility of an imaginative recuperation of subjectivity and consciousness. The protagonist's memories are not 'personal' in that, save for his grandfather, his memories of family life are restricted to a few casual references. His memories are sensate, stirred to consciousness by random connections (yams, cabbage etc.), but together they form a moral and cultural index which locate him within a powerful tradition that he is both attracted to and repelled by.

In the novel humanity is attained through memory, through stories, through responsibility. Ellison's concentration on *stories* and myths is central to the sensibility of *Invisible Man*. There can be no clean oppositions to racist paradigms, no binary oppositions of 'yes' or 'no'. There are no 'lessons' to learn, neither life affirming sentiment nor nihilistic despair. Rather, we are transported to a transitional world of fraught possibilities, where imaginative transgression attempts to redeem the illusion of hope. It is somewhat fitting, therefore, that Tarp's great sacrifice, his chain 'with a whole heap of signifying' is not utilised to continue the 'no' struggle. This historical link with revolt is 'plunged' outside history (it follows the protagonist underground) in order to facilitate the emergence of a radically discontinuous subject.

Ellison does not search for untold stories of oppression hidden in history's archive, he seeks to redeem those transcendent energies that reside in black folk culture. The purpose is redemption rather than freedom. As Charles T. Davis points out in relation to a variety of black novels of the early 1950s: 'What is prized more than anything else is an understanding of one's black self, and this requires a reconciliation of some sort with the black heritage, family and folk, in America'.[70]

However, the radical impulse at work here also threatens equivocation. The historic specificity of Tarp's chain becomes dislocated as it is incorporated into the Invisible Man's subjective quest for identity, an identity which itself, in the epilogue, threatens to become displaced into the chaos of generic mid-century American identity. The 'whole heap of history' signified in the chain threatens to become part of a metaphysical conflict. Rather than serving revolutionary ends, it is pressed into the service of epistemological ones. The trauma remains, but the dream of freedom is subsumed in the larger collapse of the dreams which structure the narrative. Tarp's defiance, as a politically-

---

69   Ellison 1965, p. 9.
70   Davis in Benston (ed.) 1990, p. 281.

conscious radical, the model of resistance which the *Liberator* fought to define and reproduce, is divested of political significance as the novel attempts to find resolution in a re-appropriation of the American dream.

This is further emphasised in the epilogue, when the Grandfather's hitherto vague advice is relocated into the dream of a lost American ideal:

> Could he have meant – hell he must have meant the principle, that we were to affirm the principle, on which the country was built and not the men, or at least not the men who did the violence. Did he mean say 'yes' because he knew that the principle was greater than the men, greater than the numbers and the vicious power and all the methods used to corrupt its name ... Or did he mean that we had to take the responsibility for all of it, for the men as well as the principle, because we were the heirs who must use the principle because no other fitted our needs? Not for the power or for vindication, but because we, with the given circumstance of our origin, could only thus find transcendence.[71]

The 'principle' of the founding fathers and the responsibility for it are finally what unite the reader and the narrator. The tacit 'contract' of the prologue reveals, not an identity based on common experience, but on common responsibility. 'We' must protect the first principles of America against corruption and manipulation:

> Or was it, did he mean that we should affirm the principle because we, through no fault of our own were linked to all others in the loud, clamouring semi-visible world, that world seen only as a fertile field for exploitation by Jack and his kind, and with condescension by Norton and his, who were tired of being mere pawns in the futile game of 'making history'. Had he seen that for these too we had to say 'yes' to the principle, lest they turn upon us to destroy both it and us.[72]

The Brotherhood is antithetical to the American dream, a dream reconfigured here as the retention of the ideal and the recognition of its debasement.[73] As the antithesis of personal responsibility and serving un-American ends, its representation serves to forge a bond between the reader and narrator. It emerges

---

71   Ellison 1965, p. 462.

72   Ellison 1965, p. 463.

73   This has echoes of Frederick Douglass's 1852 speech 'What to the Slave is the Fourth of July?', in Chesebrough 1998, pp. 109–13.

as radically other in this text, with no story to tell and no capacity to listen to other stories.

In the epilogue the Invisible Man follows the example of Trueblood. By taking responsibility for his actions and assuming control of his narrative, he places himself outside the boundaries of an authority which estranges the self and the world. The narrator eschews all the social roles he's had to play, ultimately in order to underline the centrality of a discontinuous subjectivity: a subjectivity which is constantly under attack from a powerful Communist other.

The famous last line of the novel, 'Who knows but that, on the lower frequencies, I speak for you?',[74] has been responsible for some of the more complacent, normalising interpretations of this novel:

> Because we are all members of minority groups... and because we are all used as means to the economic, political and psychological ends through which others try to define themselves, the narrator speaks for us... Because we blind ourselves to the inadequacy of the names given us by others, or exploit that inadequacy by blinding ourselves to the obligations that link us together in our invisible reality, he speaks for us.[75]

This comforting universalist interpretation relocates the narrator from his isolated cellar into a kind of metaphysical brotherhood of alienated modern subjects. Ellison barely distanced himself from such a reading. Both his critical commentaries on the book and indeed the epilogue itself (in part) demands this interpretation:

> Life is to be lived, not controlled; and humanity is won by continuing to play in the face of certain defeat. Our fate is to become one, and yet many – This is not prophecy but description. Thus one of the greatest jokes in the world is the spectacle of the whites busy escaping blackness and becoming blacker every day, and the blacks striving towards whiteness, becoming quite dull and grey. None of us seems to know who he is or where he's going.[76]

But there is more than transcendental humanism going on here. The attempt to read this novel as a universalist parable is precisely the 'spectacle of whites

---

74   Ellison 1965, p. 469.
75   Whitaker 1970, pp. 392–3.
76   Ellison 1965, p. 465.

busy escaping blackness'. Ellison is attempting to break down racial boundaries which limit possibilities of understanding the world, but that understanding is based on the recognition of the specificity of black identities. At the same time, Ellison is also negating the possibility of reading the text in ways which normalise 'blackness' as the exclusive domain of black experience.

The epilogue insists that, although the quest for black self-definition may be located in the acceptance of distinctive black cultural forms, this is the basis from which to build a truly 'American' identity rather than being the acknowledgement of an exclusively black experiential identity. In *Invisible Man*, like *Native Son*, there is no suggestion that the experience of 'blackness' is a prerequisite for resisting racism. The *experience* of race does not automatically herald racial solidarity, nor does consciousness of the structures of racism set the narrator free. Black identity as it is experienced must be deconstructed in order for self-knowledge and agency to be realised. The narrator's plea to the reader to hear his story is an acknowledgement that horrors of racist oppression in America can be comprehended by non-black Americans. Indeed, it is precisely the deconstruction of the black racially-determined self, in the context of competing beliefs and systems of power, which engenders the black modernist subject.

By the end of the novel the narrator has run through the full gamut of ready-to-wear black identities on offer in his society: the debased black of the South, the despoiler of white womanhood, the Washingtonian prototype, the black worker who threatens white jobs, the victim of scientific categorisation, the radical outsider who threatens the stability of white America, the gangster, the numbers man and the rioter. The final words of the novel are not a wry invitation to recognise the futility of all human existence. It is questionable whether they are the *final* words at all. In the prologue the narrator states the 'the end is in the beginning and lies far ahead'.[77] This is a refusal of teleological narrative and is further underlined by the allusion to Ras, Rhinehart and Brother Jack before we know who they are. The stream of consciousness narrative invites us immediately to return to the prologue at the novel's end. That this is a circular narrative is further underlined by the constant repetitions in the novel, the sense of déjà vu, the 'uncanny sense of familiarity, feeling now ... that I had been through it all before'.[78]

'Who knows *but that*, on the lower frequencies, I speak for you?'[79] is more a plea than a statement of fact. He 'speaks' for readers on the condition that

---

77   Ellison 1965, p. 9.
78   Ellison 1965, p. 243.
79   Ellison 1965, p. 469 (my emphasis).

they listen to his story and acknowledge his visibility. More specifically, this bond with the reader exists in the structure of the 'novel' itself, which posits the reader as an always present participant:

> So why do I write, torturing myself to put it down? Because in spite of myself I've learned some things. Without the possibility of action, all knowledge comes to one labelled 'file and forget', and I can neither file nor forget. Nor will certain ideas forget me: they keep filing away at my lethargy, my complacency. Why should I be the one to dream this nightmare? Why should I be dedicated and set aside – yes, if not to at least *tell* a few people about it?[80]

The 'I' who addresses us here, addresses us, however plaintively, as the 'merely human'. Despite the multiple stories in the text, we have only one distinctive voice, the literary voice. The vehicle is art, the novel, the story, the constantly repeating story. Whilst the narrator insists in the final pages that 'even an Invisible Man has a socially responsible role to play', he does not emerge from underground.[81] It is representation itself that can transcend social identity and the novel is the master discourse, within *its* margins the narrator can achieve an intimacy with the reader that is elsewhere absent in the text. The narrator himself tells us that the act of writing the story has 'negated' his anger. This may well be a conservative gesture, certainly in the context of the necessity of black rage to black liberation which attends both the other core novels of this study and the black radical Communist discourses of the Third Period. It suggests that a changed perception of the world which can channel that anger is preferable or at least more realistic than actual social change; but this 'negation' is also Ellison's insistence on the transformative power of the novel as form.

Here the novel, as the vehicle for the transmission of transcendent personal energies, is the key to constructing a dialogue across racial boundaries. Ellison's dense narrative attempts to create a site of rarefied subjectivity which resists totalisation and appropriation. This is a novel firmly rooted in its own artistic practice, carving out a space for the articulation of dislocated voices, fragmented memory and opaque narratives which underline the transformative power of the novel as genre.

For a late twentieth- or early twenty-first-century sensibility this rendering of a fragmented dislocated subjectivity is a triumph of sorts, a triumph, that is, of a post-modern rejection of any universal narrative. A moment of revelation

---

80   Ellison 1965, p. 467.
81   Ellison 1965, p. 468.

in relation to the discontinuous self which is always and never in the process of creation. In Ellison's own terms, terms he inherited from nineteenth-century realism, however, fragmentariness and dislocation signify the failure of the novel's promise (the novel as genre); a promise best encapsulated by George Eliot's idea of the genre 'as a mode of amplifying experience and extending our contact with our fellow-men beyond the bounds of our personal lot'.[82] This universal aesthetic is a disinterested one which can get to the 'truth'; Ellison retains this impulse but the universal doesn't automatically recognise the claim of difference that writing the black self necessitates. In the epilogue and prologue the novel doesn't just retain this impulse of universalism, it performs it, and performs it in all its glorious seductiveness – the we who are being addressed is the we of our 'best selves'. But the epilogue and prologue cannot be excised from the novel as a totality. Between these two direct addresses to the reader, is the story of the disintegrating black self, a self which disintegrates precisely on the denial of universal humanity to the subject.

If the novel, as the vehicle for the transmission of transcendent personal energies, is the key to constructing a dialogue across racial boundaries, then surely the representation of the Brotherhood as the antithesis of subjective personal experience confirms Communism's incommensurability with literature and, therefore, with American experience.

Invisible Man reverses the journey of *Native Son*. In the latter novel, an atomised individual who aggressively rejects society is somewhat redeemed by his recognition of a world outside his subjective experience. In *Invisible Man*, subjective experience is paramount and achievable only by repudiation of society. Where the humanitarian vision of Wright's Communists facilitates Bigger's sense of himself as a member of society, the scientific myopia of Ellison's Communists ensure the protagonist's withdrawal from society. In both novels, Communists scorn the principle of American democracy. Where Max's courtroom speech demystifies the founding principles of America as complicit in the crimes committed against black Americans, the epilogue of *Invisible Man* demands that those principles be re-appropriated by all Americans as a blueprint for a *new* understanding.

Structurally, *Invisible Man* sets up dialogical relationships between black folklore, Western mythology, Anglo-American modernism and nineteenth-century American literature.[83] Its representation of the Communist Party is

---

82   Quoted in Cooke 2010, p. 144.

83   There are numerous accounts of Ellison's relationship to black folklore, two of the most challenging accounts are Blake 1979, pp. 121–35 and Baker 1983, pp. 828–45. The question of Ellison's literary 'ancestors' is surveyed by a variety of critics in Benston (ed.) 1990, pp. 187–245.

informed by the generational experience of a variety of black writers and intellectuals who were influenced by Communist politics as well as by Ellison's own erudite philosophical beliefs. If *Native Son* charts the heady possibilities of the 1930s, and *Lonely Crusade* the confusion and bitterness of the 1940s, *Invisible Man* marks the rupture of the formidable relationship between American Communism and black radicalism.

Conclusion

This book has argued that a series of canonical African-American texts reward a textual engagement sensitive to the historicity of race politics. From Wright's sympathetic depiction of Jan and Max, to Himes's contradictory portrayal of Rosie and Luther, and Ellison's intellectual repudiation of the Brotherhood, the Communist Party constituted a powerful dynamic in the structuring of representations of African-American identity.

That this identity was fluid enough to include radical interracial class solidarity and a commitment to the prioritisation of black cultural and political struggle differentiates it from the models of African-American identity that proliferated before and since the 1930s. No previous and no subsequent political movement in the US achieved a politics which could produce an effective interracial class solidarity.

Yet, with the exception of the critics and historians I have drawn upon in this book, this confluence of race and class is still often either minimalised or constructed as a curiosity, a disjunction in the black radical tradition which serves as a cautionary tale of Marxist opportunism. In this rubric, African-American agency is necessarily absent and the impact of black Communists on the landscape of the American Left is footnoted to 'manipulation'. However, if we approach this period not as the transhistorically determined site of the failure of the Marxist dialectic, but as a dynamic, historically specific and contingent site of political possibilities, a different interpretation emerges. This book is designed to contribute to a different understanding of the relationship between African Americans and Communism. Far from being 'alien' to black traditions of struggle, Communism built on and extended the terms of that struggle. The *Liberator* turned to the black radical past, not to 'raid' it, but to find within it historically sublimated narratives of black agency which could enrich and inform an understanding of the contribution of African Americans to the contemporary fights of American workers. In *Native Son*, Wright envisions Communism as a sensitive and valuable tool to transform the dislocating energies of untargeted black rage into a meaningful model of black identity. *Lonely Crusade*, for all its disgust at Communist manipulation, presents us with a model of interracial class solidarity and a martyrological reclamation of black 'manhood' constructed through encounters with Communism. Even Ellison's parodic repudiation of Communism owes as much to the proliferation of discursive models released by Communist black political identity as it does to the traditions of high modernism which pre-occupy critics of *Invisible Man*.

It has not been my intention to glorify the CPUSA or to render insignificant the damaging legacy of the Left's illusions of Stalin. Rather, it is my argument that it was precisely the imperatives of Stalinism that generated the bitter response of many black (and white) artists and activists to Communism in the post-War era. Yet, that historical legacy has too often been conflated into a generic attack on the ability of Marxism, as an emancipatory theory and as a political practice, to speak of and to issues of race. Communists in mid-century America insisted that racism was a social construct which infected the society as a whole and that therefore anti-racist activity had to be at the centre of anti-capitalist struggle. This privileging of race generated solidarities which spoke beyond the prism of race while avoiding the liberal humanism which traditionally accompanied discourses of interracialism.

In revisiting negotiations between black activists and Communism, so as to investigate the impact of this relationship on black writers, new ways of reading black literature can be achieved. Whilst retaining a commitment to reading 'difference' in black writing, one can also place those differences within their historical context and thereby trace the struggles to form a race-conscious subjectivity which sought to deconstruct traditional racial binaries. As Manning Marable states it:

> ... if 'race' itself is a social construct, an unequal relationship between social groups characterised by concentrations of power, privilege and authority of one group over another, then anyone of any ethnic, class or social background should be able to learn the complex experiences of another group.[1]

Wright, Himes and Ellison all insist on the possibility of this commitment to find ways to communicate the experience of race which are not hermetically sealed. *Native Son, Lonely Crusade* and *Invisible Man* are novels concerned with identity where 'race' does not function exclusively in the interstitial spaces of difference. Identity in these novels is configured, crucially, not only in racial terms, but also in terms of social location and political consciousness. In this impulse alone these are not novels discussing Communism: they are novels which are made possible by the influence of Communism on black cultural and political consciousness.

---

1   Marable 1995, p. 123.

Bibliography

Abcarian, Richard 1970, *Richard Wright's Native Son: A Critical Handbook*, California: Wadsworth Publishing Company.

Ahmad, Aijaz 1992, *In Theory: Classes, Nations, Literatures*, London: Verso.

Allen, Ernest 1977, 'The Cultural Methodology of Harold Cruse', *Journal of Ethnic Studies* 5, 2: 26–50.

Allen, James S. 1936, *The Negro Question in the United States*, New York: International Publishers.

Allen, Robert 1974, *Reluctant Reformers: Racism and Social Movements*, Washington: Howard University Press.

Anderson, Bendict 1991, *Imagined Communities*, London: Verso.

Anderson, Perry 1981, 'Communist Party History', in Samuel (ed.) 1981.

Aptheker, Herbert (ed.) 1973, *A Documentary History of the Negro People in the United States 1910–1932*, Secaucus, NJ: The Citadel Press.

Arnesen, Eric 2006, 'No 'Graver Danger': Black Anticommunism, the Communist Party, and the Race Question', *Labor: Studies in Working-Class History of the Americas*, 3, 4: 13–52.

Back, Lee and Solomos John (eds.) 2000, *Theories of Race and Racism*, London: Routledge.

Bakan, Abigail B. 2008, 'Marxism and Antiracism: Rethinking the Politics of Difference', in *Rethinking Marxism* 20, 2: 238–256.

Baker, Houston Jr. 1984, *Blues Ideology, and Afro-American Literature: a Vernacular Theory*, Chicago: Chicago University Press.

Baldwin, James 1964, *Notes of a Native Son*, London: Pluto Press.

——— 1985, *The Price of a Ticket: Collected Non-fiction 1948–1985*, New York: St Martins.

——— 1999, 'History as Nightmare', in Silet (ed.) 1999.

Balibar, Etienne and Immanuel Wallerstein 1991, *Race, Nation Class: Ambiguous Identities*, London & New York: Verso.

Barrett, James R. 2009, 'Rethinking the Popular Front', *Rethinking Marxism* 21, 4: 498–513.

Bellow, Saul 1952, 'Man Underground', in *Commentary* 13: 608–10.

Benjamin, Walter 1992, *Illuminations*, translated by Harry Zohn, London: Fontana Press.

Benston, Kimberly W. (ed.) 1990, *Speaking For You: The Vision of Ralph Ellison*, Washington, DC: Howard University Press.

Bianco, Lucien 1971, *Origins of the Chinese Revolution*, Stanford University Press: California.

Blake, Susan 1979, 'Ritual and Rationalization: Black Folklore in the works of Ralph Ellison', *PMLA* 94: 121–35.

Bloch, Ernst, Georg Lukács, Bertolt Brecht, Walter Benjamin and Theodor W. Adorno 1994, *Aesthetics and Politics*, London: Verso.

Bloom, Harold (ed.) 1987, *Richard Wright*, New York: Chelsea House Publishers.

——— (ed.) 1990, *Bigger Thomas*, New York: Chelsea House Publishers.

Bloom, James D. 1992, *Left Letters: The Culture Wars of Mike Gold and Joseph Freeman*, New York: Columbia University Press.

Blount, Marcellus and Cunningham, George (eds.) 1996, *Representing Black Men*, New York: Routledge.

Boris, Eileen 1998, ' "You Wouldn't Want One of 'Em Dancing With Your Wife": Racialized Bodies on the Job in World War II', *American Quarterly*. 50, 1: 77–108.

Branch, Taylor 1988, *Parting the Waters: America in the King Years*, New York: Simon and Schuster.

Briggs, Cyril 1974 [1931], 'The Decline of the Garvey Movement', *The Communist*, June 1931, reprinted in Henrik (ed.) 1974.

Brignano, Russell Carl 1970, *Richard Wright: An Introduction to the Man and His Works*, Pittsburgh: University of Pittsburgh Press.

Brown, William Wells 1968 [1863], *The Black Man: His Antecedents, His Genius and His Achievements*, New York: Johnson Reprint Corporation.

Buhle, Paul 1980, 'Jews and American Communism: The Cultural Question', *Radical America* 23: 9–33.

——— 1991, *Marxism in the United States*, New York: Verso.

Butler, Robert 1995, *The Critical Response to Richard Wright*, Westport, CT: Greenwood Press.

Busby, Mark 1991, *Ralph Ellison*, Boston: Twayne Publishers.

Campbell, Jane 1987, *Mythic Black Fiction: The Transformation of History*, Knoxville, TN: University of Tennessee Press.

Cannon, James P. 1970, *Socialism on Trial*, New York: Pathfinder.

Carr, Edward Hallett 1982, *The Twilight of Comintern: 1930–35*, London: Macmillan.

Carr, Edward Hallett and Tamara Deutscher 1984, *The Comintern and the Spanish Civil War*, London: Macmillan.

Carter, Dan 1969, *Scottsboro: A Tragedy of the American South*, Baton Rouge: Louisiana State Univ. Press.

Chesebrough, David 1998, *Frederick Douglass: Oratory from Slavery*, Westport, CT: Greenwood Press.

Cleaver, Eldridge 1969, *Soul on Ice*, London: Jonathan Cape.

Cooke, George Willis 2010, *George Eliot: A Critical Study of Her Life, Writings and Philosophy*, Cambridge: Cambridge University Press.

Cooper, Wayne F. (ed.) 1973, *The Passion of Claude McKay: Selected Poetry and Prose, 1912–1948*, New York: Schocken.

Communist International 1920, *The Second Congress of the Communist International: proceedings of Petrograd session of July 17th, and of Moscow sessions of July 19th–August 7th, 1920*, America: Publishing Office of the Communist International.

Conney, Terry 1986, *The Rise of the New York Intellectuals: Partisan Review and its Circle, 1934–45*, Madison: University of Wisconsin Press.

Crossman, Robert (ed.) 1965, *The God that Failed*, New York: Bantam Matrix.

Cruse, Harold 1967, *Crisis of the Negro Intellectual*, New York: William Morrow.

——— 1968, *Rebellion or Revolution*, New York: William Morrow.

Davis Jr, Ben 1940, 'New York Sunday Worker', in Abcarian (ed.) 1970.

Davis, Charles T. 1990, 'Richard Wright: The Artist as Public Figure', in Bloom (ed.) 1990.

Davis, Mike 1986, *Prisoners of the American Dream*, London: Verso.

——— 1987 (ed.) *The Year Left*, Volume 2, London: Verso.

De Arman, Charles 1978, 'Bigger Thomas: The Symbolic Negro and the Discrete Human Entity', *Black American Literature Forum*, 12, 2: 61–4.

Degras, Jane (ed.) 1956–1965, *The Communist International: 1919–194; Documents*, Volumes 1–3, London: Oxford University Press

Denning, Michael 1996, *The Cultural Front: The Labouring of American Culture in the Twentieth Century*, Londo: Verso.

Dixon, Thomas 1905, *The Clansman*, New York: Grosset & Dunlap.

Draper, Theodore 1957, *The Roots of American Communism*, New York: Viking Press.

——— 1960, *American Communism and Soviet Russia*, New York: Viking Press.

——— 1987, 'The Myth of the Communist Professors: The Class Struggle', *The New Republic*, 26 January, 29–36.

Duberman, Mark 1989, *Paul Robeson*, New York: The New Press.

Du Bois, W.E.B. 1935, *Black Reconstruction in America*, New York: Harcourt, Brace.

——— 1997 [1903], *The Souls of Black Folk*, Boston: Bedford Books.

Ericksen, Thomas Hylland 1993, *Ethnicity and Nationalism*, London: Pluto Press.

Ellison, Ralph 1964, *Shadow and Act*, London: Secker & Warbug.

——— 1965 [1952], *Invisible Man*, London: Penguin.

Evans, William Barret 1964, 'Revolutionist Thought in the *Daily Worker*: 1919–1939', PhD Thesis, University of Washington.

Fabre, Michel 1985, 'The Narrator/Narratee Relationship in *Invisible Man*', *Callaloo*, 25: 535–43.

——— 1991, *From Harlem to Paris: Black American Writers in France, 1840–1950*, Urbana: University of Illinois Press.

Fanon, Frantz 1986 [1952], *Black Skin, White Masks*, London: Pluto Press.

——— 1990 [1961], *The Wretched of the Earth*, London; Penguin.

Fielder, Leslie 1967, *Love and Death in the American Novel*, London: Cape.

France, Alan 1988, 'Misogyny and Appropriation in *Native Son*', *Modern Fiction Studies*, 34, 3: 13–23.

Fink, Gary and Merle Reed (eds.) 1994, *Race, Class and Community in Southern Labour History*, Tuscaloosa, AL: The University of Alabama Press.

Foley, Barbara 1993, *Radical Representations: Politics and Form in US Proletarian Fiction*, Durham: Duke University Press.

———— 2003, 'From Communism to Brotherhood: the Drafts of *Invisible Man*', in Mullen and Smethurst (eds.) 2003.

Foner, Philip 1974, *Organised Labour and the Black Worker*, New York: Praeger.

Foner, Philip and Herbert Shapiro 1987, *American Communism and Black Americans*, Philadelphia: Temple University Press.

Freeman, Joseph 1935, 'Introduction', in G. Hicks (ed.) 1935.

Gankin, Olga Hess and Harold H. Fisher 1940, *Bolsheviks and the World War*, California: Stanford University.

Garfinkel, Herbert 1959, *When Negroes March*, Illinois: The Free Press.

Garvey, Marcus 1974 [1932], 'The Communists and the Negro', *The New Jamaican*, 5 January 1932, reprinted in Henrik (ed.) 1974.

Gates Jr., Henry Louis (ed.) 1982, *Black is the Color of the Cosmos: Essays on Afro-American Literature and Culture, 1942–81*, New York: Garland.

———— 1984, *Black Literature and Literary Criticism*, London: Methuen.

———— 1986, *'Race,' Writing and Difference*, Chicago: University of Chicago Press.

————1986b, *Figures in Black: Words, Signs and the Racial Self*, New York: Oxford University Press.

———— 1988, *The Signifying Monkey*, New York: Oxford University Press.

Gates Jr, Henry Louis and Nellie McKay (eds.) 1997, *The Norton Anthology of African American Literature*, New York: W.W. Norton & Company.

Garvey, Amy Jacques (ed) 1967a, *Philosophy and Opinions of Marcus Garvey*, Volume 1, London: Frank Cass & Co.

———— (ed.) 1967b, *Philosophy and Opinions of Marcus Garvey*, Volume 2, London: Frank Cass & Co.

Gayle, Addison 1971, *The Black Aesthetic: Blueprint for Negro Writing*, New York: Doubleday.

———— 1975, *The Way of the New World: The Black Novel in America*, Garden City, NY: Anchor Press/Doubleday.

———— 1980, *Ordeal of a Native Son*, New York: Anchor Press.

Genovese, Eugene 1971, *In Red and Black*, London: Penguin Press.

Gibson, Donald B. 1995, 'Wright's Invisible Native Son', in Butler (ed.) 1995.

Gilroy, Paul 1993, *The Black Atlantic*, London: Verso.

Goodman, James E. 1994, *Stories of Scottsboro*, New York: Pantheon.

Gordon, Lewis R. (ed.) 1997, *Existence in Black: An Anthology of Black Existential Philosophy*, New York: Routledge.

Gorman, Robert A. 1989, 'Black Neo-Marxism', *Rethinking Marxism*, 2, 4: 118–140.

Gottesman, Ronald (ed.) 1971, *Studies in Invisible Man*, Columbus, OH: Charles E. Merrill Publishing Company.

Guttman, Sondra 2001, 'What Bigger Killed For: Rereading Violence Against Women in *Native Son*', *Texas Studies in Literature and Language*, 43, 2: 169–93.

Hall, Stuart 1994, 'Cultural Identity and Diaspora', in Willams and Chrisman (eds.) 1994.

———— 2000, 'Old and New Identities, Old and New Ethnicities', in Back and Solomos (eds.) 2000.

Hall, Stuart and Paul DuGay (eds.) 1996, *Questions of Cultural Identity*, London: Safe.

Harper, Phillip Brian 1996, *Are We Not Men: Masculine Anxiety and the Problem of African-American Identity*, New York & Oxford: Oxford University Press.

Harris, Trudi 1990, 'Native Sons and Foreign Daughters', in Kinnamon (ed.) 1990.

Haywood, Harry 1978, *Black Bolshevik, The Autobiography of an Afro-American Communist*, Chicago: Liberator Press.

Henrik, John (ed.) 1974, *Marcus Garvey and the Vision of Africa*, New York: Random House.

Hicks, Granville (ed.) 1935, *Proletarian Literature in the United States: An Anthology*, London: Lawrence and Wishart.

Hill, Robert A. (ed.) 1985, *The Marcus Garvey and Universal Negro Improvement Association Papers Volume I*, Berkley: University of California Press.

Himes, Chester 1973, *Quality of Hurt: The Autobiography of Chester Himes*, London: Michael Joseph.

———— 1975, *Black on Black: Baby Sister and Selected Writings*, London: Michael Joseph Ltd.

———— 1986 [1945], *If He Hollers Let Him Go*, New York: Thunder's Mouth Press.

———— 1997 [1947], *Lonely Crusade*, Edinburgh: Payback Press.

Hobsbawn, Eric 1995, *The Age of Extremes: The Short Twentieth Century, 1914–1991*, London: Abacus.

Hoch, Paul 1979, *White Hero Black Beast: Racism, Sexism and the Mask of Masculinity*, London: Pluto Press.

Hogue, W. Lawrence 2009, 'Can the Subaltern Speak? A Postcolonial, Existential Reading of Richard Wright's *Native Son*', *Southern Quarterly*, 46, 2: 3–9.

Holt, Thomas C. 2000, *The Problem of Race in the Twenty-First Century*, Cambridge Massachusetts: Harvard University Press.

hooks, bell 1991, *Yearning: Race, Gender and Cultural Politics*, London: Turnaround.

———— 1992, *Black Looks: Race and Representation*, London: Turnaround.

———— 1996, *Killing Rage*, London: Penguin.

Hord, F. Lee 1991, *Reconstructing Memory: Black Literary Criticism*, Chicago: Third World Press.

Howe, Irving 1970, 'Black Boys and Native Sons', in Reilly (ed.) 1970.

Howe, Irving and Louis Coser 1962, *The American Communist Party*, New York: Praeger.

Hughes, Carl Milton 1967, *The Negro Novelist: A Discussion of the Writings of American Negro Novelists 1940–1950*, New York: Books for Libraries Press.

Isserman, Maurice 1982, *Which Side Were You On?*, Connecticut: Wesleyan University Press.

Jackson, Lawrence P. 2000, 'The Birth of the Critic: The Literary Friendship of Ralph Ellison and Richard Wright', *American Literature*, 72, 2: 321–55.

Jacobson, Julius (ed.) 1968, *The Negro and the American Labour Movement*, New York, Anchor Books.

James, C.L.R. 1937, *World Revolution 1917–1936: The Rise and Fall of the Communist International*, London: Martin Secker & Warburg.

———— 1996 [1940], 'On *Native Son* by Richard Wright,' in McLemee (ed.) 1996.

———— (ed.) 1980, *Fighting Racism in World War II*, New York: Monad Press.

Kanet, Roger 1973, 'The Comintern and the "Negro Question": Communist Policy in the United States and Africa, 1921–1941', *Survey* 19, 4: 87–122.

Kazin, Alfred 1942, *On Native Grounds: An Interpretation of Modern American Prose*, New York: Harcourt Brace Jovanovich.

Keady, Sylvia 1995, 'Richard Wright's Women Characters and Inequality', in Butler, (ed.) 1995.

Kelley, Robin D.G. 1988, ' "Comrades, Praise Gawd for Lenin and Them": Ideology and Culture among Black Communists in Alabama, 1930–1935', *Science and Society* 52, 1: 59–82.

———— 1990, *Hammer and Hoe: Alabama Communists during the Great Depression*, Chapel Hill: University of North Carolina Press.

———— 1993, ' "We Are Not What We Seem": Rethinking Black Working-Class Opposition in the Jim Crow South', *The Journal of American History*, 80, 1: 75–112.

———— 1994, *Race Rebels*, New York: The Free Press.

Kelly, Brian 2001, *Race, Class and Power in the Alabama Coalfields, 1908–21*, Urbana: University of Illinois Press.

Keith, Michael and Steve Pile (eds.) 1993, *Place and the Politics of Identity*, New York: Routledge.

Kinnamon, Kenneth 1990, *New Essays on Native Son*, Cambridge: Cambridge University Press.

Klehr, Harvey 1984, *The Heyday of American Communism*, New York: Basic Books.

Klehr, Harvey and William Tompson 1989, 'Self-Determination in the Black Belt: Origins of a Communist Policy', *Labor History* 30, 3: 354–66.

Kresser Cobb, Nina 1978, 'Richard Wright: Individualism Reconsidered', *CLA Journal*, 21, 2: 346–8.

Lee, A. Robert 1999, 'The Novels of Chester Himes', in Silet (ed.) 1999.

Lenin, Vladimir I. 1964a, *Collected Works*, Volume 20, Moscow: Progress Publisher.

———— 1964b, *Collected Works*, Volume 22, Moscow: Progress Publisher.

Lemann, Nicholas 1991, *The Promised Land: The Great Black Migration and How it Changed America*, London: Papermac.

Lewy, Gunther 1990, *The Cause that Failed*, New York: Oxford University Press.

Lichenstein, Nelson 1982, *Labor's War at Home: The CIO in World War II*, New York: Cambridge University Press.

Lubin, Alex (ed.) 2007, *Revising the Blueprint: Ann Petry and the Literary Left*, Jackson: University Press of Mississippi.

Lukács, Georg 1971 [1923], *History and Class Consciousness*, translated by Rodney Livingstone, London: Merlin Press.

Lundquist, James 1976, *Chester Himes*, New York: Frederick Ungar Publishing Co.

Margolies, Edward 1990, 'Native Son and Three Kinds of Revolution', in Bloom (ed.) 1990.

McDermott, Kevin and Jeremy Agnew 1996, *The Comintern: A History of International Communism from Lenin to Stalin*, London: Macmillan.

McLemee, Scott (ed.) 1996, *CLR James on the Negro Question*, Jackson: University Press of Mississippi.

McSweeney, Kerry 1988, *Invisible Man: Race and Identity*, Boston: Twayne Publishers.

Majors, Richard and Janet Mancini Billson 1992, *Cool Pose: The Dilemmas of Black Manhood in America*, New York: MacMillan.

Marable, Manning 1981, *Race, Reform and Rebellion* London: Macmillan.

———— 1983, *How Capitalism Underdeveloped Black America: Problems in Race, Political Economy and Society*, Boston: South End Press.

———— 1986, *W.E.B. DuBois: Black Radical Democrat*, Boston: Twayne Publishers.

———— 1993, 'Beyond Racial Identity Politics', *Race and Class*, 35, 1: 112–30.

———— 1996, *Speaking Truth to Power: Essays on Race, Resistance and Radicalism*, Colorado: Westview Press.

Marriott, David 2000, *On Black Men*, Edinburgh: Edinburgh University Press.

Martin, Charles H. 1979, 'Communists and Blacks: The International Labor Defense and the Angelo Herndon Case', *Journal of Negro History*, 64: 131–41.

———— 1985, 'The International Labor Defense and Black America', *Labor History*, 26, 2: 165–94.

Marx, Karl 1983 [1867], *Capital*, Volume 1, translated by Moore and Aveling London: Lawrence & Wishart.

———— 1970, *On Ireland*, London: Lawrence and Wishart.

Maxwell, William J. 1999, *New Negro Old Left: African–American Writing and Communism Between the Wars*, New York: Columbia University Press.

Meier, August and Elliott Rudwick 1976a [1966], *From Plantation to Ghetto*, New York: Hill and Wang.

——— 1976 [1969], *The Making of Black America: Essays in Negro Life and History*, New York: Atheneum.

——— 1982, 'Communist Unions and the Black Community: The Case of the Transport Workers Union', *Labour History* Spring: 165–97.

Milliken, Stephen F. 1976, *Chester Himes: A Critical Appraisal*, Columbia: University of Missouri Press.

Moretti, Franco 1983, *Signs Taken For Wonders: Essays In The Sociology Of Literary Forms*, London: New Left Books.

Morgan, Stacy I. 2004, *Rethinking Social Realism: African American Art and Literature 1930–1953*, Athens: University of Georgia Press.

Mullen, Bill 2001, 'A New Blueprint for African-American Literary Studies', *Modern Fiction Studies*, 47, 1: 148–9.

Mullen, Bill and James Smethurst (eds.) 2003, *Left of the Color Line: Race, Radicalism and 20th Century Literature of the United States*, Chapel Hill: University of North Carolina Press.

Munck, Ronaldo 1986, *The Difficult Dialogue: Marxism and Nationalism*, London & New Jersey: Zed Books.

Muraskin, William 1972, 'The Harlem Boycott of 1934: Black Nationalism and the Rise of Labor Union Consciousness', *Labor History*, 13, 3: 361–73.

Murphy, James F. 1991, *The Proletarian Moment: The Controversy over Leftism in Literature*, Urbana: University of Illinois Press.

Naison, Mark 1985, *Communists in Harlem During the Depression*, New York: Grove Press.

Nelson, Bruce 1993, 'Organized Labor and the Struggle for Black Equality in Mobile during World War II', *Journal of American History*, 80, 3: 952–88.

Nelson, Cary 1989, *Repression and Recovery: Modern American Poetry and the Politics of Cultural Memory, 1910–1945* Madison: University of Wisconsin Press.

Nimni, Ephraim 1991, *Marxism and Nationalism: The theoretical origins of the political crisis*, London: Pluto Press.

North, Joseph (ed.) 1969, *New Masses: An Anthology of the Rebel Thirties*, New York: International Publishers.

O'Meally, Robert G. 1980, *The Craft of Ralph Ellison*, Cambridge, MA: Harvard University Press.

Painter, Nell Irvin 1979, *The Narrative of Hosea Hudson: His Life as a Negro Communist in the South*, Cambridge, MA: Harvard University Press.

Parry, Benita 1987, 'Problems in Current Theories of Colonial Discourse', *Oxford Literary Review*, 9: 27–58.

Patterson, Haywood & Earl Conrad 1950, *Scottsboro Boy*, New York: Country Life Press.

Peddie, Ian 2001, 'Poles Apart? Ethnicity, Race, Class and Nelson Algren', *Modern Fiction Studies*, 47, 1: 118–44.

Pells, Richard H. 1973, *Radical Visions and American Dreams: Cultural and Social Thought in the Depression, Years* New York: Harper.

Pinkney, Alphonso 1976, *Red, Black, and Green: Black Nationalism in the United States*, Cambridge: Cambridge University Press.

Preis, Art 1974, *Labor's Giant Step: Twenty years of the CIO*, New York: Pathfinder.

Pudaloff, Ross 1983, '*Native Son* and Mass Culture', *Studies in American Fiction*, 11, 1: 3–18.

Rabinowitz, Paula 2001, 'Domestic Labor: Film Noir, Proletarian Literature, and Black Women's Fiction', *Modern Fiction Studies*, 47, 1: 229–54.

Rampersad, Arnold 1988, *The Life of Langston Hughes Volume II*, New York: Oxford University Press.

Reckley, Ralph 1999, 'The Use of the Doppelganger or Double in Chester Himes' *Lonely Crusade*', in Silet (ed.) 1999.

Record, Wilson 1951, *The Negro and the Communist Party*, Carolina: University of North Carolina Press.

Reed, Christopher 1997, *The Chicago NAACP and The Rise Of Black Professional Leadership: 1910–1966*, Bloomington: Indiana University Press.

Reilly, John M (ed.) 1970, *Twentieth Century Interpretations of Invisible Man*, Englewood Cliffs, NJ: Prentice Hall.

Robinson, Cedric 1983, *Black Marxism: The Making of the Black Radical Tradition*, London, Zed Press.

———— 1997, *Black Movements in America*, New York: Routledge.

Rosen, Steven J. 1999, 'African American Anti-Semitism and Himes's Lonely Crusade', in Silet (ed.) 1999.

Rosengarten, Theodore 1974, *All God's Dangers: The Life of Nate Shaw*, New York: Knopf.

Rosenhaft, Eve 1983, *Beating the Fascists? the German Communists and Political Violence, 1929–1933*, Cambridge: Cambridge University Press.

Sallis, James 2000, *Chester Himes: A Life*, Edinburgh: Payback Press.

Samuel, Raphael (ed.) 1981, *People's History and Socialist Theory*, London: Routledge and Kegan Paul.

Schraufnagel, Noel 1973, *From Apology to Protest: The Black American Novel*, Florida: Everet/Edwards.

Shannon, David A. 1959, *The Decline of American Communism*, London: Atlantic Books.

Silet, Charles (ed.) 1999, *The Critical Response to Chester Himes*, Westport, CT: Greenwood Press.

Sivaandan, Ambalavane 1983, 'Challenging Racism: Strategies for the '80s', *Race and Class*, 25, 2: 1–11.

—— 1990, *Communities of Resistance: Writings on Black Struggles for Socialism*, London: Verso.

Slaughter, Joseph 2007, *Human Rights, Inc.: The World Novel, Narrative Form and International Law*, New York: Fordham University Press.

Smehurst, James Edward 1999, *The New Red Negro: The Literary Left and African American Poetry, 1930–1946*, New York: Oxford University Press.

—— 2001, 'Invented by Horror: The Gothic and African American Literary Ideology in *Native Son*', *African American Review*, 35, 1: 29–40.

Smith, Dennis 1988, *The Chicago School: A Liberal Critique of Capitalism*, London: Macmillan Education.

Smith, Jeremy 1999, *The Bolsheviks and the National Question: 1917–1923*, London: Macmillan.

Solomon, Mark 1998, *The Cry Was Unity: Communists and African Americans, 1917–1936*, Jackson, MI: University of Mississippi Press.

Soja, Edward and Barbara Hooper 1993, 'The Spaces that Difference Makes', in Michael Keith & Steve Pile (eds.) *Place and the Politics of Identity*.

Spero, Sterling and Abram L. Harris 1968, *The Black Worker*, New York: Atheneum.

Starobin, Joseph H. 1972, *American Communism in Crisis*, Cambridge, MA: Harvard University Press.

Staub, Michael E. 1994, *Voices of Persuasion: Politics of Representation in 1930s America*, Cambridge: Cambridge University Press.

Torigian, Michael 1989, 'National Unity On the Waterfront: Communist Politics and the ILWU During the Second World War', *Labor History*, 30, 3: 409–23.

Trotsky, Leon 1974 [1924], *The First Five Years of the Communist International*, Volume 2, London: New Park Publications.

—— 1976, *On China*, Monad Press: New York.

—— 1978, *Trotsky on Black Nationalism and Self-Determination*, New York: Pathfinder.

Van Deburg, William L. (ed.) 1997, *Modern Black Nationalism: From Marcus Garvey to Louis Farrakhan*, New York: New York University Press.

Vincent, Theodore 1975, *Black Power and the Garvey Movement*, New York: Ramparts Press.

Wald Alan M. 1987, *The New York Intellectuals: The Rise and Decline of the Anti-Stalinist Left from the 1930s to the 1980s*, Chapel Hill: University of North Carolina Press.

—— 1994, *Writing From the Left: New Essays on Radical Culture and Politics*, London & New York: Verso.

—— 2003, 'Narrating Nationalisms: Black Marxism and Jewish Communists through the eyes of Harold Cruse', in Mullen and Smethurst (eds.) 2003.

Wallace, Michelle 1996 [1978] *Black Macho and the Myth of the Superwoman*, London: Verso.

——— (ed.) 1992, *Black Popular Culture*, Seattle: Bay Press.

Wells, Ira 2010, ' "I Killed for, I Am": Domestic Terror in Richard Wright's America', *American Quarterly*, 62, 4: 873–95.

West, Cornel 1991, *Breaking Bread: Insurgent Black Intellectual Life*, Boston: South End Press.

Whitaker, Thomas R. 1970, 'Spokesman for Invisibility', in Reilly (ed.) 1970.

Wiegman, Robyn 1995, *American Anatomies: Theorizing Race and Gender*, Durham & London: Duke University Press.

Williams, John A. and Charles F. Harris (eds.) 1970, *Amistad 1*, New York: Vintage Books.

Williams, Patrick and Laura Chrisman (eds.) 1994, *Colonial Discourse and Post-colonial Theory: a Reader*, London: Harvester Wheatsheaf.

Wolters, Raymond 1970, *Negroes and the Great Depression*, Westport, CT: Greenwood.

Wood, Marcus 2000, *Blind Memory*, Manchester: Manchester University Press.

——— 2003, *The Poetry of Slavery*, Oxford: Oxford University Press.

Wright Richard 1951, *Twelve Million Black Voices*, New York: Viking.

——— 1963, *Lawd Today*, New York: Walker.

——— 1964, *White Man Listen!*, New York: Anchor Books.

——— 1977, *American Hunger*, New York: Harper & Row.

——— 1990 [1940], *Native Son*, London: Picador.

——— 1993 [1952], *The Outsider*, New York: Harper Perennial.

——— 1997 [1937], 'Blueprint for Negro Writing', in Gates Jr. and McKay (eds.) 1997.

Young, Roert 1990, *White Mythologies*, London: Routledge.

Zumoff, Jacob 2012, 'The American Communist Party and the "Negro Question": from the Founding of the Party to the Fourth Congress of the Communist International', *Journal for the Study of Radicalism*, 6, 2: 53–89.

Index